TESTIMONIALS FROM READERS OF THE FIRST EDITION

"Helge's work contributes to our health, joy, freedom, and peace. Since that is what we all want, this book is a road map home."
Aquarius Magazine

"A startlingly practical self-help book featuring thoughtful explorations of our own emotions and how we can focus our risk taking to accomplish results that matter."
Bookman News (Bookman Book Review Syndicate)

"Helge's unorthodox self-help book is not comprised of nebulous concepts. She spent years formulating concrete steps that people can follow to become happier and healthier."
Texas Alcalde

"A heart-felt, practical guide to managing life's challenges—a most welcome contribution to the personal growth field."
Tom Kenyon, psychotherapist and author of *Brain States*

"Readers at all levels of personal growth will find great value in this book. Helge shares powerful techniques for experiencing and dissipating emotions. This book is an excellent resource of strategies and exercises that work with people of all ages."
Tony Cecala, Ph.D., Publisher, *The Holistic Networker*

"Dr. Helge shows us how to embrace our humanity so that we can open the door to our divinity. Her work is deeply personal, helpful, and sincere."
Dr. Rudy Scarfalotto, D.C., author, *The Alchemy of Opposites*

"Yes! Yes! Yes! You have touched me so deeply."
Carol Keeffe, author of *How to Get What You Want in Your Life With the Money You Already Have*

"A masterpiece whose time has come, written with love and compassion."
Don Petrocelle, author, *Poetic Odyssey*

"Your great book made a splendid addition to our magazine. Keep up the wonderful writing."
Personal Transformation Magazine

"Powerful insights, valuable exercises, and unique tools for facing our personal challenges and our inherent resistance to the inevitable changes in our lives. Helge writes with an articulate passion born of personal experience, a candid self-assessment, and research with clients. This book is highly recommended."
The Midwest Book Review

"Doris leads those with broken wings through her wise counsel, love, and practical techniques. She is touching hearts and changing lives. If you are ready to change old patterns and walk through the desert to the oasis with grace, treat yourself!—Read this book."
Beth Franklin, Executive Director, Literacy Council of Alabama

"This is the 'bible of personal growth!' . . . A breakthrough book in understanding who we are and how we can realize the wonderful, divine, and perfect person we are all becoming."
Edward A. Thomas, Attorney at Law, Quincy, MA

"Practical, simple, and powerful — the Zen of transforming pain into powerful change in your life."
Victor S. Sierpina, M.D., University of Texas Medical Branch at Galveston

"Our office worked with Doris' techniques, and now our employees are energized, motivated, and de-stressed."
Lawrence M. Sinclair, Floor Supervisor, Royal, Inc., Chicago

"If you'd like to know why God allows painful events in all of our lives, read this book."
Rev. Dave Logan, First Memorial Church, Los Angeles

"If these ideas were made available to all of those who feel disempowered, violence—in the workplace and in homes—would cease to exist."
Brenda Holbrook, Director, N.Y. Violence Prevention Center

"Trying to let go of or release emotions like anger and fear guarantees that they'll keep reappearing. Doris' work is the missing piece I share with my clients. When they use her techniques, they watch their self-judgments melt, their anger turn into love, and their fear become self-confidence."
C. Dana Roberts, psychologist, New York City

"The most liberating, magnificently simple and thoroughly helpful (yes, REALLY helpful) book on the market. Unlike your usual self-help tomes, there are no mantras to say, no affirmations to intone religiously three times a day, and no exercises that must be done before going to bed. Thank you! With Doris' work, your feelings fall into proper perspective and stop draining your energy, and this happens SPONTANEOUSLY. We urge you to buy this worthwhile book as soon as possible."

Joanna and Richard Swanson, CEO and owner, Mountain Mist Resort, NC

"Now, I trust myself even when my life feels stagnant. Doris' work brought multiple benefits to my audience. I've learned to see the transformation that is taking place even when things feel stuck and the tendency is to panic."

Elizabeth Ann Wright, Host, "Ultimate Solutions," WGUN, Atlanta, GA

"When we discovered that our child had A.D.D., we began a ride on the emotional roller coaster. The ideas in this book allowed us to take ourselves off."

Paul and Lynnette Oliver, parents of a child with A.D.D.

"I am proud to endorse your work . . . It was enlightening as I was going through some fearful and exciting times . . . Reading your work helped me recognize and accept my feelings and know that I am OK and in the flow of life. It has helped me."

Sue Bailey, board member, Society of Government Meeting Planners, Washington

"I don't know of anyone who won't find value in this book. It has helped me tremendously and is my standby in tough times. You will help many people with this information."

Doug Gazley, Director of Music, Unity of Gwinnett, Atlanta, GA

*"This was a wonderful **next step** for me after I worked with my 12-step program. I feel very empowered, and I know I'm in charge of my own life."*

C. L. Monroe, New Orleans

"Doris touched and changed my life forever."

Mollie Jo Rogers, President, ABWA, Houston, TX

TRANSFORMING PAIN INTO POWER

MAKING THE MOST OF YOUR EMOTIONS

Doris Helge, Ph.D.

Shimoda Publishing   Ontario, Oregon

TRANSFORMING PAIN INTO POWER
Making the Most of Your Emotions

by Doris Helge, Ph.D.

Published by: Shimoda Publishing
251 W. Idaho Avenue, Ste. 126
Ontario, OR 97914
shimodapub@mindspring.com
http://www.mindspring.com/~shimodapub/

Printed and bound in the United States of America
10 9 8 7 6 5 4 3 ②1

Publisher's Cataloging in Publication
(Prepared by Quality Books Inc.)

Helge, Doris
Transforming pain into power : making the most of your emotions / by Doris Helge.
p. cm.
Includes bibliographic references and index.
Preassigned LCCN: 96-69333
ISBN: 1-8855-98-88-2 (pbk.): $16.95
1. Self-actualization (Psychology) 2. Emotions—Therapeutic use 3. Attitude (Psychology) 4. Choice (Psychology)
I. Title.
BF637.S4H45 1998   158'.1
QBI98-40351

WARNING—DISCLAIMER

This book is designed to provide information regarding the subject matter covered. It is sold with the understanding that the publisher and author are not engaged in rendering legal, psychological, or other professional services. If legal, psychological, or other expert assistance is required, the services of a competent professional should be sought.

It is not the purpose of this publication to reprint all of the information that is otherwise available to the author or publisher, but to complement other texts. You are urged to read all of the available material, learn as much as possible, and tailor the information to your individual needs.

Every effort has been made to make this document as complete and accurate as possible. Its purpose is to provide an additional point of view for educational purposes. The author and publisher shall have neither liability nor responsibility to any person or entity with respect to any loss or damage caused, or alleged to be caused, directly or indirectly by information in this book.

IF YOU DO NOT WISH TO BE BOUND BY THE ABOVE, YOU MAY RETURN THIS BOOK TO THE PUBLISHER IN GOOD CONDITION FOR A FULL REFUND.

CONTENTS

LIST OF FIGURES

DEDICATION

This book is dedicated to the liberation of the people on this planet. Once tasted, we all hunger voraciously for a level of freedom that can only be gained by accepting responsibility for our own lives. The bliss that it provides to us generates a drive beyond any description other than we just want *more of who we really are*. My dream is that we will awaken one incredible day and discover that we are living in harmony with each other. We will have so much self-love that we treat every living thing with the utmost respect. They are all aspects of ourselves.

ABOUT THE AUTHOR

Doris' prestigious career began by completing her Ph.D. at the age of 25. She launched and directed two national organizations. She taught, conducted research, and held faculty and administrative positions at universities in three states before beginning her own consulting business. The national studies she conducted were frequently used in Congressional testimony and influenced legislation at the federal and state levels.

She has authored publications on the subjects of personal empowerment, child abuse, self-esteem, winning strategies for business, health care, and special education. She is an internationally known speaker, and her work has assisted thousands of individuals in propelling themselves toward their personal empowerment.

Her speaking style is dynamic, interactive, and thought-provoking. Because of the special nature of her message, her work is sought by a variety of groups. In fact, Doris was recently selected by a group of peers in the National Speakers Association as a "Showcase Speaker."

Doris has appeared on over 150 TV and radio programs. She and her partner, William Richards, conduct seminars on a variety of topics. The tools that Doris presents in this book were successfully field-tested in seminars in various locations across North America.

FOR INFORMATION OR SPEAKING ENGAGEMENTS

Persons wishing more information about Doris' speaking engagements, seminars, and additional publications may send a #10 self-addressed envelope to Dr. Doris Helge, c/o 1225 E. Sunset Dr., #317, Bellingham, WA 98226-3529.

ACKNOWLEDGMENTS

So many people contributed to this book. The most special thanks are for William, my sweetheart and treasured friend. He ever so gently, sweetly, and carefully pried open my heart and stretched my mind. William, I'm so glad it's you!

Many thanks to the *real* Lee Harris, whom I will love forever and ever.

Mom, thank you for all of the difficult roles you played so that I could become who I am today.

Special thanks to the reviewers for their careful proofreading and helpful suggestions: William, Janine Parker, Richard Lacey, Sara Bingham, Roanne Hoglund, Bianca Braden, Katherine McAllister, Valerie Smith, and Terry Garrett.

So many others—Michael, Melony, Linda, Herb, Mark, K.B., Janene, and Sandy.

I thank you and I love you. There is nothing more to say. There is only more to experience and to be. So out of this "funnel" and into the next.

OTHER CONTRIBUTORS TO THIS BOOK

Cover Design

Carey Klein designed the book cover for this edition. He is a freelance graphics artist who resides in Bellingham, Washington.

Text Layout and Design

Brian Smith was a pioneer in the field of personal computers and is well-known for his expertise in layout and design of text and illustrations in books, journals, newspapers, newsletters, and other print media. Brian resides in Olympia, Washington.

Copyediting

Nancy Gordon is a freelance editor who specializes in copyediting and proofreading. Nancy may be contacted via The Gordon Group in Boise, Idaho.

GOING THE DISTANCE—WITHOUT RESISTANCE

Do you know anyone who has repeated the same painful experience over and over?

Why would we all have painful events in our lives if they didn't serve us in some way?

Would you like to learn how to stop *trying* to change things about yourself and your life—and experience *spontaneous* change?

YOU WILL FIND SPECIAL VALUE IN THIS BOOK, IF:

♦ You've ever tried to release or let go of "negative" emotions such as anger, fear, or sadness, only to find them returning to your doorstep.

♦ You would like *even more* valuable tools for your personal growth toolbox.

♦ You'd like to *USE* your emotions to bring yourself greater energy, easier relationships, and improved health.

♦ You would appreciate new ways to handle stress at work and at home.

USE THIS BOOK TO:

♦ Drop self-judgments.

♦ Allow yourself to be as powerful (capable) as you really are.

♦ Learn to *USE* painful experiences—instead of feeling used by them.

♦ Safely and constructively experience anger, fear, and sadness—and watch them spontaneously change into love, happiness, and self-confidence!

♦ Develop so much self-love that your relationships reflect that back to you.

- *Naturally* increase your energy level—and your health.

- Discover that anger, sadness, and fear are just raw, neutral energy that you can *use* to *improve* your life.

- Learn new ways to deal with your frustrations at work instead of lugging them home—and protect your immune system in the process.

- *Develop your innate emotional power.*

THIS BOOK OFFERS UNIQUE TOOLS THAT WILL HELP YOU DISCOVER:

- Why there is nothing wrong with your life.

- Why nothing about you needs to be fixed or changed.

- How all of your experiences and emotions are essential for your personal growth—and your eventual happiness!

Waking up to see life as it really is.

ONE

NEW PIECES FOR THE PUZZLE OF LIFE

Birth canals are small, uncomfortable passageways which simultaneously produce almost indescribable joy and pain. As humans, we are always giving birth to new aspects of ourselves. We walk down frightening paths only to discover new layers of self-confidence. Our self-doubts arise specifically so that we can give birth to heightened degrees of self-love and empowerment. An uncomfortable feeling such as anger, fear, or sadness rears its head, and many of us want to numb, disguise, or deny it—anything to get rid of it! *That doesn't work.*

We travel down the path of life only to discover that our feelings continue to demand our attention. Since we didn't heed their call the first time, they scream louder. Our painful situations magnify so that we can gain the personal growth available from them. Have you ever known someone who left an unpleasant job or relationship only to re-create it? Although the characters and setting may change, the new situation is very similar to the old. I cannot tell you how many clients have told me that after the (job or personal) honeymoon was over, they woke up with the stark realization that "the person had a different name, but I realized, I've been here before, and it's even worse this time!"

The popular recommendation to counteract our insecurities by "faking it 'til you make it" may temporarily suit our desire not to feel uncomfortable, but it is not a long-term solution. *If that was the answer, we wouldn't have to keep faking it.* The messages in this book can help you "make it," and the methods for doing so are field-tested. They can help you allow your life to change permanently, versus settling for Band-Aids.

Keep in mind that the suggestions in this book are based on case studies with both genders and with people in all walks of life, from teenagers to senior citizens. I've worked with persons of extraordinary achievement levels and those who considered themselves low achievers.

I also know the techniques work because I have practiced them for many years. There was a time in my professional speaking career that I had spoken to several hundred people at a time but never to several thousand. Because speaking to a larger crowd was a new challenge, my insecurities became apparent close to curtain time. When a runner came backstage to announce, "Guess how many tickets have been sold!," I didn't share his enthusiasm. Instead, my self-doubt soared. Rather than lying to myself about how I felt, I allowed myself to be aware of what existed—an agonizing sense of unworthiness and the fear that I would go "braindead" on stage. The thought, "I have nothing of value to offer them," wafted through my consciousness, even though I knew better. The sensations were quite intense.

Now, for the good news. Just as I advocate in this book, that was the ticket to my freedom. I fully experienced the feelings of insecurity, allowing myself to sink to the "bottom of the bottom" (see Figure 5, chapter 6). It's important to note that this process took very little time. By the time I needed to walk out on stage, I felt more self-confident than I ever had. Now, I can speak to large crowds without feelings of self-doubt and unworthiness surfacing.

Why didn't the process take very long? Because we really do love ourselves enough to provide our next challenge. We don't brutally shove ourselves farther out on a limb than it is beneficial for us to go. As Figure 5, chapter 6 indicates, we meet our challenges (including feeling difficult emotions) by degrees. You can use the material in this book to prove this principle to yourself.

It is important to understand that pain and pleasure are side by side in our brains. If we allow our unpleasant feelings (in this case, fear and self-doubt) to be experienced, new levels of their opposites (higher levels of self-confidence and self-love) are immediately available to us. Our "gremlins" are merely tools for our personal growth. They can only be "conquered" by befriending them because they truly are our friends. They are leading us to higher levels of self-actualization, even though the sensations they produce are sometimes uncomfortable.

If I had attempted to dodge the challenge (denied my fear), I would have re-created the scenario later—in a magnified manner. The anxiety level and the challenge would have felt even more intense. When we choose to work with uncomfortable feelings the first time they surface, we shorten the time we are engaged in a particular challenge and propel ourselves into new levels of self-love and happiness.

I have shared the above example with you because many studies indicate that public speaking is the worst fear of many people and second only to a dental visit for other individuals. The true story illustrates that the process of transforming pain into power can be much quicker than we sometimes think. It is not an "endless journey," yet it has incredible rewards. When we allow ourselves to complete the personal growth spiral depicted in Figure 5, chapter 6, we are ready for new challenges, versus continuing to battle the same insecurities over and over.

Please note that *I experienced, versus judged, the feelings,* even though they were quite uncomfortable. Resisting or repressing emotions causes them to park their RVs, turn on their generators, and plan to spend more time with us. Simply experiencing them allows them to spontaneously transform into their opposites.

In addition, the effects of hiding from our pain can have tremendous implications for our health. When we repress our feelings, we stifle the flow of energy through our bodies. We inadvertently suppress our immune systems, and we perceive events as more stressful than they really are. We feel confused and less connected to those we love. Whether we are avoiding our anger or our love, the price of our unwillingness to be honest about our feelings can be quite high. On the other hand, allowing life to touch us has tremendous benefits.

Studies that have chemically analyzed tears have indicated that they cleanse stress hormones, so we feel less fatigued after crying. Our sobs are an innate gift, as tears assist the body in washing away toxins. Many recent studies are investigating the fact that men tend to die seven years earlier than women partly because most men seldom cry. Even when they allow tears to well up in their eyes, they rarely shed these very precious, innate rejuvenators. It seems that we forgot to tell our little boys that the strongest trees—those that tend to live the longest—bend with the wind.

Many women would rather cry or feel hurt than express anger. Just as men were told, "big boys don't cry," most women were conditioned to believe that anger is unbecoming or "not lady-like." Some women fear anger because they have been in hurtful situations when others were enraged. Some take pride in the fact that they put the needs of others before their own but secretly resent doing so.

Gender-related patterns of hidden anger or sadness are associated with the physical diseases we tend to develop. Recent studies have begun to examine why women tend to develop higher percentages of chronic fatigue syndrome, fibromyalgia, and arthritis while men have higher percentages of other diseases such as heart attacks.

Many people advocate "releasing" or "letting go of" painful experiences or emotions. Feelings such as anger, sadness, and fear have been viewed as "negative" or toxic emotions. Yet, our creator placed pain and pleasure side by side in our brains. Anger cuddled up next to love and happiness. Fear nestled next to self-confidence, and sadness snuggled up to joy.

The objective of always operating from love and joy is admirable, yet most of us would like to omit an essential step that is necessary to reach that point. The physiology of the brain allows us to experience the feelings we dislike, when they are present, or cheat ourselves out of the opportunity to experience their opposites—like love and happiness.

Consider the example of anger, which is passion for ourselves ("I deserve better than that" or "I want more out of life"). When we embrace anger (experience it), more self-love appears. Once we express our irritations in a safe and constructive way, we discover that we have been angry with ourselves because we positioned ourselves in an unfavorable situation. We stop blaming others, our compassion for them increases, and forgiveness becomes automatic.

Most parents love their children too much to try to protect them from painful learning experiences. Wise parents shield their children from *unnecessary* pain or danger by teaching them how to be physically safe and develop decision-making skills. However, parents with foresight know that efforts to guard their children from *any* pain would cheat them out of developing their abilities to meet life on its own terms. They would grow up as shallow adults totally unprepared to solve problems or empower themselves by meeting new challenges. The same is true for us as adults, and this book can assist you in finding value in *all* of your painful experiences.

Discover the hidden gifts of anger (empowerment and self-love), and find out how energizing—and even fun—it can be to safely and constructively experience it. Learn to feel the sweet memories that are hidden within your deepest grief. Find out what a friend your fear is. Like the first robins of spring, it arrives to announce the imminent arrival of something new—your new layers of self-confidence.

- It is our discomfort in life that drives us onward.
- Where there is fear, there is self-confidence.
- Where there is pain, there is power.
- Where there is anger, there is love.
- Where there is sadness, there is joy.
- Where there are no victims, there can be no tyrants.
- The road to pain is paved with our judgments and expectations.
- The road to success is paved with "failures."
- Emotions are our personal language . . . sensation . . . *energy in motion.*

If you want *even more* happiness and love in your life, allow life to touch you.

CAUTION:

This book can empower you to deal with the self-doubt and fears that surface when we approach new challenges. You will soon learn that fear is a formidable *source* of new power.

TWO

CHANGE IS GAIN—NOT PAIN

Our worst fear is not that we are inadequate.
Our deepest fear is that we are powerful beyond measure.
Marianne Williamson

The last 20 years of my research and work with clients have made it clear to me that most of our critical social problems are related to our inability to safely and constructively express our feelings. Our emotions will be a key topic of concern during the next millennium. We are discovering that our painful feelings and experiences, even those that we have judged most harshly and have tried to forget, can be one of our most valuable resources.

We can learn to use our "negative" emotions such as anger, fear, depression, and sadness as resources to bring what we *want* into our lives. We can also learn to more effectively use our "positive" emotions including love and joy to allow ourselves to live our most pleasurable dreams. Even though we have approached our feelings as a foreign language, we will discover that they are truly our best friends. They are the language of *me talking to me*, and they are magnificent tools for achieving our personal empowerment.

This book is experientially based and contains unique knowledge gleaned from my work in the fields of business, psychology, and education. It is replete with examples based on actual case study materials. The messages in this document add to so many other useful tools that are available. I wrote it because it was my next step in being more fully who I am.

7

If you read statements that contradict your belief system, I ask only that you **consider the possibility that most of what we have been told about life is upside down and backward.** If the material in these pages "pushes your buttons," it is feasible that this information may be presenting significant tools to you.

All of the distortions we have believed have served a purpose. Whatever your truth is at this time is meaningful for you. We are all masterful enough to know exactly what we are doing and to discern our next steps in life (even when we are not aware of our inherent wisdom).

Many of the tools provided in this publication are distinct. There is nothing wrong with other techniques or approaches. They have all been utilized because they work, at least to some degree and for some people. This publication contains additional tools so that you can have *even more* of what you want in your life.

The following introductory story is shared to provide a frame of reference for some of the concepts in this book.

After years of research—collecting case studies, conducting seminars, and recording insights, I began writing this book with a burst of excitement. Authors always write for themselves, and I was eager to achieve even more clarity by putting my thoughts and conclusions on paper. As the pile of rough drafts grew, my emotions began to shift from excitement to fear. What if I ended up feeling that the manuscript wasn't good enough? What if no one read the book?

I felt really vulnerable. Here I was writing a book about using painful emotions and experiences as resources, a subject that was as dear to my heart as any but my sweetheart, William. Completing this book would be one of the biggest challenges of my life because it led me through a series of growth experiences so that I could finally resolve for myself some of the same questions the book addresses.

The writing progressed, and preliminary feedback at seminars and talks at bookstores indicated that I should go ahead with the project. There were times when I wrote in circles and felt I knew nothing about life. I was in a key growth experience, described as a *funnel* in Chapter 16.

I wasn't ready to finish the book, and my procrastination was evident to me. I diverted myself into another career venture rather than allowing myself to be successful in the completion of this publication.

Periodically, I received telephone calls from seminar participants asking if the book was available. They wanted to buy a copy, and I had none. I couldn't seem to find time to finish it. Finally, William and I made a decision to isolate ourselves in a cabin for the winter so that I could complete this manuscript while he worked on other projects.

We chose a remote area that was inaccessible by standard vehicles during its long season of ice and snow. It could be accessed by four-wheel drive on endless miles of precarious washboard roads with frequent snowslides. There were fewer than 30 people within a five-hour drive from our home, and the region had no grocery store or gas station.

The area offered very few distractions from my work. I had placed myself in the enviable position of having the time and the location to write as much as I wanted to. It was up to me to provide the necessary focus and passion. There were no schedules to meet, and we had elected not to have a telephone, TV, or VCR.

Nature provided the finest entertainment in this beautiful mountain area with lots of fresh snow. There were gorgeous high mountain views, herds of elk, cross-country skiing right outside of our doorstep for several months of the year, and hiking to a lovely cascading river. There were even natural hot springs for breaks.

So how did I procrastinate? I became an ardent mountain cook! William didn't know I possessed any degree of culinary skill because I had never exhibited it before. It was further evidence that we can always find ways to delay our success just a little bit longer.

I also delayed completion by writing a frenzy of short stories and articles as the days on the calendar drifted by, one by one. I noticed myself allured by small community distractions. I asked myself, "Where am I off track? What am I not willing to see?" I was beginning to feel crazy. How could I complete a book about how to bring what we want into our lives by working with our feelings when I wasn't moving forward in my own life?

Yes, I was definitely feeling my emotions and consciously experiencing each day. New insights were flooding in, and my creativity level and my relationship with myself were constantly being enriched. However, I couldn't seem to discern the missing piece about why I wasn't completing the book. We were financially supported just enough to get by comfortably, but we were living in a simple rustic cabin and had given up a large pleasant home to take this step so that I could complete the project.

Yet my relationship was and is awesome. All of my life, I've wanted to love myself enough to be loved by another. (In the early days of my pain, I didn't know that's how it really works.) I had traversed in life from being successful and well-known in my field to the opposite polarity. (Chapter 6 fully explains the concept of polarities.) By age 25, I had completed my Ph.D. and was teaching at a university. At age 26, I was directing a national program headquartered at another university. In my early thirties, I directed national agencies, testified at Congressional hearings, authored research publications influencing legislation, brought home a sizable income, and owned an expensive 3,700 square foot home with a swimming pool. There was one significant catch. I had never experienced a loving relationship.

I divorced and lived the chapters in this book. Eventually, I developed self-love that was then reflected back to me by a mate.

So much did I cherish this relationship that I wasn't about to give it up for anything! That was the key to why I was procrastinating about making another major change in my life.

There are parts of all of us that fight our changing, no matter how much a modification will improve our lives. These elements are our Guardians, core components of our personalities that we gave birth to when we were young children. Our Guardians were designed to protect us—to keep us from fully experiencing life until we were big enough and strong enough to confront our major challenges. They shielded us from harm or social disapproval by reminding us (instilling fear) that we weren't powerful enough to do certain things.

Our Guardians became the parts of our identities that still fear that we are not powerful or deserving enough to have everything we want in our lives. Because we have fed them with our belief systems and developed defense mechanisms to support them, the Guardians became our masters instead of our servants. When we are unaware of their persistent and wily ways, they unduly influence us. We self-sabotage and push away the very things we say we want! Our Guardians fight to preserve the status quo in our lives, even when our circumstances feel painful to us. This allows them to function in comfort zones of familiarity and to feel in control of our lives. The Guardian is more fully described in Chapter 16.

My Guardian had experienced tremendous difficulty as William and I grew closer together. She kicked and screamed during the entire journey of our increasing intimacy. Having never experienced real love or a successful relationship before, there were many, many baby steps along my path. My Guardian repeatedly feared her death because I was changing. As a result, I waged many wars inside of myself.

Finally, my love for myself (that was reflected in my love for William) won the battles. My Guardian had no choice but to give up her fight regarding that particular issue. As described in Chapter 6, there really is a "bottom to the bottom" of our fear of giving and receiving love. Yet there is no ceiling to the highs of loving your mate or yourself.

Now the Guardian was using every iota of strength to resist this newest change in my life. Although William and I had both experienced worldly success before we met, during our lives together, our joy and focus had been our relationship. I knew that my previous success had been possible because I had focused 100% of my efforts in that direction. That had been my compensating strategy—a defense mechanism designed to offset my feelings of insecurity. I had so little self-love that no external love was reflected back to me.

My Guardian sat on my shoulder 24 hours a day, whispering softly and steadily in my ear that it was impossible to have external success and real love at the same time. Now that I had tasted the bliss of a genuine connection with the other part of myself named William, I knew that I would never give up my love, no matter what that meant.

Day after day, I watched the neighborhood children drive their snowmobiles around and around the same snow-covered field. I wondered why they didn't venture out of their habitual routines into other fields that were equally simple to travel. Finally, I understood that they were providing me an opportunity to see that I was spinning my wheels in my own known reality. My Guardian may have been crooning sweet nothings in my ear, but her hands were simultaneously applying pressure around my neck. She was choking me!

Once our thinking is clear because we have identified the mechanism that is holding us back, it spontaneously begins to transform. A distortion cannot stand to be perceived. When the fear surfaced in my body so that I could feel it, I understood. Neither William nor I had yet experienced the new *balance* of love and external success we were about to embark upon. I finally realized that I would have to give up another layer of being a "victim" in life, and my Guardian was frightened simply because this meant change. It was out of my comfort zone. Was I really ready to fling myself off yet another cliff into unfamiliar territory? Was I willing to let in more of my personal power and let go of an additional layer of blaming anyone or anything for the circumstances of my life?

Our love was so strong that we had happiness even if we had nothing else. It was obvious to me that I was self-sabotaging, instead of knowing that I could have love *and* success. I had been unconsciously saying, "I don't want success again, or I'll have to change my lifestyle. What would I possibly do if I had more money and additional choices in my life?"

I simply had to be willing to allow my reality to change. I was in one of the tightest parts of a funnel of personal growth, and my inner conflict was prohibiting me from moving forward with my life. My next step was to be willing to let in more of my power and to allow the changes that would occur as a result of having done so.

Life is a series of illusions. It is rarely about the surface reality. This external reality is simply a tool to push our buttons so that we will make some decision that will facilitate our continual change and growth in this journey called life. It became abundantly clear to me that I had been using every excuse possible not to put my focus on completion of this book and advance another step in my life. So I felt my panic, kept my eyes open, and moved through an additional phase of development.

One night, I knew I was within a few weeks of completing the manuscript. I was filled with relief and excitement, but the feeling in my belly told me that the Guardian hadn't yet finished fighting. I watched myself continuously changing a chapter, knowing that I could be moving a lot faster with the task but not judging my slow progress. My delay was serving some purpose. I just didn't yet know what it was.

I asked for the wisdom to be revealed to me and went on with my work. The next day, my dog, Sugar, and I left home for our usual morning outing in the snowy woods and mountains before beginning work. I thought we'd only be gone for 30-45 minutes and planned to be seriously editing chapters by mid-morning. I had forgotten that I had posed the question the night before in an attempt to understand my procrastination.

Another dog in the neighborhood joined us as we strolled across a meadow and up a winding trail into a mountain basin. It was about 20 degrees and the night before had been quite cold, so the ice and snow on the ground were easy for all three of us to negotiate. I was waking up more than thinking about anything in particular except that I was eager to make substantial progress editing the book on this day.

I let the dogs lead me instead of encouraging them in any specific direction. They began climbing up a long steep hill. I debated and then decided that I was willing to exert that much effort. The deep breathing that was required felt good, and I knew the exercise would fully wake me up.

After about a half hour of climbing, I decided I was ready to return home and get to work. I looked for an easy trail downhill because some of the pathways had so much snow covering fallen trees that it was easy to inadvertently place a foot in a "snowhole" and fall through several feet of false ground. Being in snow up to my hipline is fun, but it wouldn't have accelerated my trip home if I had waded in the fluffy white stuff on that morning, so I avoided the areas that would have contained the greatest number of invisible cavities.

My gaze began to be drawn across the hill rather than down, and I've learned to trust my instincts, especially in nature. So I trekked across the hill and then upward to the top of a ridge that I had never anticipated climbing. Some internal part of myself was beckoning me to experience something at the top of the ridge, so I obeyed, curious to discover the reason for the inner command. Time was moving on, and it was now clear to me that part of my real work on that day was in this snowy, wooded place. It had to be done before the editing. "So be it!" I said to myself, knowing that these innate nudges bring in a new piece of ourselves when we allow ourselves to follow them.

I followed my instincts with precision. My body was quite excited about something and wanted to express its delight with the new clarity that was about to surface. In response, I cried out, "Yes!" and then "Freedom!" I felt wonderful, even though I didn't yet consciously know what had transpired within my psyche. Both of the dogs backtracked to discern the reason for the excitement, provided encouragement, and then went about their business of investigating the new fragrances that nature shares each day.

A new level of awareness began to pour through my body as I wandered wherever I felt drawn to climb on the hillside. I was ready to do what I hadn't done before—to follow some unexplored path in life. I had been a successful author before, but something different was unfolding that I didn't yet consciously comprehend.

Attempting to figure it out would have confined it to my current understanding and impeded its progress. **The only requirement was to be open to the change and expansion that was already in process. When we fight change, change fights us.** My job was to follow my instincts and consciously participate in this flow of the river of life. I had been so afraid of owning my full power because of my mindset that change meant loss.

I felt my heart opening and my breath becoming fuller and deeper. I chose a sunny area at the top of the ridge and lay down so that I could fully experience the sensations in my body. The cold floor of the earth cared for me by providing air conditioning for my overheated body. I began to laugh and rolled over and sat up.

My heart was continuing to open, and tears were streaming down my face as I felt a profound sense of new freedom. I finally understood. My fear of being more fully who I am (owning my power) was because I was afraid of being lonely again. This was my Guardian speaking. In the past, when I had been quite successful in the world, I had not had a relationship with my Self, so I had been desperately lonely.

Each of us walks a different path in life. My particular journey involved leaving worldly success and my other comfort zones behind. It was only then that I gradually developed such a loving relationship with myself that this was reflected back to me externally by William. We both knew that I had been avoiding completing this book partly because I feared that it would alter our connection in some way. There was no objective basis for my fear of losing the relationship, but our Guardians fight change, no matter how much it will benefit our lives. The Guardians are quite happy with the status quo. It is all they know, and our stagnation allows them to feel in control.

William and I had discussed what we knew—*transitions are a continuous part of life, and they bring gain, not loss. I knew this intellectually, but the full wisdom hadn't yet been accepted by my body.* That was the piece that was being integrated this morning. The cellular structure of my body was rapidly reformulating because now it knew at the deepest levels that I wouldn't lose myself or my relationship if I allowed myself to be even more of who I really am.

The experience reminded me of a comment made by a dear friend, "The changes in our lives aren't about giving something

up. We just move from cube steak to châteaubria
to meatloaf!"

Our obsessions with security and our striving for perma...
contradict the very principles of life itself. Because our insecurities are deeply rooted in a lack of self-knowledge and self-confidence, we experience difficulty accepting change. Only when
we embrace it do we allow inner peace and personal sovereignty, the only true forms of security that exist.

The Tao Teh Ching eloquently sums up the principles of change:

> Those who want to conquer the world and make it con-
> form to their own desires will never have success, for the
> sovereignty of the world is a subtle thing. He who tries to
> shape it spoils it; he who tries to hold it, loses it.
>
> Hua-Ching Ni, 1995, *The Complete Works of Lao Tzu*

I was finally ready to let myself have what I wanted in life—a
nurturing and constantly growing relationship *and* financial success. A remarkable sense of freedom flowed through me, and
the two dogs came over to frolic wildly in the snow and contribute to the celebration.

I was now ready to descend and return to our cabin. As soon as
I turned to face the valley and had taken a few steps, my instincts said, "No, not yet." Evidently, there were more insights to
be revealed this morning. I pivoted to face the next ridge and
wondered if I would feel compelled to climb it. Waiting for inner
direction, I was reminded once again what a splendid teacher
nature is. I was still at the top of the first crest. As with most
summits, it was merely a plateau—an invitation to climb yet another peak that would provide an additional opportunity to advance in life.

There are so many mountains to climb in our lives, and all we
ever need to do is place one foot in front of the other. Unlike in
earlier years of my life when I was always seeking some endpoint, now I find it quite rewarding to spend time at the plateaus

ιd receive the clarity that is always available to us in those places.

Today the message was that I was finally ready to climb another mountain, and I had a choice about when to do so. The exhilaration of the knowledge that I would no longer hold myself back was followed by a flash of panic in my heart. I was afraid I hadn't turned the woodstove damper down, and chimney fires are always a possibility in cabins. What if my book burned? I had no backup disks, and the only hard copy was in the cabin. This was merely an old layer of fear, and I could smell its release in my body.

Mentally retracing my steps before leaving the cabin reassured me that I had taken the necessary precautions with the fire. My heart wasn't quite finished feeling the panic, so I stood still as it concluded this layer. After a couple of moments it was complete, and I was fully ready to proceed.

I didn't descend along the route I had climbed. I was hungry to know what was over the next ridge in life and honored that. The dogs reflected my desire to experience unexplored territory. They leaped down steep snowy banks with lighthearted abandon, as if they were young puppies. I followed, appreciating tree branches that graciously reached out, letting me know they were available to steady my progress through the steepest areas if I needed them.

We were heading in the opposite direction from the cabin into an unfamiliar area that I felt would loop back into the main canyon road that ran by our home. As I hadn't planned to be out long, I was unprepared for my growing thirst. Although I knew I could make it back to the cabin without water even if my perceptions of distance and time were distorted, a drink would be exceptionally sweet at this time.

We skirted a huge pile of fallen trees that I knew would contain masses of deceptive air pockets in the snow. Suddenly, I heard the most wonderful melody—liquid gold—the sweet flow of a natural spring just waiting to be discovered in this frozen jumble of hills, valleys, and fallen trees. My ears led me right to the source of the gush of water.

The spring was underground and completely surrounded by huge snowbanks, fallen trees, and gigantic icicles. Except for the sound of its music, it would have remained undetected. Its narrow entrance to the world was open, welcoming me to its nurturing flow. It wasn't until after soothing my parched throat that another level of awareness emerged. I realized that I had spontaneously received the answers to the question I had posed the night before concerning my self-sabotage. How powerful we all are! We get everything we ask for in life, as long as it is for our good, and we remain open to the message and the messenger.

Our life's events build upon themselves with ingenious and flawless precision. As you consider the story you have just read, use it as a mirror to reflect on the perfect unfolding of your own experiences. It may even assist you in recognizing a process you are currently going through. It will be an honor if it does.

EXERCISES

Questions and exercises are periodically inserted in this book to assist you in relating the content of the manuscript to your own life.

1. Record some of the changes that are emerging in your life.

2. What are your greatest fears about these changes?

3. Can you think of an example of how one step in your life led to the next, with flawless precision?

THREE

ALLOW THE CREATIVE POWERS WITHIN YOU TO EXPLODE WITH AN AWESOME FORCE

Our humanity would be a poor thing were it not for the divinity that stirs within us.

Francis Bacon

Break through to the other side.

Jim Morrison

As individuals, we are no longer satisfied to function at a survival level. We want to thrive. We want it all—love, satisfying work, health, supportive friendships, and wealth.

All of us have part of what we want in our lives. We also want even more. However, there is a component of each of us that does not yet believe that we can have it all. We don't have many role models to show us that we can have love *and* wealth as well as happiness at work *and* at home.

> Having what you want in your life requires only one thing—developing an excellent relationship with your Self.

EVERYTHING BEGINS WITH YOUR *SELF*

In truth, there is nothing outside of you *because your external world* (whether personal or business) *reflects your internal self.* It also magnifies your current circumstances so that you can see yourself clearly. Sometimes you can see your immediate past.

When those in my household are vibrant and alive, filled with joy and love, they reflect that part of me. When they are fearful or angry, I have an opportunity to see and express those feelings within myself.

When the people in my business life are procrastinating or frazzled, that is a reflection or magnification of my own ineffective functioning. It shows me the places where I am not willing to allow myself to be truly successful. When I am willing to function in a way that is more consistent with my true abilities, the commercial printer finishes my jobs early and impeccably. Unsolicited business and leads for work that I truly enjoy flow into my reality.

THERE IS NOTHING TO DO IN LIFE BUT WATCH OURSELVES CHANGE

Life is all about change and growth. We perch at the brink of one steep overhang after another and discover that we already know how to fly—or we teach ourselves in midair. After a brief time of savoring our new feat and integrating what we have learned, this experience is followed by yet another venture into an unexplored realm. An excellent relationship with our Self enables us to flow from the known to the unknown, over and over again. This is one of the most critical skills involved in our success.

The reasons that most adults seek assistance from others include the following:

Emotional:	grief, fear, anger, sense of loss, feeling powerless or out of control
Monetary:	financial crisis or desire for more money
Health:	crisis
Relationships:	painful or unfulfilling personal or professional relationships
Sexual:	lack of satisfaction

Legal:	difficulties
Habit:	use or abuse of tobacco, alcohol, or drugs; weight control; sexual addiction
Career:	loss of employment, desire for new challenges, need for skill development, difficult work relationships, problems with pay level or communication, need for assertiveness

Most of us seek assistance to *resolve a problem* instead of just because we want *even more* joy, love, health, or success. We haven't yet learned that we can realize all of our dreams.

To solve business problems, many people attend seminars or workshops, buy books, or take courses. Experts are available to share information on virtually every aspect of our working lives.

A smorgasbord of options is also available to deal with our personal stresses, including counseling, stress reduction techniques, expressive therapies, and spiritual practices. Most adults seek to meet their personal needs through other people, and relationships are their primary vehicle for accomplishing this.

Too often, "solutions" encourage dependency vs. self-sufficiency. Individuals go from one seminar, consultant, counselor, or book series to another. Frequently, those seeking assistance never learn that they are their own best resources. Many find that they are unable to wean themselves from external support systems or outside expertise. This is not bad. However, it's important to be conscious that we are seeking answers from someone outside of ourselves.

You already practice approaches that are useful, at least to some degree. The knowledge in this book provides a foundation so that your existing techniques will be even more effective. In addition, new strategies and perspectives are offered to facilitate your process.

THE APPROACHES IN THIS BOOK ARE UNIQUE

♦ Simplicity

This publication presents simple, unique tools that you can begin to use immediately to develop an excellent relationship with yourself. The techniques are easy to understand, and you can receive rapid results by using them. They have been comprehensively field-tested in seminars and other activities with clients. This document also contains extensive case study materials from private consultations.

Most of us have already graduated from a course taught in our society. It was contributed to America by the Puritans, although many other cultures espouse the same tenet. The course description is, "Life is difficult and must be endured. If we suffer long and well enough, we *may* be entitled to a joyful afterlife."

This book takes exactly the opposite approach. It is possible to obtain personal empowerment, insights, and joy from even the most difficult circumstances if we are open to the wisdom available in every experience in our lives.

♦ Polarities

This concept is an important cornerstone of this book because polarities are an essential tool for our personal empowerment. Polarities are the naturally occurring opposites in life such as happy/sad and self-hatred/self-love. The function of polarities in our lives is quite simple. As an example, after we feel fearful of a new challenge and consciously face it, we feel empowered.

Experiencing the polarities in life enables us to *thrive* vs. survive. Once we have fully experienced one side of a polarity (unpleasant feelings such as self-doubt or fear), we can fully experience the other side (pleasurable emotions such as self-confidence or empowerment). This concept is fully explored in chapter 6.

Most of us have already learned to feel unfulfilled, be unhappy, or to operate at an emotional survival level. (Henry David Thoreau said "most people lead lives of quiet desperation.") We have a choice to allow ourselves to be all that we truly are and to have what we want in our lives. All that is necessary is to have the desire for even more of our real selves. We just have to make an internal commitment to live consciously. We don't have to "be there." That way we don't miss the lifelong journey we are here to experience.

◆ Nothing to "Fix"

Contrary to what we have been taught, there is absolutely nothing wrong with our current circumstances. Life is a journey, and we are always where we are supposed to be, at any particular time. **When we understand that, we stop struggling, and our paths become much easier.** Neither is there anything wrong with your existing tools or approaches to life. You have been using them because they work, at least to some extent. This book describes *additional* tools to add to your existing toolbox.

Even if our present situations feel uncomfortable, they are the perfect ways for us to learn more about ourselves so that our next adventures can naturally unfold. Our stresses are essential to the process of change and are the ideal steppingstones so that we can achieve self-actualization. The tools presented herein provide clarity and reduce our resistance to life's experiences so that we can fully gain the value available from them. Therefore, individuals have discovered that using the methods in this book *spontaneously* alleviated situations in their lives that felt painful.

◆ Nothing to "Get Rid Of"

A key principle of this book is that there is nothing to get rid of. This includes emotions that we label as negative or perceive as painful and characteristics about ourselves that we judge as bad. It also includes past events in our lives. All of our previous experiences made us who we are today. When we attempt to deny or eliminate elements of our past, components of our personalities, or our emotions, we are in resistance. We are battling parts of our Selves. This creates energetic blockages in our bodies, and less energy is available to experience our lives.

This book advocates *experiencing* instead of attempting to let go of or get rid of our uncomfortable feelings. Most of us judge our anger, grief, depression, and fear so harshly. These emotions are actually very powerful tools for learning about ourselves and for becoming more whole and complete. The chapters that follow provide tools for expressing emotions in safe and constructive ways. The only way to let go of our emotions, past experiences, and "undesirable" personal characteristics is to embrace them, without judging them.

Most people do not allow themselves to fully experience their love, joy, and other sweet sensations. Sometimes this is because they feel they don't deserve to be loved or to experience true happiness. At other times, it is because of our misperceptions that we can only experience limited quantities of joy and bliss.

If the knowledge in these pages appeals to you, you will be able to fully use your past and present so that you can have what you want in your life. Past experiences that our society has defined as failures or hurtful will become catalytic. You will find that they are powerful tools to assist you in becoming whole and releasing the shame and blame that create your energetic blocks. A vast increase in self-love, personal empowerment, and a healthier body are by-products of not judging yourself and your experiences.

We love ourselves when we learn to accept all parts of ourselves. This includes the aspects that we love, hate, are afraid of, and empowered by. It involves embracing where we are victim as well as where we are perpetrator.

Struggle-free living requires *mining the gold in the darkness.* This concept is explained in detail in chapter 8. Eventually, we discover that we have mislabeled some experiences in our lives as dark. There truly is no such thing. Every incident in our lives is a tool for getting to know ourselves and growing to be all that we truly are. We can struggle with and resist our learning experiences, or we can simply consciously experience them, without judgment. It is all a matter of choice, and it is essential that we be aware as we make our choices.

◆ Emphasis on the Unknown

The principles in this book do not fit into existing categories. They are not associated with a specific religion, philosophical group, dogma, or belief system. They are not in conflict with, or in lieu of, any of these frameworks.

Labels and classifications can separate us from each other, and we are all more alike than different. The very process of labeling can perpetuate the deception that categories are pure, and this is very seldom true.

Categorical groups and divisions also limit us to our present knowledge. We have been taught from an early age to analyze, classify, and define our experiences via a linear thinking model. We have learned to interpret new events in ways that are consistent with our existing thinking patterns. Yet, regardless of how much we resist the forces of change, they flow through us, with or without our approval. A significant thrust of all of our lives is to grow beyond our comfort zones and identities.

Because we are always moving toward our next unknowns, the amount of time that we spend resting in any comfort zone decreases. Each time we trust and leap from the familiar to the unexplored, we have an opportunity to do so consciously or unconsciously—with more or less fear. We have an opportunity to be aware of fears that arise and to allow ourselves to experience rather than repress them.

Our choice is to flow with the river of life or to resist and fight the new. This book can assist you with your choices by making each step of your journey a more conscious one.

♦ Beyond Judgment

Although many readers will naturally change some of their life patterns or habits while reading this book or afterward, the intent of this work is to increase our awareness of our existing behaviors and patterns. It is not designed to induce change. Change occurs naturally. *Trying* to alter any behavior sets up resistance to what currently exists, and resistance *inhibits* change. By simply *noticing* our current behaviors and *not judging them*, they will shift as needed, on their own.

♦ Self-Love and Empowerment Are Not Taught

Self-love and empowerment are *natural by-products* of using the tenets explained in this book. Self-love and empowerment happen spontaneously when we live consciously, without judging ourselves or our experiences. They happen automatically when we have the courage to feel and express our emotions. That is the primary reason that this book does not focus on teaching or learning self-love or empowerment per sè.

When we experience our emotions in any given moment, life takes care of itself. As the concept of polarities stresses, only by honoring our existing feelings of fear, sadness, or self-loathing, can we fully participate in their counterparts, including self-confidence, joy, and self-love.

♦ Truth vs. Self-Manipulation

We all deserve the truth. Although our society teaches us to fear being "too honest" or vulnerable about our emotions and desires, it is time to move beyond the days of hype and lies. In truth, we find that each time we are more *real* (honest and vulnerable), we give permission to those around us to also be who they are.

If you need to present a mask to others, just do so consciously. Never lie to yourself. Gradually you won't need the facade anymore.

The polarities of life must be felt, or we will continue to re-create opportunities to experience our painful emotions. Living with polarities involves accepting our current circumstances and feeling what we truly feel. Thus, we do not create resistance to what exists. We liberate and energize ourselves, and this allows us to bring what we want into our lives. We no longer feel that we have to motivate ourselves or manipulate our behaviors and our lives.

When we have productivity blocks, we notice them rather than judging them. Then, they change on their own, when the time is right, because we haven't been fighting the realities of our lives. We no longer berate ourselves, wondering how to change what is "off track." Instead, we recognize that whatever exists is serving a purpose.

Everything in life contains wisdom for us if we are open to it. By trusting our internal wisdom and thus giving up control (our *attempts* to control our lives), we eventually find that we are always the directors and projectionists of our own lives. Our internal guidance is always present, even when we feel the most out of control. Sometimes, we just can't comprehend the wisdom at the time. I know that if I do not receive what I think I want, it is because part of me is aware of something that is better for me at this particular time. It's usually something that I had never dreamed of! You've heard the expression, "Let God unfold the magic!"

When I've reflected on my career and relationship goals that didn't evolve, I've been filled with gratitude. The profession that emerged was so much more rewarding than what I was attempting to create. That was also true with relationships. Once I didn't try to establish an external connection, I developed a much stronger bond with myself. Eventually, I enjoyed a relationship that far surpassed any expectations I would have had, *without trying to develop anything.* Since we consciously create from our known reality, our attempts to program our future generally result in more of what we have experienced in the past.

◆ Beyond Blame and Victimization

This book is not about assigning blame, and the ideals espoused can assist individuals to cease playing the role of victim. Self-responsibility is a major tenet of this publication. Accepting personal responsibility and not judging ourselves are primary sources of our freedom. Using the principles discussed herein can rapidly accelerate our emancipation. *We* are responsible for our lives, and *we* are also totally responsible for our reactions to everything that happens in them. Blaming others or situations in our lives inhibits our personal growth. If we don't judge our experiences, we have no reason to blame anything or anyone for our circumstances, and this is truly liberating.

◆ Focus on Self

Self-focus is healthy. Only if I love myself do I have anything to offer others. It is solely when I love myself that I have any compassion for others because I treat them only as well as I treat myself. When I am impatient with myself, I judge others as being slow or inept. When I am patient and nurturing with myself, I spend very little effort focused on the speed or efficiency of someone else. I understand that they are doing what is right for them at this particular time.

When I acknowledge my emotions and gain the wisdom they bring to me, I have compassion for my employees and others who are experiencing painful situations. On the other hand, when I am in judgment of my own lethargy about working on one of the first days of spring, I judge my employees and co-workers as lazy. When I am willing to be where I am, (e.g., not quite ready to leave an unpleasant job situation because I want to cling to a security blanket,) I am compassionate with my friend who complains about being in an unrewarding relationship but is not ready to leave it.

There have been times when I have respected my desire to "hang out in this place just a little longer" because I was the happiest I had ever been. My thoughts were, "How could it get any better?" or "I don't want a new challenge yet." I allowed myself to savor the present, without judgment, knowing it would change in its own perfect time. Because of this, I could easily and compassionately deal with an associate's resistance to leaving his comfort zone and moving on to his next challenge.

A common expression in the personal growth field is "we can't change anyone but ourselves." In truth, we can't even change ourselves! The more we refuse to embrace who we are in a given moment, the more this staunch soldier stands squarely in front of us, clamoring for our attention and defending our right to learn from every part of our lives. The only way we alter ourselves is by being aware and not judging who we are in this moment. We transform *automatically* when we live consciously and do not resist what exists. There is no need to *try* to change *anything* or *anyone* because everything in our lives serves a purpose. Insights and new understandings are available in every situation, no matter how subtle they may be.

A miracle occurs when I cease my attempts to change people, circumstances, or events. I give myself the utmost freedom because I discover that my only "job" is to live my life, to be fully me in every situation, and to learn as much as possible. When I live my own life in a 100 percent conscious manner and focus on being all that I truly am, I don't try to alter anything or anyone. I am never disappointed when I do not expect a specific reaction from others. I am *self*-validating. Yet, wherever I go, things change. My associates improve their performance just as I do.

Our relationship with our Selves is reflected in our interactions with others because we are remarkable mirrors for one another. We are all affected by changes in those around us because we are so connected. (Concepts in the field of quantum physics explain these linkages.)

WHAT TO EXPECT FROM THIS BOOK

This book offers practical knowledge and tools that can increase your self-sufficiency, your success, and your relationships. Simple principles are described that can *spontaneously* enhance your self-love and empowerment. Consistently using the tools in the book will offer you opportunities to:

♦ Gain passion for your Self and thus for other areas of your life, including your work and your associations with other individuals.

♦ Improve your relationships in all areas of your life because they will reflect your enhanced connection with yourself.

♦ Own your full power instead of buying into our society's addiction to powerlessness.

♦ Take healthy risks so that you can more easily move beyond your comfort zones.

♦ Experience the exhilarating freedom of self-responsibility.

♦ Use your emotions as *resources*.

♦ Practice *the affluence of Self-influence.*

♦ Experience greater energy.

There are extensive descriptions of tools in the chapters that follow, as well as actual case study materials. Questions and exercises are provided to enhance your ability to practice the principles presented. Occasionally, stories are included in the text to illustrate key concepts. The book may "strike a nerve" as you move conceptually and experientially out of your current comfort zones. However, you wouldn't be reading these pages if you weren't seeking a greater understanding of how to mine the gold in the darkness of life. Since there is no way to escape change in life, consider allowing yourself to be even more open to new ideas and perspectives.

UNLEASH YOUR NATURAL CREATIVE POWERS

Note that you have selected a book subtitled *Making the Most of Your Emotions*, because our emotions are major creative forces in our lives. This is why they are our best friends, even when we shun their company. I believe that they are the most overlooked and the most profound personal development tools that exist. They are more powerful and faster than conscious creating techniques such as affirmations and visualizations.

Similar to exhausted parents who unconditionally love their children even when they test every boundary, our emotions are natural tools and are always available to us. We just have to be aware that they are our friends rather than unwelcome relatives.

When we take advantage of these essential and ever-available raw materials, we no longer attempt to manipulate our consciousness. By simply learning to trust ourselves and our experiences, without judging either, we cease our self-defeating battles to change what exists.

Life wasn't meant to be a struggle, in spite of the fact that the people on this planet have made toil and strife an art form. There is so much more to life than fear and pain, although they are essential to our evolution. The tools in this book will assist you in finding the wisdom and therefore the joy in the trials that we all face. You can discover that the experiences you have judged as the most negative have the potential of producing the most joy and the greatest personal expansion.

Our emotions are a key topic of concern because we are learning to stop *attempting* to avoid our pain and instead are developing passion for fully experiencing life. We are discovering that our painful feelings and experiences—even those that we have judged most harshly and have tried the most to suppress—can be some of our most valuable resources for bringing what we want into our lives. Learning to safely and constructively express our feelings will eliminate many of our physical diseases. It will also inhibit the crime and violence around us. (Techniques for expressing emotions are discussed in later chapters.)

Although we will inevitably encounter personal challenges, we can understand that they are simply continuous, natural growth processes. They require us to change internally so that we can experience success in business and relationships.

Most of our battles are internal and self-imposed. They usually occur because we are unwilling to acknowledge our capabilities and fully experience our lives. By living consciously and not judging ourselves and our experiences, we can have fun, while taking seriously all of the learning experiences involved in this incredible playground we call life.

EXERCISE

1. We are always involved in a creative process because our intentions are *powerful*. Record what you would like to accomplish by reading this book.

FOUR

WHY ARE WE SO AFRAID OF OUR EMOTIONS?

What we resist, persists!
Virginia Satir

WE HAVE BEEN TAUGHT TO VALUE OUR INTELLECT AND TO DEVALUE OUR EMOTIONS

Our social programming has taught us that our intellectual knowledge and our linear thinking processes are superior to our emotional experiences. There is a *reason* that we have right and left brain capacity. Both are essential to fully experience life. We need both for self-actualization, lasting happiness, and a sense of fulfillment.

WE HAVE MISTAKENLY ASSUMED THAT WE CAN SOLVE PROBLEMS BY INVOLVING ONLY OUR INTELLECT

Particularly in the Western world, we have been taught that emotions are a time-consuming nuisance that can slow down our useful, rational problem-solving processes. We have been taught that emotions can lead us off course and distract us from our *real* work. This is the basis for expressions such as the following:

> "Use your head, not your heart."
> "Think, don't feel."
> "Don't get distracted by irrationality."

Being a product-oriented society, it is difficult for many of us to perceive that a process has real benefits. Feeling our fears and crying our tears consumes time that has never been programmed into a flowchart. We are busy people! How can we defend taking the time to feel emotions and release blocked physical energy and intellectual capacity? "I'll deal with it later," is our common response to our feelings when they beckon us to experience more richness in our lives, more personal freedom.

The belief that we can meet our challenges by involving only our intellect is the basis for many programs based on goal setting and positive thinking. Most affirmation, visualization, and Neuro-Linguistic Programming (NLP) procedures deal only with an intellectual concept. Because we are holistic beings, such programs provide useful tools but not complete answers.

WE WOULD RATHER *ANALYZE AND TALK* ABOUT OUR EMOTIONS THAN *EXPERIENCE* THEM

We are more comfortable *talking* about our feelings than *experiencing* them. When we finally give ourselves permission to know that we have emotions, most of us focus on analyzing, defining, labeling, and categorizing them. Our intellects are more familiar than our hearts; we feel safer.

Trying to figure out why we are the way we are (why we feel the way we do) is more comfortable than simply feeling how we feel, without judgment. Analyzing and labeling emotions and defining *why* we feel the way we do inhibits the natural flow of our lives. It delays the process of being real with ourselves, of simply feeling. It also limits our understandings to our known realities—what we have already experienced.

We have assumed that we feel only one end of a polarity at a time, such as fear about a new adventure. In truth, we frequently feel both ends of the polarity simultaneously. For example, when we are faced with a new challenge, we usually feel fear and excitement at the same time. *By focusing on analyzing and labeling our feelings, we miss subtleties and clues that are leading us directly into our next steps in life.*

WE ARE NOT FAMILIAR WITH THE LEVEL OF SENSATION AND PASSION FOR OURSELVES THAT OUR EMOTIONS PROVIDE TO US

Simply feeling how we feel *in our bodies* is one of the greatest ways to achieve our freedom. Physical sensations keep us connected to who we really are. They are our individual language. Each of us sometimes has a special warm sensation in our heart, butterflies in our stomach, weak legs, or an inner voice sending us messages. When we ignore our personal signals about life, we miss vital clues about our best plans of action, and we shut down elements of ourselves. We set ourselves up for disease because we foster resistance in our physical systems. Social programming has encouraged us to focus on *achieving* and to ignore our bodies' needs to freely move themselves in full expression of life.

Our feelings are the essence of fully experiencing life; essential tools for our passionate journeys to achieve our freedom, and we are not familiar with that level of expressiveness. We have suppressed it because we have not felt safe allowing ourselves to be that alive.

WE LACK ROLE MODELS AND SUPPORT SYSTEMS

As we make field trips into the strange world of feeling our emotions, most of us begin to experience them and then retreat back into our intellects. We do not have social support systems available to us as *emotional* beings although we are validated for being intelligent creatures who can psycho*analyze* themselves. Although we have access to advocates if we say we are victims who have been wronged by others, **there are few support systems for us as powerful individuals, totally responsible for our lives and our actions**. There are precious few role models providing examples of our being the dynamic creators that we really are.

We lack role models who can show us by example that safely and constructively feeling our emotions brings freedom to us as individuals and empowerment to all of society. Feeling the level of sensation in our bodies that accompanies our full emotional release also makes us more fully present, more able to function as all that we truly are. Yet *that level of sensation is not understood or supported in our society.*

SOME HAVE PROPOSED THAT WE WORK ONLY WITH LINEAR PROCESSES

While a number of valuable insights and tools have come from an emphasis on linear (intellectual) processes, they are an incomplete answer to our search for wholeness. Yes, thoughts create your reality. It is also true that our emotions, based on our subconscious material, either support or sabotage our thoughts and our creative processes. We undermine our efforts to create what we think we want in our lives so that we can provide ourselves additional opportunities to feel our repressed emotions. We will continue to do this until we have resolved whatever emotional material prohibits us from knowing that we deserve to have what we want in our lives.

We are multifaceted beings, composed of intellectual, emotional, physical, and spiritual properties. Any tool that is not holistically based will not have lasting results. In fact, techniques that are not balanced can actually backfire. This includes programs that overemphasize working with our intellects because they can ignore or attempt to negate what exists inside of us at the emotional or physical levels. Such denial creates internal barricades that inhibit our progress.

Our subconscious minds are much too brilliant to believe what is not true, including unrealistic "wish list" affirmations. We may rebel by digging ourselves into deeper pits of denial. The resistance covers up our denial, and a vicious cycle ensues. Emotions surface because of the inconsistencies between the real world and our affirmations. It is wise to be conscious of this possibility if you choose to do affirmations or visualizations. (This concept is discussed in depth in chapter 10.)

WE FEAR SOCIAL DISAPPROVAL IF WE FEEL OUR EMOTIONS

Beginning in childhood, we were taught not to feel. (Chapter 16 describes how we created our Guardians to help us live in society.) We learned quickly that many adults usually viewed our emotions as a nuisance. When we are in the company of *others who are uncomfortable with their feelings* or for some other reason don't want us to feel our emotions, we hear expressions like those listed below.

♦ "Now, you know we don't have time for that stuff."

♦ "Don't feel that way."

♦ "You'll get over it."

♦ "Get a grip!"

♦ "You don't *really* feel that way."

♦ "Big girls don't cry."

♦ "Big boys don't cry."

♦ "Now, don't be an ugly boy/girl."

♦ "Dry those tears and put a smile on your face."

♦ "When you act right, I will let you _____."

If the individuals making these statements were to state the truth, they would say:

♦ "I'm uncomfortable with your feeling that way."

• "Your feelings mirror to me how I feel, and I'm unwilling to experience that right now."

• "I don't have time or the compassion to be around you right now."

♦ "I'm withdrawing from you."

• "I'm pushing you away . . . I'm withdrawing from you . . . The only way I know how to do this is to tell you that you are wrong."

- "I'll reject you because I think I have to prove that you are wrong. This is the only way I will be able to justify that my position on this issue is OK."
♦ "I'm telling you not to feel the way you feel."
  - "I don't want you to be honest about your feelings or to experience your truth because I am not able to do so."

When we have experiences like these, we learn:

♦ I can't feel this way, or I will make someone else uncomfortable.

♦ People won't like me if I am not nice, sweet, happy, compassionate, and fun to be around . . . or *however* they expect me to be.

If we think that we need the approval of such individuals, we abide by unwritten or written social codes regarding our emotions. Just like them, we are *not* real and vulnerable. We are untrue to ourselves. *We sacrifice part of ourselves in an attempt to gain social approval. This is how we perpetuate the social myth.*

The truth is:

♦ The more I give myself permission to feel how I feel, instead of betraying my Self, the more I love myself.

♦ The more I am willing to be real, honest, and vulnerable, the more I give others permission to be so.

This is true even though breaking social mores and traditions can be difficult for those who are in the forefront of social change. Sometimes we plant seeds and are not always understood. By the time the seeds sprout, we may not even be around. We may never be understood or even remembered. That is why *it is so important that we do these actions for ourselves, not with the goal of changing anyone or anything.*

Remember that the job of our Guardians is to stop us from fully experiencing our emotions. As we decide to open up to our full potential, our Guardians will still try to protect us from genuinely feeling. They will fight for their lives and their jobs until we have become comfortable with emotions and have given our Guardians new job descriptions.

WE HAVE JUDGED EMOTIONAL EXPRESSION AS A WEAKNESS

Social programming has taught us to project an image, to have an identity. The "appropriate identity" we mastered incorporated attributes that helped us be successful and fit into society. Such characteristics included appearing self-confident, intelligent, competent, and "together" (in control of our emotions). Generally, we adapted to this programming quite well. We learned to be controlled. Most of us are not passionate about ourselves, our lives, or other individuals.

Men, in particular, have been conditioned not to publicly feel their emotions. In fact, emotional expression has been viewed as a weakness of women. To ensure opportunities for promotion, many professional women have attempted to emulate businessmen. Therefore, some career women have tended to be less emotional than nonprofessional women. (Of course, this is an illusion when their feelings are actually being repressed.)

WE HAVE LABELED OUR EMOTIONS AS POSITIVE AND NEGATIVE

Our society has labeled feelings such as those listed below as negative, painful, or uncomfortable.

Anger	Rage	Depression	Grief	Hatred
Insecurity	Sadness	Fear	Terror	Jealousy
Guilt	Lust	Numbness	Self-hatred	Loneliness

Most people are uncomfortable when others fully express emotions such as those listed above. Contrary to social perceptions, there is no reason to try to eradicate these feelings. They serve us quite well. Properly used, they empower us, enhance our awareness, and are sometimes essential to warn us of danger. They indicate our next areas of growth and assist us in understanding our current comfort zones. What I fear the most clearly signals to me where my next challenge will be. Fear and anger are powerful motivators for action. They are tools for learning more about ourselves and becoming more fully alive.

Guilt, lust, hatred, and other feelings listed above are not negative; they are simply a part of *each* of us. Owning this will eventually stop the cycles of violence in ourselves and in all of society because we will experience, versus repress, our emotions. When we welcome or accept all of our emotions, we embrace all of ourselves.

Neither our emotions nor our thoughts are bad or good. Judging our thoughts and feelings is self-defeating. *We* judge them, and then *we* suffer because of our labels. They are just part of us, and labeling them creates shame, guilt, and separation. The separation is both within ourselves and from others in society. Internally, we attempt to segment ourselves, classifying parts of ourselves as good and parts as bad. We feel separate from others in society who we feel are better than or not as good as we are. Eventually, we feel inferior to some individuals and less powerful than others. This spirals into "powerlessness" and feeling like a victim.

Sometimes we choose to resist our feelings because we want others to like us or approve of us. In such cases, it is important to be conscious that we are slicing off entire components of ourselves, freezing the natural flow of our powers. We are sacrificing essential elements within us, and this is self-betrayal and abandonment. When we make such a choice, we need to know that we have consciously decided to reduce our passion for our Selves.

WE HAVE BELIEVED A MYTH THAT SELF-ACTUALIZED OR SPIRITUALLY DEVELOPED INDIVIDUALS DON'T EXPERIENCE "NEGATIVE" EMOTIONS

During the last three decades, our society has become increasingly interested in spiritual development. A myth has been promulgated that spiritually developed individuals don't experience "negative emotions." Many individuals have sought to learn meditation specifically as a vehicle to let go of negative feelings.

There are no negative emotions. There are only emotions, and they are here to be experienced, in safe and constructive ways. (Chapter 20 provides examples of techniques.) If I do not judge my sadness, hatred, fear, and anger, I am acknowledging all parts of myself. I simply express these feelings in safe and constructive ways so that I have even more energy available to be all that I truly am. *It is not necessary for me to process my emotions endlessly, to try to get rid of them, or to change them. It is only necessary to consciously experience them.*

If I attempt to deny that I am jealous of my friend, I am not being truthful, and I prohibit us from being as close as we would be otherwise. If I simply tell her I am jealous of her, there are no secrets between us. I discover that my feelings are only of concern to me. She has no judgment of them. My willingness to directly and honestly communicate with her cleared the issue for me, and this allowed my full energy to be available rather than using part of it to suppress or battle my feelings.

If I tell my spouse that I feel insecure about our relationship, I open myself up to work on this challenge. If I attempt to conceal it, I am using part of my energy to hide something from him, and I am not fully present when we are together. We are all interconnected, and he is too smart not to sense that I am holding back part of myself from our relationship. Because of my fear and insecurity, I am keeping us separated when it is more important than ever for us to connect so that I can advance through my insecurity. Whether or not I choose to stay in this relationship, my self-doubt is an essential tool to build additional self-confidence and self-love. The "darkness" of my insecurity is gold waiting to be mined; it is the doorway to my next level of self-actualization.

Spiritual development is not about wearing white robes and halos. It is not about separation from others by attempting to feel better than they are (because we feel insecure). It is about connecting so deeply with our Selves that we experience wholeness of body, mind, and spirit. This accomplishment is not an endpoint or an achievement level. It is an endless series of growth progressions. As we take each step, we become even more united with our Selves. We therefore develop healthy relationships with other parts of ourselves, other individuals, our mirrors. We love ourselves enough that we become our own cheerleaders. Eventually, we are willing to be totally who we are without regard to the social context or the specific individuals present.

If I deny my fear, I do not deal with it. If I do not feel and express my anger or sadness, I am using a portion of my energy to repress valid pieces of myself. I have arrested essential components of my vitality that would otherwise fuel my passion for my whole self—my passion for living. There is nothing to "move beyond."

Many individuals have learned relaxation therapies and meditation techniques in an attempt to control their emotions. They are inadvertently turning their emotions in on themselves, cutting off some of their life forces. The truth is that there is nothing to control. All feelings can be safely and constructively expressed.

If I hold my anger or rage in check, sooner or later, I may explode and be as capable of violent behavior, of being totally out of control, as the most reprehensible murderer. There is no place for the rage to go if I control it. It will continue to ferment in my system until it finally discharges in a way that will hurt others or myself.

If I consistently misuse a meditation or relaxation technique to deny my feelings, I create an energetic constriction in my body. This will form a perfect habitat for birthing disease (dis-ease). "Stuffing" anything is never a long-term solution. Buried feelings never die. They chisel away at our psyches, diligently searching for opportunities to be acknowledged so that we can allow ourselves to become whole.

We need to be *in* our bodies versus trying to meditate our problems away. When we are not consciously experiencing our bodies, we don't have access to the clues that they provide. These include those knots in our stomachs telling us we are afraid, the lumps in our throats when we want to cry and don't, and the rush of blood to our faces because we are enraged or embarrassed. We neglect our physical systems and make them vulnerable to illness when we don't express ourselves. Our bodies are always talking to us; all we have to do is listen.

Meditation and relaxation techniques are highly valuable. They can be used for self-discovery. They should not be misused just because we have learned to hide from ourselves and our feelings.

WE ARE AFRAID THAT OUR EMOTIONS WILL CONTROL US

Our work ethic is one of the strongest in the world, and most of us think that we cannot feel our emotions *and* be productive. The intangible results of fully experiencing our Selves are greater than any tangible items that could be produced. Acknowledging our feelings enhances our functioning so that we can create virtually anything we desire because our feelings unleash energy—the raw ingredient we need for better physical, intellectual, and emotional performance.

Our Guardians, originally thought forms designed to protect us until we were big and strong enough to meet life's challenges, have developed lives of their own. They encourage our misperceptions that we are incapable or powerless, and they thrive on controlling our behaviors.

Here are some of the "tapes" that our Guardians sometimes play when we begin to express our emotions:

- ♦ "It's not safe."
- ♦ "You won't be able to stop (crying, etc.) if you start."
- ♦ "Your emotions will control you, and you'll embarrass yourself and others."
- ♦ "You will lose your friends and loved ones. They won't want to be around you because you will make them feel uncomfortable."
- ♦ "You don't have time for this stuff."

The following dialogue emerged from a case study of a situation in which I served as a consultant. The client was just beginning to allow her emotions to flow.

Client: "I feel so out of control. Ever since I started allowing myself to feel, I haven't been as productive as I used to be. I'm afraid I'll never be the way I was again."

Consultant: "You're right! You're not functioning as a robot anymore. And you never will again."

Client: "But, I'm afraid I won't get anything done this way."

Consultant: "You'll have a more balanced life now. You won't *just* work. You'll take time to *live,* because you won't always be working so that you can hide from yourself. You'll also produce more in shorter periods of time because your mind will be clearer."

Outcome: After a transition phase of a few months, the client did indeed far surpass her previous work productivity (and income). She chose to decrease the number of her public speaking engagements so that she had more time to be with herself instead of always being on the road. She published one nonfiction book and one novel in a year's time—double her normal productivity.

Each time we feel our emotions deeply, especially when we are dropping our old armoring, we gain more self-trust. A domino theory often activates. We feel our emotions and become vulnerable and real with ourselves, and many individuals around us also feel more comfortable doing so.

Sometimes we silence or numb ourselves out of concern that others will be uncomfortable if we deeply feel and express ourselves. This is "caretaking," which means placing someone else's comfort before their wholeness. What right have we to make a determination regarding what is in their best interests, to inadvertently inhibit their next steps by being dishonest? The only valid solution is to be ourselves and to allow them to experience whatever emotions arise in their lives.

The irony is that we fear being controlled if we experience more of our Selves (our emotions).

In reality, the control is of us and by us! Our Guardians are directing our functioning even though they are merely tired, outmoded components of our identities.

The scenario can be viewed as quite comical. We fear being controlled by our emotions, and they are just part of us.

We fear change simply because we are afraid to be as capable as we really are.

We haven't yet totally understood that there really are safe ways and places to experience our emotions.

WE FEAR WHAT WE WILL DISCOVER WHEN WE EXPERIENCE OURSELVES MORE DEEPLY

We fear that we will discover parts of ourselves that we would identify as ugly. Surprisingly enough, we also fear that we will identify components of ourselves that are truly beautiful and powerful. These discoveries will dramatically alter our self-images. Such transformation entails lifting our veils of self-deception, and our Guardians do not like exposure, change, or adventure. They have an investment in maintaining our current self-images, instead of uncovering the truth and risking change. Thus, we feel a need to see ourselves as right or wrong, as victims or tyrants, or as good or bad. These inaccurate perceptions are based on the concept of duality. They contribute to our suffering rather than to our wholeness.

SELF-DISCOVERY

Will you leave me if you see who I really am?
Will you leave me if I *don't* allow you to see who I really am?

How passionately real and alive I am,
how raw and connected to myself,
the parts of me that hate and those that love,
the victim and the tyrant who live within this body.
The parts of me that fear and the parts that know
I am totally awesome.

Will you leave me if you see who I really am?
Or will you leave me if I am not fully present when I am with you?

It really is of no consequence as I reflect upon it,
for I am who I am,
and I am giving myself no choice
but to wholly discover
the fullness of my being.
So be it.

MANY PEOPLE ARE AFRAID OF PASSIONATE EMOTIONS

Over the centuries, passionate emotions have been used to destroy as well as to create, to kill as well as to birth. This is because, as a civilization, we haven't yet learned to safely and constructively express ourselves. Thus, many people are afraid of intense emotions of any kind. When they consider going deeply into themselves, whether to feel love, fear, joy, or anger, they become afraid of being hurt. They fear being out of control and hurting others or themselves.

Our Puritan heritage provided us rigid rules for emotional expression. It's OK to cry a little, but to cry a lot, we need an excuse, so we go to a sad movie or a funeral. Be careful there, because it's a public arena, and you don't want to be accused of being overly sensitive or holding onto your grief. It's OK to laugh, but not too loudly. It's best not to become angry to begin with, but if you do, don't be direct about how you feel with the person involved. It's not nice. If the pressure builds within you and you explode outwardly (e.g., violent behavior) or inwardly (e.g., depression or a suicide attempt), please be discreet.

Long-term solutions require a different approach. You can sign up for a simple course described below:

SELF-ACCEPTANCE 101
This course includes the following laboratory experiences:

♦ Embracing/loving all parts of yourself

♦ Being *real*, honest, and vulnerable with yourself first and then with others

The students who diligently tune into SELF-ACCEPTANCE 101 discover that they are *automatically* enrolled in and graduate from SELF-LOVE 202 and PERSONAL EMPOWERMENT 203. All they have to do is show up for the course. This means being conscious as they live each day.

These courses are the key to creating what you want in life. Those who sign up for SELF-ACCEPTANCE 101 are fully committed to self-discovery. They are eager to be *all* of who they really are, and they have the courage to self-actualize.

Instead, most of us unconsciously graduate from courses that are more consistent with our social programming. The titles of some of these courses include:

♦ Letting Go of Fear
♦ Controlling Negative Emotions
♦ Managing Anger
♦ Getting Rid of Depression
♦ Be Happy Now!

The objectives of these courses include getting rid of or letting go of emotions that our society has labeled as negative or painful. The paradox is that *attempting to get rid of emotions is one of the biggest obstacles to our success.* The more we try to eradicate or block our awareness of our feelings, the more resistance we build to what exists. This resistance is manifested in our physical bodies and emotions. Our intellectual processes also become less clear because our denial drains our vital forces.

Anger and fear are the two most harshly judged emotions in our society. These natural and valuable feelings have been labeled dangerous, evil, and inferior personal qualities. "Cures" for them abound and are promulgated by books, tapes, seminars, and counseling designed to control our emotions and to get rid of them.

Anger and fear are not going to go away. This is why control of anger and other emotions does not work on a long-term basis. There *are* safe and constructive ways to express anger. (Chapter 20 provides examples.) The emotions we have labeled as negative are part of who we are, and they serve a critical role, assisting us in being more alive and real.

Our emotions can't hurt us in any way. Experiencing them can only help us tremendously. Anger is passion for our Selves. Anger is also fear, just as it is the other side of love. When we express our anger, we allow ourselves to be more fully open to life. Our hearts reopen. All emotions must be felt. Polarities must be experienced.

Whenever I avoid feeling my emotions, I bar part of myself from being present, so I am not fully alive. I forfeit life force that would otherwise be available to me. If one-fourth of my energy is consumed by repressed feelings and one-fourth of my energy is being used to dam these emotions, I am operating with only one-half of my energy. No wonder we're so tired!

Feeling buried emotions allows me to decide if I want to continue to create experiences in my life that result in those feelings. When I avoid feeling suppressed emotions, I *unconsciously* re-create opportunities to feel them. If I don't feel what is already present, I can't fully develop the empowerment and self-love that would come from doing so. My choice is to either shut down and not feel what is there, or to travel through the desert so that I can enjoy the oasis.

There is nothing to fix, move beyond, or get rid of. Everything in life is simply a tool so that we can be more of who we really are.

WE HAVE ALSO BEEN CONDITIONED NOT TO FULLY FEEL OUR JOY

We have been told:

♦ Pride comes before a fall.

♦ When things are going "too well," a flock of birds will fly over us and drop greetings on top of our heads.

♦ We should feel guilty if things are easier for us than for others.

♦ Other people won't like us if we are happier than they are.

Therefore, many of us cheat ourselves out of fully feeling some of our most joyful occasions. We push away love and happiness as an expensive and distorted insurance policy designed to avoid our anticipated pain.

It's upside down and backward! Happiness can be quite contagious. Remember the times you have laughed uncontrollably, and most individuals around you have begun laughing, too, even though they didn't know why?

WE HAVE DEVELOPED *JOY ALARMS*

When we are in unfamiliar arenas, such as extended periods of bliss, we are out of our comfort zones. Our Guardians crank up their stereos and play tapes like the following:

TAPE 1:

> "This is fun. I feel really good!"

> "Is this OK? I've never felt like this before."

"It's scary. If I let myself feel this good, I won't be able to live without it, and I know life can't be this way all of the time."

"It's not safe to feel this good. You know what always happens when things are like this. Something goes wrong."

"There must be a problem here."

"I know what it is . . . "

NOTE: At this time, our Guardians create reasons for us to feel worried or to project our past pain into our future. Once we allow this, we sigh with relief as we slither back into the pits of our comfort zones.

"I knew it couldn't last. Oh well, back to the *real* world."

Our Guardians relax. Things are back to normal. The Guardians are in control again.

TAPE 2:

"I feel great!"

"Is it OK to be happy? Other people aren't. Maybe it isn't fair for me to be happy when they're not."

"I feel guilty having such a good time when not everyone else has it this good."

"Will it ever be any better for them? I just can't be happy until I know they are."

The Guardians relax and croon to themselves, *"Ahhhhhh . . . control is such bliss. I love job security."*

It's important to understand several things here. First of all, this is an "apples and oranges" argument. The starving children of the world don't know if we clean our plates or if we leave food on them so that we don't distend our stuffed bellies and cause them to ache. Anytime we descend from our highs to be on the same emotional level as someone we sympathize with, we've done them and ourselves a distinct disservice. Happiness and well-being are just as contagious as gloom and doom. The choice is ours. Rather than judge that it is bad for a person around us to feel dejected, we can recognize that unhappiness is serving that individual. It is allowing them the possibility of consciously experiencing one end of a polarity and then mining the gold in their darkness. Instead of prostituting ourselves, we can hold the focus by living what we believe and feeling our joy. Then others can also move into the space we're enjoying, if they choose to do so.

QUESTION

1. What are your fears concerning feeling and expressing your emotions?

2. Have you ever denied your feelings and become ill?

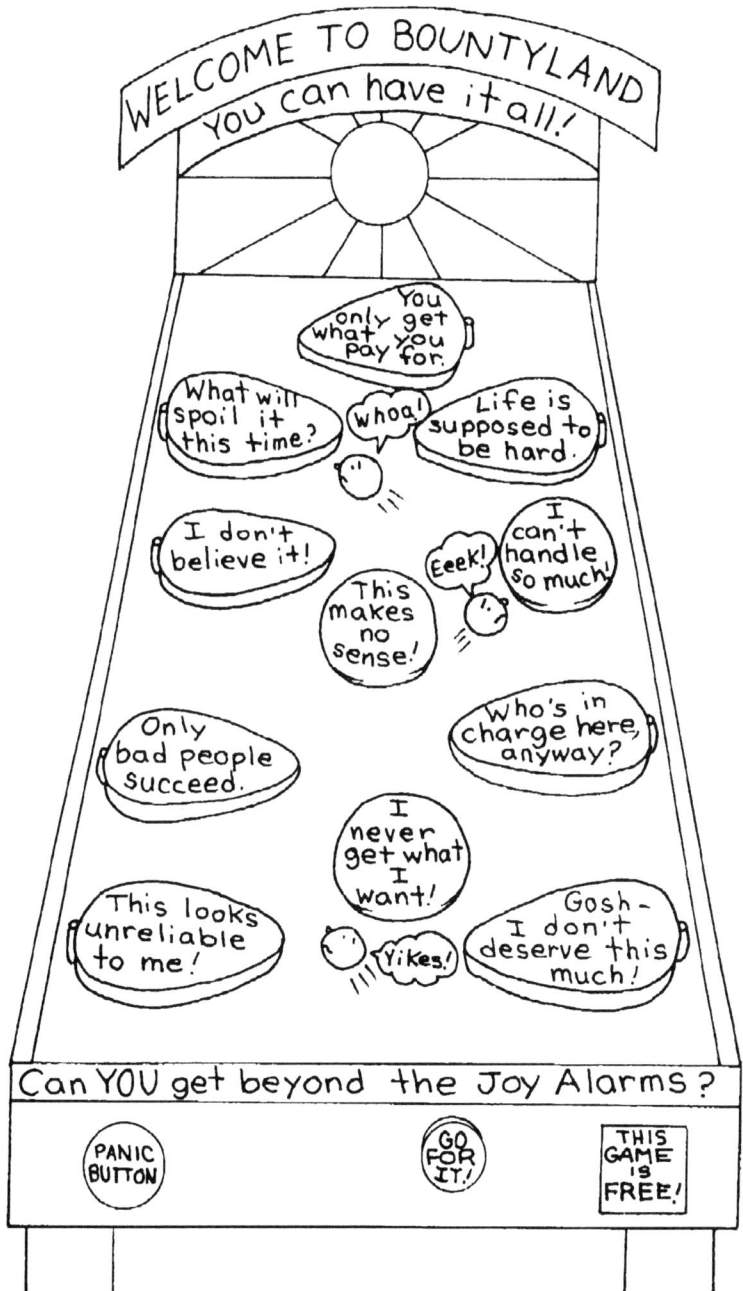

FIVE

FROM BLAME AND JUDGMENT TO EMPOWERMENT

Life has taught me to think,
but thinking has not taught me to live.
Alexander Herzen
19th Century
international
journalist

Sleep no more.
William Shakespeare

GOOD MORNING, AND WELCOME TO MORE OF THE SAME

Our alarm goes off and we awaken to the 7:00 a.m. news broadcast.

Here are today's updates:

Regarding the latest string of convenience store burglaries, three men in face masks have now robbed eight chain stores in the greater metro area. There were no deaths reported, although there were several injuries. Police state that there are no suspects at this time.

An oil spill from a ship coming into the harbor was reported at 5:46 a.m. this morning. Details are not available, but all volunteer groups have been summoned for cleanup duty as the area affected is more than one mile wide. The spill has now been contained, but there is an above normal level of concern because spring nesting has already begun in the area. Stay tuned for an update during the next hour's broadcast.

The man who terrorized and held hostage 57 workers in the County Convention Center for 16 hours beginning yesterday afternoon has now been booked in the county jail without bail. The hostages were released at 6:12 this morning when the terrorist was captured. Although most of the hostages were not physically harmed, eight people were admitted to County Memorial Hospital for treatment. As we reported yesterday, one man died from a heart attack during the ordeal, and his identity has not been announced. Police also have not released the identity of the suspect, but there is reportedly a connection between the bombing last week of the County Memorial Office Building and yesterday's terrorist attack.

The County Convention Center is expected to reopen by noon today. Two major events were temporarily placed on hold yesterday when the center was closed due to the attack. The events are now back on today's calendar. The regional Ethics in Business Conference will proceed on time. The National Symposium on Child Abuse was delayed and will now begin at noon today. Those registered to attend may call the County Convention Center for additional details. That number is 642-8801.

Clear skies today and HOT! Thunderstorms tomorrow.

Stay tuned for a complete weather report, immediately after this brief announcement.

WE SAY WE WANT MORE AND BETTER

Most of today's approaches to our personal, business, and social problems aren't working. Record numbers of individuals are seeking counseling and are engaged in self-help groups. The abuse, violence, crime, and pollution that have existed since the beginning of civilization are now being exposed.

A higher proportion of individuals than ever before want to understand the deeper meanings of their existence. They search for their purpose in life. They want to understand and deal with their personal growth issues. Even those who are already successful in their personal and business affairs want *even more* enjoyment and satisfaction.

Social changes are also being reflected in today's business world. The list below, comparing some of the hot topics in business seminars in the '80s and '90s illustrates this point:

IN THE '80s:	IN THE '90s:
Sales	Values and ethics
Time management	Belief systems, integrity
Stress management	Personal growth issues
Quality control	Total quality management (TQM)
Excellence	Moving beyond excellence

During seminars I've conducted during the last few years, I've asked participants from all walks of life to delineate what they want even more of. The topics most frequently listed are itemized below.

Love	Health	Money	Success	Friendships
Play	Joy	Motivation	Empowerment	Productivity
Time	Awareness	Understanding	Community	Wisdom

WE REFUSE TO OWN OUR POWER

As the preceding list clearly illustrates, we are seeking to experience more of the aspects of ourselves that we value. A parallel social trend is particularly disturbing. At the same time that we say we desire additional personal growth and empowerment, most individuals look outside of themselves for solutions to their problems.

Owning our full power is difficult for most of us because it involves taking personal responsibility for our lives. How easy it is for us to ask the government to protect us by issuing more regulations that dictate how we are to live our lives. How many times each month is there a call for more regulations to provide censorship, to tell us how to raise our children, to determine what we can buy, and so forth? It is so easy to ask the government to curtail our constitutional rights instead of taking personal responsibility for solving our own problems. How simple would it be for us to unintentionally slip into some of the characteristics of a totalitarian society? Because of this, I find it necessary to ask myself two basic questions:

♦ What will it solve for me to give my power away and ask someone else to "do it for me" or to resolve my problems?

♦ What will I cheat myself out of if I give away my responsibility (my power)?

Through my journey in life, I have dealt with what I called low self-esteem, evidenced by characteristics such as workaholism, perfectionism, over-achieving, and seeking external approval. My low self-esteem could have been indicated by characteristics such as underachievement, dropping out, acting a-socially, or substance abuse.

Over the years, I tried many types of empowerment techniques ranging from assertiveness training to expressive therapies. It finally became apparent that, for me, there really is no such thing as low self-esteem. There is only the refusal to own my full power.

WHAT HINDERS OUR SELF-ACTUALIZATION?

♦   *Self-judgment*

Judging ourselves as inadequate creates turmoil inside of us that blocks our personal development. It guarantees that we will continue to go around and around the wheel of life in a vicious cycle. The cycle involves trying to fix ourselves and criticizing others because we disapprove of ourselves.

Of course, we are our own worst critics. We are all walking around rating and downgrading ourselves—partly because we fear that others are evaluating us. Most people are so busy degrading themselves that they don't have the time, focus, or energy available to judge us. Those who do are avoiding feeling their own self-judgment, so they disapprove of us. Take note when you aren't finding fault with yourself how few people have any opinion of you at all.

Pause a moment to consider how ludicrous it really is that we judge ourselves. We are only responsible to ourselves. We are not experiencing life to please anyone else. The purpose of life is to learn and grow. How can I achieve anything if I don't take risks and expand beyond my comfort zones? This naturally entails making what we have considered to be mistakes. Failures are essential to our success. As the Japanese proverb states, "Fall down seven times; stand up eight."

Consider how preposterous it is to wonder so often what others think of our appearances and our actions. Where do we draw the limit? If we don't ask others to grade us when we conduct our most intimate personal affairs, why do we expect or allow them to do so when we are in public?

♦ Not experiencing our emotions

Emotion is "energy in motion," an energizing force within us. When we feel our emotions, we have the purity of a baby. Babies laugh and then cry, laugh and then cry, without judgment. Emotions are just part of their lives, and living is what babies do. They have not been programmed to avoid their feelings.

When we repress our emotions, we curb our zest for life. We toss away one of our most valuable tools for flourishing, versus simply staying afloat, when we feel overwhelmed by the waves of the sea of life. We lie to ourselves about how we really feel. There is a direct correlation between repressed emotions and crime, physical diseases, substance abuse, child abuse, domestic violence, and other social problems.

♦ Not owning our power

Owning our power means consciously making decisions and choices that affect our lives. When we do not own our power, we expect someone else to take care of us or solve our problems. We then blame those individuals or events that occur for the conditions in our lives.

One of the greatest inhibitors to our self-actualization is that we simply do not want to be as powerful as we truly are. We don't want to be fully responsible for our lives, even though there is no way that we can make a mistake. Life is like a continuous experience on trapeze bars. We always either catch the bar or it swings back around for us to try again. If we were ever to fall, a big surprise would await us. There would be a giant, fully reinforced net waiting to catch and cradle us until we were ready to once again venture from the net to acknowledge more of our capabilities.

♦   *Judging our experiences*

The roads to our pain are paved with our judgments and expectations. When we judge our experiences, there is usually someone (ourselves or another person) whom we choose to blame for our situations. Judging our experiences creates a civil war in our psyches because we are resisting our circumstances. This precludes our ability to remain open to receive the wisdom available from them.

IN TRUTH:

> ♦ There is nothing to fix. Every experience in our lives serves a purpose.
>
> ♦ It is time to own our power and to acknowledge our capabilities.
>
> ♦ There is nothing to do but to feel our emotions and not judge them.

The strategies in this document will empower you to deal with the self-doubt and fears that automatically rear their heads when we approach challenging new endeavors. Remember, your fear is an awesome *source* of new power.

WHY IS IT SO FRIGHTENING FOR MOST OF US TO BE AS POWERFUL AS WE REALLY ARE?

The American media promulgates victimhood, and most people in our society are addicted to "playing victim." Why? It is easier for us to blame others than to take responsibility for our own growth and learning. Whether we blame the traffic for making us late or blame another person for inflicting a psychological wound, we all play victim.

The paradox and the illusions here are quite fascinating. We all have astonishing capabilities. Yet, as a society, we are addicted to feeling powerless. Why are we so afraid to feel and be as capable as we are? Is it because we have incorrectly defined power?

Webster's New World Dictionary (10th ed.) defines power as the ability to do or act, vigor, strength, influence, and authority. All of these qualities are internal attributes. Even "authority" must be an intrinsic characteristic. As evidence of that, witness those who are promoted to positions of authority and cannot maintain them because they do not feel worthy or are not effective.

Our society has promoted the illusion that being a powerful person means having power over others. This refers to external authority, such as a person in a certain position who controls or manipulates people so that they will do something that they wouldn't otherwise do.

It is not true that one person must be disempowered for another to be fully empowered. It is the *insecure* person who feels the need to dominate others and attempts to disempower them.

Such a person portrays society's distorted image of power. In truth, this is a person who *feels powerless*. The most powerful individuals I know express their power by being vulnerable. They are so *self*-secure that they are real and honest with themselves and with others. They are true to themselves. They do not need to prove themselves or their abilities to others, nor do they make personal choices designed to gain external approval. They may not always be liked by others, but they are generally respected by them. Frequently, they are not identified in our society as powerful individuals. Many have such soft qualities of real power that they are never noticed or understood by mainstream society.

Genuine power is an innate quality. It embodies tenderness, compassion, and sensitivity, as well as the ability to be firm and tenacious. It includes the ability to be who we really are, no matter who is in our presence. Compare this to "power over" which involves a facade of power that comes from feeling inadequate; in such a case our self-doubts cause us to demean others or demand that they succumb to our point of view.

Once we understand how powerful we really are, we know that our next step is to accept full personal responsibility for our lives. All of our social training has been antithetical to this concept. Our society, including the news media, glorifies playing victim.

I was once director of a national rural development organization. A reporter with one of the major news networks sought my assistance. He flew from New York to the West Coast to meet with me and also to interview the mother of a rural child who had been raped and killed. After we had met his agenda, half a day was available before his plane departed for the East Coast. I asked him if he would visit a program we were conducting in a local school system. It involved middle school children who had been sexually and physically abused. We were conducting research on specific techniques with which the children who had been abused could empower themselves. The results of the program were excellent, and we had significant data to substantiate this claim. Our office staff wanted the reporter to broadcast the results so that more children could benefit from the techniques that worked.

He was as impressed with my naiveté as I was with his refusal to visit the program and interview the staff and some of the participants. He finally leveled with me, saying, "The networks don't cover good news. What sells is victim, sex, and violence—not what works. We simply give the American people what they want."

In essence, yes. In truth, no. As William Randolph Hearst proved beyond a shadow of a doubt with the initiation of the Spanish-American war, the media are extraordinarily influential. The news and entertainment networks program society much more than we program them, and we have been conditioned to play victim.

> Accepting total responsibility for our lives is a challenge for most of us. It is much easier to feel inadequate than to be as magnificent as we truly are.

It is easier to join a self-help group and to commiserate with others who also feel impotent than it is to be self-responsible. Although I don't judge the time and energy I spent doing this, I do remember having a lucid realization one day that I was surrounded with mirrors of others who were still blaming the past. It struck me that I was the only person who could put my life in forward motion, no matter how frightened I was of that task.

> Once we are more aware of our power, we require ourselves to be more conscious, more consistently awake and aware. It is a hefty responsibility and one of the greatest joys in life.

PARADIGM SHIFT

The fact that you are reading this indicates that you are interested in stretching your comfort zones. Understanding a paradigm shift that is occurring in our society will assist you as you exit your current reality and move into your next level of experiencing life.

There is an old paradigm in our society that consists of principles such as blaming others for our lives and our circumstances. We all operate in this paradigm some of the time. When we do, we aren't accepting personal responsibility for ourselves, our situations, or our feelings.

We are cheating ourselves out of the incredible freedom that emerges when we acknowledge our choices in life and consciously make decisions. When we don't trust ourselves to make a decision, knowing that all of our actions inevitably just lead to another learning experience, we stand paralyzed at another crossroad in life. We freeze action and blame someone or something else for our lack of progress.

We don't really lose anything because that's impossible. However, we "create time," which makes it seem like we lost something. We invent other opportunities to go around the wheel again, instead of going forward with our lives.

> When we blame others, we give away our power. We indirectly or unconsciously ask others for permission to live a certain way. We are inadvertently saying that we are incapable of making our own decisions and choices.

In the Old Paradigm, we also depend on others to comfort, heal, and entertain us. We blame others because they don't fit our pictures of how they should perform in our lives. They should be happy, encourage us, love us, etc. The list is endless. In short, it's someone else's responsibility to "make our day."

The truth is that those who surround us are the individuals who resonate with us, and they are our mirrors. They show us what we don't always want to see about ourselves. How many times have we shunned one human mirror, only to walk down the street and come face to face with another individual displaying the same characteristics? How many times have we left one relationship only to create another with the same challenges?

Our civilization is now moving into a new paradigm where we take responsibility for our own lives. The New Paradigm empowers us and gives us tremendous freedom of choice in our lives. It also stretches our comfort zones because we are not used to acknowledging how capable we are. We sometimes find ourselves engaged in skirmishes in our inner combat zones.

Our egos fight our changing, even when change is for our benefit. Our known realities are challenged because we are used to discomfort, and we have learned how to act when in pain. We find ourselves experiencing "approach-avoidance." (Our behaviors are inconsistent—we both approach and avoid allowing ourselves to have what we have said we desire.)

On the other hand, self-responsibility results in personal freedom, and that is accompanied by feelings of bliss. Most of us have conditioned ourselves to accept occasional bouts of joy or bliss, but it threatens our egos to invite them as permanent guests in our psyches. It sets off *joy alarms*, and we become anxious. Sometimes we re-create pain so that we can dive back into our comfort zones!

The following pages contrast the Old and New Paradigms.

THE OLD PARADIGM
(The framework in which most of us function)

♦ We live in a *Victim Mentality*.

♦ We prefer to blame others for our circumstances.

♦ We judge our feelings as positive or negative. We want to avoid our painful feelings, but they are part of who we are. Thus, we are always battling ourselves (and therefore each other).

♦ We use most of our energy to repress and deny our feelings and experiences.

♦ We rely on elements and people outside of ourselves to comfort, heal, entertain, and empower us.

♦ We endure life and feel isolated from ourselves and each other.

Old Paradigm

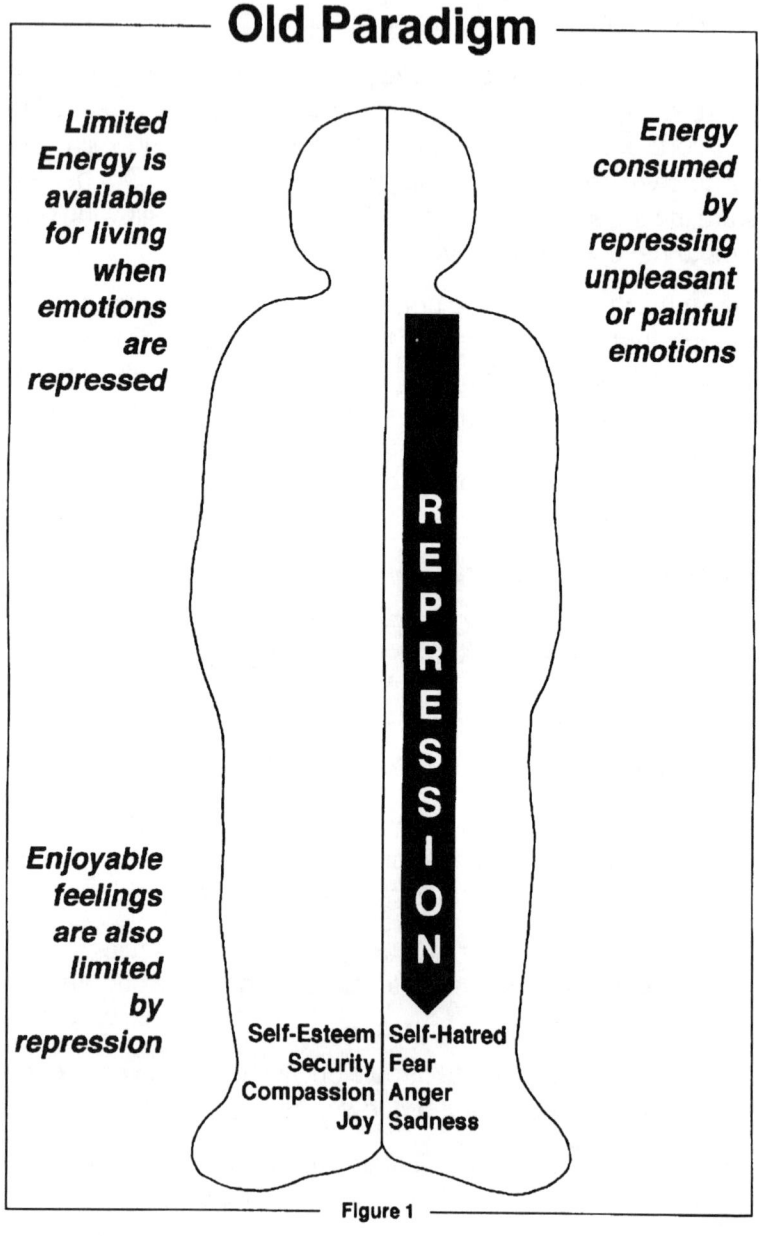

Limited
Energy is
available
for living
when
emotions
are
repressed

Energy
consumed
by
repressing
unpleasant
or painful
emotions

R
E
P
R
E
S
S
I
O
N

Enjoyable
feelings
are also
limited
by
repression

Self-Esteem	Self-Hatred
Security	Fear
Compassion	Anger
Joy	Sadness

Figure 1

In the Old Paradigm, our judgments of our experiences or feelings as negative or positive create self-perpetuating cycles. We repeat our painful experiences because we keep trying to justify our evaluations of them as negative. We attempt to eradicate our unpleasant feelings or experiences. We either do not express our feelings (we stuff them) or we express them in ways that are not safe to ourselves or others. Examples include being numb to life (the walking dead), withdrawing from others instead of solving our problems, covert passive-aggressive actions, and hiding our problems in drugs or alcohol. As the pattern continues, we may engage in violence, substance abuse, suicide attempts, anorexia/bulimia, or other self-abuse.

These behaviors result from our inaccurate perceptions. Some of us fear anger because we believe its natural consequence is violence. We may think grief culminates in the destruction of our open hearts. Many people assume that fear automatically results in shame or running away from a situation or person.

In the Old Paradigm, we cheat ourselves out of experiencing the present. We live in the past or the future because we haven't resolved the issues from our past. We feel victimized by other people or life's circumstances. If we are using half of our energy to live in the past, only half of it is available to function in the present. We incorrectly assume that our earlier experiences will automatically be extrapolated into the future.

We allow the past to continue to pull at us like an expanded rubber band, and we are afraid that the band will snap at any moment, causing unbearable pain. If we don't spend some time with our suppressed feelings, we remain half of a person because we don't accept these emotions as parts of ourselves. It is essential to process our old issues, whatever they are. The secret is that it is not a life-shattering process to visit with our feelings. All that is required is to feel our repressed emotions. When we do so, the past and the old feelings of hurt become *just experiences.*

In the Old Paradigm, we think that we must fix or change ourselves. We over-analyze how our personalities and characteristics emerged. We may spend years trying to decide if our insecurities or our fears of intimacy originated because of abuse or neglect. We label ourselves as victims because we assume someone or something else is responsible for who we are in the present. It is important to feel the emotions that are inside of us, particularly those that have been trapped or suppressed in our bodies. It is also important to advance to our next levels of Self as soon as the time is right for us, and each of us knows that precise time.

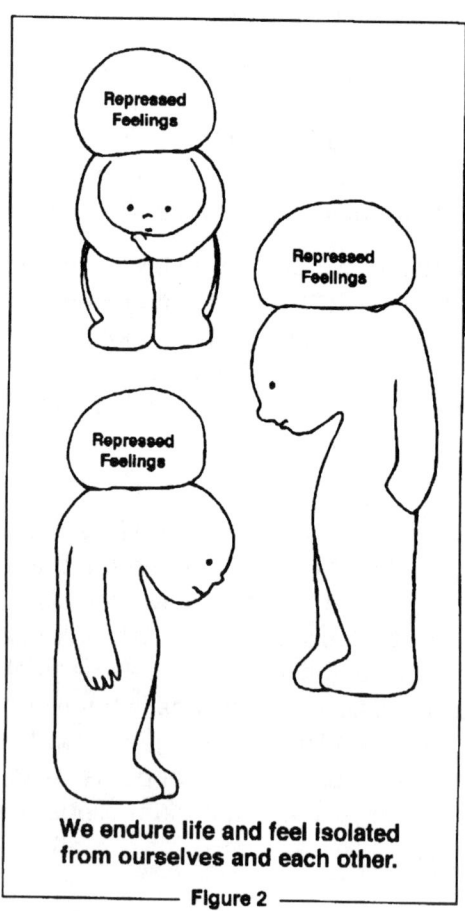

We endure life and feel isolated
from ourselves and each other.

Figure 2

THE NEW PARADIGM
(What we are working toward)

◆ We live in a creative mentality.

◆ We choose to take responsibility for the realities of our lives.

◆ We allow ourselves to feel and express all of our feelings, and we know how to do this in safe and constructive ways.

◆ This energizes us and allows us the freedom to be the powerful beings that we are.

◆ We know how to comfort, heal, entertain, and empower ourselves.

◆ We know we each have the choice to be as whole, real, and alive as we are willing to be.

◆ We welcome life. We feel connected to ourselves and to each other.

◆ We look forward to the next moment in our lives while fully experiencing the present.

In the New Paradigm, we understand that all experiences in life are purposeful. We know that pain is just a wake-up call and that we label experiences as painful simply because we wish they were different. Once we integrate the wisdom from an experience that feels unpleasant or painful, there is no pain.

We don't feel a need to fix or change ourselves because we no longer resist or deny who we are. Because we don't judge ourselves, we accept all of our characteristics. Owning our individual attributes, instead of disputing who we are, brings our freedom right to our doorstep.

This means that we have our full energy available to us; we are whole instead of half. We have the highest levels of self-respect because we are self-responsible. Therefore, self-love and self-trust continue to blossom in our lives.

We have moved beyond blaming others because we have recognized that all of us on this planet are still in school. Everyone is learning by experiencing life, even though some people are more consciously involved in the process than others. Once we recognize that all of us are doing our best given our state of maturation, we feel a deep sense of relief.

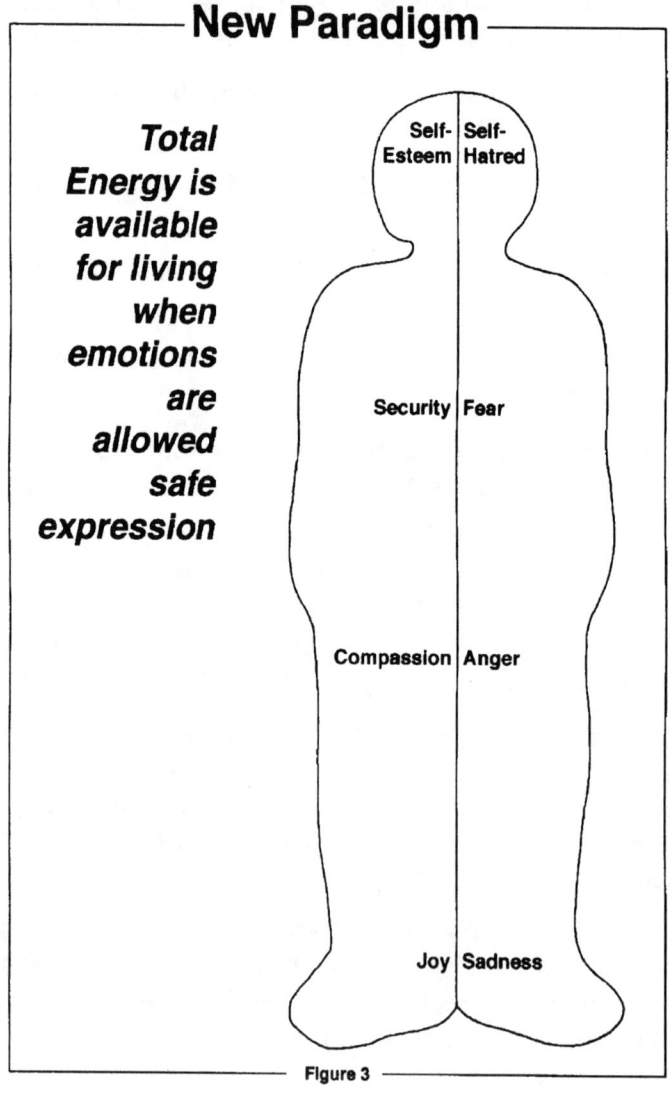

New Paradigm

Total Energy is available for living when emotions are allowed safe expression

Self-Esteem | Self-Hatred

Security | Fear

Compassion | Anger

Joy | Sadness

Figure 3

We have learned the value of experiencing polarities. We know that when we allow ourselves to feel the unpleasant side of a polarity, its opposite will immediately follow. So we embrace, or at least accept, our uncomfortable feelings.

We feel our fears and continue to move forward in our lives. We know we have an option to celebrate when we feel our fears and self-doubts because every time we shake hands with "Fear," "Personal Power" walks up and asks for our other hand. The twins travel together. This is the beauty of polarities.

We are willing to feel all of our emotions, no matter what they may be, because we have learned that they enrich our lives and empower us. We feel and express our emotions in ways that are safe to ourselves and others. We are honest, real, and vulnerable. This automatically gives other people permission to be who they are. Thus, the mirrors surrounding us are individuals who are also consciously growing.

We deal with "Insecurity" and "Fear" by owning them. They don't threaten us because they are just a component of all of us. Neither do we adopt them as core identities; we simply acknowledge and feel them. As a result, their traveling companions, "Personal Power" and "Self-Confidence," automatically become more visible parts of us.

We fully use our past, so it no longer controls our lives. It has become the catalyst that moves us right into the core of ourselves so that we can take a good look at ourselves and gain valuable insights and understandings. All of a sudden, the experiences we previously labeled as painful have lost their emotional charges. They have become *just experiences* that we learned from. The energy that was bound up in repression or judgment is now available for use. It was released as pure neutral energy, and it burst into a profound sense of personal freedom and empowerment.

Because of our courage and our understandings of life, we have now allowed ourselves to fully live each moment as it occurs. We no longer live in the future by wishing it were now. Neither do we extrapolate our past into events that are approaching. We have provided ourselves the freedom of a newborn infant kicking its legs, waving its arms, and announcing, "Stand back, world. This is now, and I am fully here!"

Neither paradigm is better than the other. They are simply different, and there is nothing right or wrong with either one. Each brings different results and feelings, and fully experiencing the Old Paradigm is the only way to fully experience the New. (Chapter 6 described the concept of polarities.)

Both paradigms offer wisdom for all of us, and they are not in competition with one another. The Old Paradigm is based on fear, and the foundation for the New Paradigm is self-love. Sometimes we choose one and sometimes the other. Insights and clarity emerge when we consciously choose one or the other and do not judge our decisions or ourselves for making specific choices.

The Old Paradigm brought me tremendous gifts. It was essential to fully experience it before participating in the New Paradigm. Because I know how to be and feel like a victim and come out the other side, I have the ability to stand with one foot in both worlds and speak from that place. I have felt both ends of the polarity.

I know how to come beyond the pain because I have done it. There are two options I know. One is pain, and the other is wisdom. Both are acceptable, and both serve a purpose. The critical variables in making our decisions are choice and timing.

We feel victimized as long as we need to, and that serves a valuable purpose in our personal growth cycles. Each steppingstone in our lives is essential, and it is important not to judge any of them. *We will experience any phase as long as it has insights and clarity to offer us.*

COMPARISON OF THE TWO PARADIGMS

Old Paradigm	New Paradigm
Live in a victim mentality.	Live in a creative mentality.
Attempt to get rid of our past.	Fully *use* our past to empower ourselves.
Blame others for our circumstances.	Take responsibility for our realities.
Judge our feelings as positive or negative. Attempt to avoid feeling painful or unpleasant emotions.	Feel and express our emotions in safe and constructive ways, without judging them as positive or negative.

Old Paradigm	New Paradigm
Use most of our energy to repress and deny our feelings and experiences.	Our self-expression energizes us and provides us freedom to be the powerful beings that we truly are.
Rely on others to comfort, heal, entertain, and empower us.	Comfort, heal, entertain, and empower ourselves.
Endure versus enjoy life.	Welcome life and know we have the choice to be as whole, real, and alive as we are willing to be.
Feel isolated from ourselves and each other.	Feel connected to ourselves and to each other.

It is useful to be aware of the two paradigms and to notice when we are functioning in each of them. If my personal identity is "victim," I am unable to become all that I can be. I will blame others and avoid accepting personal responsibility. When I know that I am accountable for my own happiness, I can always choose whether to accept that responsibility or blame others when I am unhappy. That's personal freedom!

> Where we focus our attention reflects our self-images.
> When I feel like a victim, I continue to re-create perpetrators in my life to validate my perception.

It doesn't really matter how I learned to feel powerless or victimized. What does matter is that, when I am ready, I focus my attention on feeling my emotions and moving through my growth cycle so that I can also feel the joy in the other ends of the polarities.

It is my birthright to learn self-love and self-trust, if I choose to. Conscious growth felt more difficult at first than being a victim. I found that I had an addiction to powerlessness instead of accepting total responsibility for my life and circumstances. If our personal growth processes are our focus, our lives become exciting cycles of self-discovery, even during the parts that we perceive as painful. After a while, we comprehend that everything in our lives is based on choice, and we become more excited about rediscovering all parts of ourselves. Our relationship with our Selves bursts with self-love and self-trust, and that is mirrored back to us by our external relationships.

As illustrated below, conscious choices made without self-judgment initiate a self-perpetuating process that facilitates self-trust and self-love. If our focus, intentions, and passion are to fully live and experience joy, we can mine the gold in the darkness of *any* of life's experiences. Every event in our lives is a tool to get to know ourselves and to grow to be the best that we can be. We can struggle with our learning experiences or not. Life is filled with one choice after another.

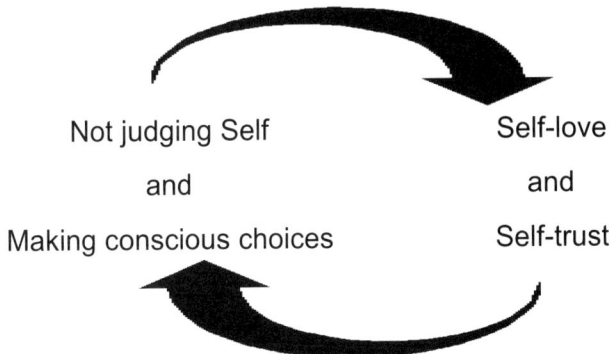

Not judging Self

and

Making conscious choices

Self-love

and

Self-trust

The self-perpetuating process of self-trust and self-love
that ensues when we make conscious choices
without self-judgment

Figure 4

It becomes clear that we are not trying to eradicate anything that exists in our lives. *Anger, fear, and other emotions are our power.* They are access points to learn more about ourselves

so that we can more fully live. The
only way to let go of any emotions
or experiences is to embrace them,
without judgment.

Instead of getting rid of our past,
we can fully *use* it. We can open
ourselves to our past pain, and it is
guaranteed to be a catalyst so that
we become more whole by releasing the blocks within ourselves. The
creative energies within us will explode with an awesome force that
will bring what we *want* into our
lives.

GRADUATING FROM VICTIM 101

Learning to take self-responsibility and move from victimhood
into personal freedom is a major process in life, so we might as
well enjoy the journey. All we really have to do is be conscious
and observe our approach-avoidance without judging ourselves.
We continue to refine the lessons and the learning which take
place as our lives progress.

At first, we feel victimized without perceiving our roles in setting
up the situations. As we become more conscious, we comprehend our performances more clearly and easily. We also recognize when we take things personally that have nothing to do
with us. We aren't loving other individuals enough to allow them
to be where they are in their lives without our interference. We
don't always understand that they need the freedom to make
"mistakes" and grow.

Graduating from Victim 101 involves a sequence of events and
realizations. Most of us blame others quite unconsciously, at
first. Then we consciously watch ourselves not being self-responsible. Next, we watch our approach-avoidance and recognize the areas where we are simply afraid to be as powerful as

we are. We understand how we are hanging onto old patterns and our identities of "powerless." We feel our fear of losing that worn-out badge. It is familiar to us, and we know how to function within the tightly constricted boundaries it provides for us. Then, we begin to more frequently accept personal responsibility. We grow, and we expand our comfort zones. We allow more freedom and bliss into our lives for increasing periods of time. Our challenges become more and more subtle.

I remember so vividly when I was first becoming aware of the degree to which I played victim and of tools for living in a conscious manner. I was experiencing a painful divorce and was just beginning to move beyond programming myself to be a victim.

It was a time of deep introspection. Where was I setting myself up? Where was it easier to blame someone else for my unhappiness than to take responsibility for my own life? What did I need to learn from this event so that I didn't re-create my pain as an additional learning experience? The answers provided a great deal of clarity and direction for my life.

Life is a series of illusions. There is always more going on than meets the eye. Thus, we may feel victimized; we may even want revenge, but the truth is that there can only be a tyrant if there is a victim. People and animals that exert an energy of self-confidence or fearlessness are rarely, if ever, attacked.

It is so important to move beyond our judgments of each other and of life's experiences. There are no accidents in life, and we have a choice to take responsibility for having consciously or unconsciously set up our paths.

> We are all simultaneously teachers and learners. When it is time for us to have particular experiences that will enhance our growth, our teachers appear and present our next challenges. If we feel powerless, our teachers present situations in which we are challenged to move beyond victimhood into assertion and self-confidence. All of life's experiences serve a purpose, no matter how dismal they may feel in the moment.

WITHOUT BLAME, THERE IS NOTHING TO FORGIVE

Some time back, I took something personally that had nothing to do with me. My friend handled a situation in a way that resulted in my feeling hurt because she didn't deal directly with me. She was under a great deal of stress as she was trying to work through a difficult situation with her family. I had an image of how I should have been treated, and it wasn't fulfilled. Instead of just living my own life, I found myself in emotional turmoil about the situation.

I saw the mechanism. If I had loved myself enough at the time, I would never have felt offended. If I had loved Janet unconditionally, I wouldn't have had a vested interest in how she did anything. I saw where I wanted to control things—to have them be the way I wanted them to be. I was expecting perfection from Janet at a time that she needed the freedom to grow without my interference.

For weeks, I harbored my resentment and anger, knowing that there was some place that I hadn't yet gained the wisdom available from the experience. I thought I had graduated from Victim 101 long ago, and yet I was feeling victimized.

I knew that we continue to harbor resentments when we haven't gained the wisdom from the experience or because we want to protect ourselves by holding a self-image of having been wronged by someone else. Of course, this is an illusion. In reality, we are using the experience as an excuse for not taking self-responsibility and getting on with our lives. Our egos want us to play victim and blame others for our circumstances.

It finally became clear to me that I was at a major turning point in my life. Rather than just focusing on my next step and getting on with my life, I was procrastinating by focusing on Janet's behavior and how she hadn't met my needs. It was a very humbling experience.

It caused me to reflect on some basic tenets about forgiveness. *Webster's (New World Dictionary, 10th ed.)* definition of forgiveness is to give up resentment or the desire to punish an offense or offender. This assumes that the other person has wronged us. As individuals and as a collective society, we often need someone to be wrong so that we can be right. This gives us "power over" them, even if it is just a psychological edge inside of us.

> When each of us simply owns our innate power, freedom will reign in our entire society. This major transition will occur as each of us transforms our own patterns. It will happen, one by one, two by two, four by four, etc. We are all connected to each other.

We already have proof of this phenomenon as indicated by the Hundredth Monkey Study reported by Ken Keyes. Scientists studied monkeys living on one island and determined that when one breed of monkey began washing its fruit before eating it, monkeys of the same breed who lived on surrounding islands did the same thing. It's important to recognize that there was no physical interaction between the animals. There is a magical number in consciousness where all of society changes, even though major social transformations begin with only a few individuals.

With regard to the concept of owning our power versus playing the "blame and forgive game," forgiveness is an unnecessary phenomenon if we understand the mechanics of life. *Since ev-*

erything in life is perfect, there is never a reason to forgive anyone for anything. We sometimes need to remind ourselves not to expect others to fit our images of how they "should be."

When we forget how life really works and judge someone else for simply being who they are, forgiveness brings us tremendous personal freedom. Dropping our resentment and anger toward others brings us more energy and focus to advance in our own lives.

But forgiveness is not a charitable thing to do. It is not an action that we initiate for someone else's benefit. We forgive others because harboring anger and resentment saps our energy and causes disease in our bodies. Forgiveness allows us to stop judging ourselves for setting up painful learning experiences or repeating old patterns in our lives.

MOVING FROM JUDGMENTS TO CELEBRATION

It's important not to judge ourselves when we notice that we are blaming others or not being self-responsible. Our familiar patterns are just old friends. They change spontaneously when we live our lives in a conscious manner and are open to our personal transformations.

Self-judgment, on the other hand, creates resistance to change. When we judge ourselves, we create our own prisons. We even handcraft and position each bar on our self-imposed cells. We work overtime, serving as both our judge and our jury. With each new sentence that we adjudicate, we securely fasten another lock on our cells.

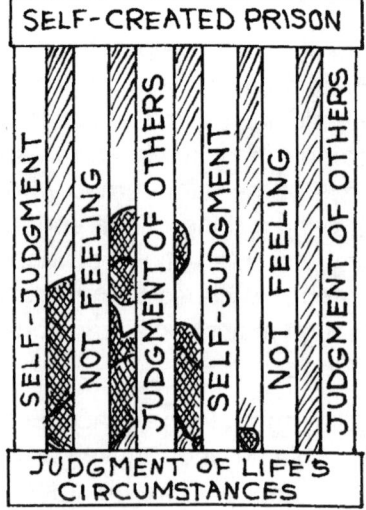

SELF-CREATED PRISON

SELF-JUDGMENT   NOT FEELING   JUDGMENT OF OTHERS   SELF-JUDGMENT   NOT FEELING   JUDGMENT OF OTHERS

JUDGMENT OF LIFE'S CIRCUMSTANCES

It is important to use the instances in which we judge others as tools for self-awareness. When I notice my judgment of another individual, it triggers a response like the following:

Oh, I'm still judging other people for being _____. Since we're all mirrors for each other, this must be a reminder that I'm still _____ myself. I'm glad I see this in the mirror they provide to me. Now I don't have to waste energy denying that I'm still _____.

Fill in the blanks above with the names of things we judge about other people. For example, we judge and label others as:

* *insecure*
* *frightened*
* *unmotivated*
* *arrogant*
* *easily offended*

* *closed-minded*
* *angry*
* *insensitive*
* *projecting personal issues on others*

The most profound changes occur when we stay open to the wisdom that is available in all of our experiences, no matter how dreary they may feel on the surface. When we *try* to transform our patterns, we create more internal opposition to change. Instead, we can ask ourselves questions like these: What was my role in creating this situation? Who is my mirror? How is it easier for me to blame someone else instead of being as powerful as I really am? What can I learn now so that I don't re-create this learning experience?

When we feel and express our related emotions, we feel an extraordinary influx of new energy. We begin to focus on our own lives instead of fretting because someone else didn't meet our expectations.

We choose our life circumstances. When I am focused on my own path and loving myself, I have no energy available to judge the actions of others. I also don't expect anyone else to meet my needs, so I don't feel the necessity for them to be a certain way.

The situations that promote our resentment or anger are illusions. They are actually just opportunities to learn something about ourselves. They are feedback loops, indicating that it's time once again to expand our comfort zones.

When we are tempted to judge another individual, we can understand that we have just drawn a mirror into our lives. Looking closely at this mirror (the other person), we can graduate ourselves from Judgment 101 by being conscious of our judgments before they take place. Then, we can plan a celebration. The situation we just encountered was a challenge to remember that it's time to allow more bliss and empowerment into our lives!

EXERCISES

1. What are the areas about yourself that you judge the most harshly?

2. How is that a self-created prison for you?

3. What aspects of your past do you still judge instead of using them as catalysts for achieving more empowerment and self-love?

4. Would you feel more freedom in your life if you understood that nothing about your life needs to be fixed or changed because it all serves you?

5. In what areas of your life is it easier to blame others than to fully own your power?

6. In what areas of your life are you willing to take more self-responsibility versus "playing victim" or blaming others for your characteristics or circumstances?

7. What emotions are the easiest for you to feel and express?

8. Outline some ways you can safely and constructively express your frustrations at work.

   Examples:

   a) Punch, mold, or shape a small ball of clay you keep in your desk. Notice that you can still carry on your normal work day while expressing yourself.

   b) Tense the muscles throughout your body during a meeting or while working at your desk. Hold your breath for a moment. Then release your breath and your tension, de-stressing your entire body. Notice that you didn't deny your frustration—you simply experienced it in a safe and constructive manner. Does your body feel more energized or less tense?

SIX

POLARITIES: FULLY EXPERIENCING LIFE

To live is the rarest thing in the world.
Most people exist; that is all.

Oscar Wilde

The wild horse of life prances in front of us, flaunting his splendid mane, his lustrous coat, and his spirited passion for life. Full of himself, he rears up and paws the air, snorting and tossing his mane. His hot breath steams the atmosphere and flares his nostrils as he stamps the ground with his powerful hooves. His vitality and his zest for life are almost overwhelming because he graduated himself long ago from ordinary existence. Each day, this passionate and liberated being embraces new challenges, savoring the thrills of truly living. His motto appears to be, "Now is the time," and he is impatient to proceed with his journey.

His fiery eyes and forceful whinny beseech us to claim *our* freedom, and his mere presence shatters our shallow pretenses. With our heads down in shame, we run to our safety zones, secure our blinders once again, and breathe a sigh of relief that we have avoided uniting with this radiant reflection of who we really are. With his head held high and his focus on the highest summits of life, the gleaming wild horse races away from us to meet his destiny.

Most of us exist rather than allowing ourselves to truly blossom. Polarities allow us to fully experience life, and they are one of the most important concepts in this document.

Polarities are naturally occurring opposites in life. They are contradictory life circumstances and emotions. *Webster's (New World Dictionary, 10th ed.)* defines polarities as the property of opposites; the tendency to grow, turn, think, etc., in contrary directions as if because of magnetic repulsion.

Almost everything in our lives has an opposite—hot/cold, alive/dead, young/old, health/sickness, wealth/poverty, self-doubt/self-confidence, happy/sad, fear/empowerment, love/hate, etc. Just as a battery requires a positive and a negative charge to operate, consciously experiencing polarities empowers us to thrive.

Once we have fully experienced one side of a polarity—unpleasant feelings such as insecurity or sadness, we can fully participate in its counterpart—emotions such as self-confidence, fearlessness, and joy.

We fear a new challenge and consciously walk through our fears. No matter what the outcome of that specific situation, we *automatically* feel increased self-confidence and empowerment because we were courageous enough to *attempt* our next step in life.

> Our judgment of our emotions and experiences is
> a self-created prison.

We have been taught that some emotions are good and some are bad. For example, love is "good" and hate is "bad". It's fun to feel joy and empowerment, but we shy away from sadness, fear, loneliness, and anger. Because we don't want to visit with our own unpleasant emotions, we tell our friends and loved ones, "It's OK. Don't feel that way."

We have labeled some of the most natural components of ourselves as positive and some as negative. We hate feeling our fear, and we love feeling happy. There's a catch! We can't feel the full extent of our joy and empowerment without feeling the depth of their respective opposites. Polarities provide a frame of reference for measuring our experiences, not as good or bad but by the distinct difference between each pair.

It is impossible for us to fully love ourselves or others if we are in denial of our feelings. The positive and negative charge of a battery are *both* essential to its functioning. Likewise, it is necessary for us to honestly feel *whatever* we feel—pain *or* pleasure.

Anger is the other side of love. Denying our anger disrupts the electrical circuit within us. This closes our hearts to others and therefore to ourselves. Expressing our anger in safe and constructive ways allows us to reopen our hearts to others so that we can fully love ourselves again.

As much as we sometimes wish it were different, the twin emotions of love and hate sit side by side within our brains. They get along quite well together unless we refuse to acknowledge that one of the twins exists. If we do, one will protect the other by burrowing with it into the cocoon of denial that we have created. Then they will both be equally repressed. Our resistance to what exists within us will cripple our ability to experience our greatest joy, love, and empowerment.

The truth is that we all sometimes feel sad, lonely, depressed, and angry, as well as a myriad of other feelings that we so wish to avoid. It's part of being a human being. If we hadn't experienced day, how would we understand night? If we had never felt sad, how would we have a basis of comparison that would allow us to fully appreciate and experience joy?

We all have opposites within us. We are all both fighter and lover, victim and tyrant, adult and child, etc. We all have female and male characteristics. We are all equally as capable of being the kindest person on the planet as we are of being the most heinous criminal. Our characteristics and behaviors are based on the choices we make.

As parents, we would be amazed if our children did not experience fear of new challenges such as learning to walk, ride a bicycle, or interview for a job. We encourage them to walk through their new and scary experiences. Why is it that we lack the self-love required to be just as tender with ourselves? What are the ways that we don't encourage ourselves as we journey through our unfamiliar and frightening experiences?

We tell ourselves that we aren't afraid. We repress our fear, wad it up, and ram it into an already overflowing stuff bag. With great vigor and health, "Fear" tenaciously leaps out of the bag and jumps up and down on top of it as if it were a trampoline. "Fear" just wants to be acknowledged, and it will stop at nothing to get our attention. Over and over, it cries out, "Can't you see me? Can't you feel me? Listen to me. I'm just part of you! I'm the doorway to your new empowerment!"

In the meantime, we have buried our senses in the same way that ostriches are said to hide their heads in the sand. We pull on a full bodysuit with a built-in face mask. The designer brand of the body suit is "Denial," and that label is plastered all over the garment. We begin to run away from the stuff bag as fast as we can, pretending not to notice "Fear" as he continues to jump and scream for our attention.

Since "Fear" and the stuff bag are inside of our consciousness, our tactics don't work, so we rush around re-creating experiences that challenge us to feel our insecurities. "Fear" assists us by calling in obstacles for us to face so that we will finally acknowledge him. This part of us really is our friend, and he will do whatever it takes to get us to recognize him so we can graduate to our next levels of empowerment.

Our fears simply need to be experienced. They will not control our lives if we feel them. However, they will be fierce dictators if we attempt to deny their existence. They will eventually control every action we take.

We play a game with ourselves that we must be perfect in every situation and not fail. Although everything in life is just a learning experience and there is no such thing as a genuine failure, we constantly judge our performances in terms of success or failure. Our terror of feeling our fears becomes more profound than our original anxieties. Our fears become our masters instead of the true friends that they are.

In reality, fear is an ally. It warns us of things we should know about, such as how to be on guard while driving in a storm. It also alerts us so that we know our next steps in life. When I'm living consciously, I know that whatever I am afraid of (assuming I am physically safe) is my next step.

Most of us cheat ourselves out of achieving some of our greatest successes because we are so frightened of failure. After Thomas Edison had tried over 1,000 times to develop a light bulb, several people asked him why he kept trying. He replied that he knew so much about what didn't work that he must be quite close to success. His self-esteem was so high that he continued to trust himself, and he discovered volumes of knowledge as he progressed through his failures. Most millionaires in America have made a fortune three times before they are able to maintain their financial success. American ideals are based on individualism and an entrepreneurial spirit. Do we as individuals really understand that if we are not failing regularly, we are not learning? Do we comprehend that we are blocking our eventual success when we are stagnant?

The walking dead have made their choices. They have elected not to feel their *highs* because they are unwilling to feel the *lows* that are a part of human existence. They literally cheat themselves out of some of the most pleasurable parts of life by not feeling and guarantee themselves the opportunity to re-create pain. It is a choice. The walking dead have not yet realized that there really is a "bottom to the bottom" of the lows. At some point, we reach the depths of fear, anger, or pain about a particular concern. Then, it is not necessary to delve into that issue again. There is even better news! The highs in life have no ceiling. As we graduate from level to level, we find that the amounts of joy, empowerment, and love that we feel far surpass our wildest dreams.

The following are examples of polarities in life. Each individual will experience a given pair of opposites to a different degree. This will depend on their core issues, previous life experiences, and maturational level. It is paramount to keep in mind that we feel polarities over a period of time. We don't feel all of the lows at once. Instead, we feel graduated degrees of any polarity.

LOWER SIDE OF POLARITY	HIGHER SIDE OF POLARITY
♦ Fear	♦ Empowerment, Self-Confidence, Feelings of Safety and Security
♦ Anger, Rage	♦ Compassion
♦ Sadness	♦ Joy
♦ Insecurity	♦ Self-Confidence
♦ Victimization, Powerlessness	♦ Empowerment
♦ Grief	♦ Joy, Sweet Memories
♦ Guilt	♦ Compassion for Self
♦ Judgment	♦ Acceptance
♦ Self-Hatred	♦ Self-Love, Self-Worth, Self-Esteem

Polarities are one of the few areas of living for which we have been provided a map. It is a very simple map that we can choose to follow as we advance from one level of a polarity to the next. Unlike other areas of life, we can even choose to have a destination.

If we want to open our full creative forces in life, we can follow a circular path to feel the highs and lows associated with a specific polarity. Eventually, we will exhaust the depths of the lower end of it. Then, all that will continue to be available for us to feel will be ever higher levels of the upper end of that polarity.

The map for attaining your highest joy, love, empowerment, and wisdom is depicted in Figure 5 on the following page.

Graduating from level to level can be as simple or as difficult as we would like. It is all personal preference and choice. If we want the game to be difficult, all we have to do is deny or resist our feelings. This will create more wars (internal battles) than in a science fiction series. Our emotions will continue to demand to be noticed so that we can eventually win the game. If we don't experience our lows, we will continue to re-create opportunities to do so until we feel them. Resisting our lows will negate opportunities to experience our highs.

If we want to play the easier version of the game, we can merely watch ourselves play it. All we have to do is show up, be conscious, and experience life. We will automatically graduate from one level to another with an easy and graceful flow, collecting multitudes of insights with even the slightest turns on the map. During the times that we don't judge our emotions, we will speed our progress even more. To introduce conflict, internal battles, frustration, resistance, struggle, and to slow down our process, all we need to do is be unconscious and judge our emotions.

Just remember the following:

◆ The way to the oasis is through the desert.

◆ Our lows are the compost pile that supplies the nutrients for our highest highs.

◆ The only way to reach our highest highs is through feeling our lowest lows.

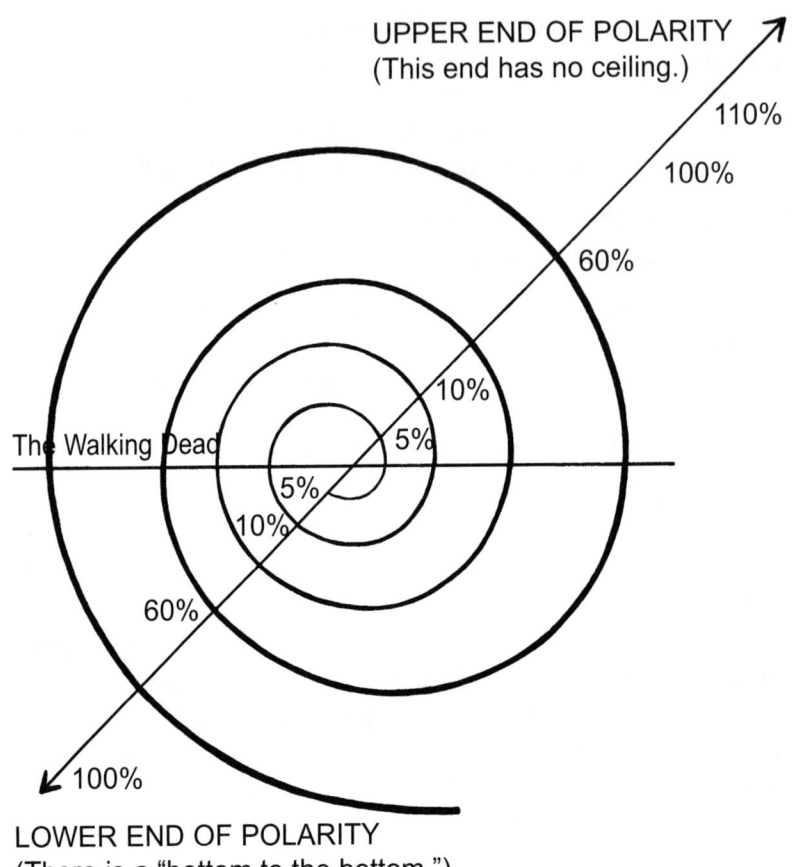

LOWER END OF POLARITY
(There is a "bottom to the bottom.")

Figure 5
POLARITY MAP

This is a map for attaining your highest joy, love, empowerment, and wisdom. It will assist you in advancing from one level of a polarity to the next. Note that we experience polarities in degrees. For example, when we feel 5% of the lower area of a specific polarity, we earn the right to feel 5% more of the upper extremity. Then we repeat this with increasing percentages until we have completed the lower end, and all that remains to be experienced are ever-increasing percentages of the upper end.

Growing through experiencing the polarities within us is a critical tool for our full empowerment. Why would we have such a broad scope of emotions if they weren't all useful to us? How could we comprehend cold if we hadn't experienced hot? How interesting would life be if everything we touched was lukewarm? The battery simply operates by having opposites—a positive and a negative charge.

We don't try to change this or judge the negative charge in a battery as bad. We simply understand that we can't get power without both the positive and the negative charges. (Keep in mind that electricity flows from negative to positive.)

If I don't allow myself the experience of feeling fearful or powerless, how can I feel and experience the full breadth of my power? It is our judgment of feeling our pain or unpleasant emotions that robs us of experiencing the pleasurable ends of polarities. We can never get rid of our pain. However, we can feel it and integrate the wisdom that it offers us. We merely have to recognize the parts of ourselves that we are attempting to avoid when we hide from our discomfort.

> We can't be fully empowered and we can't fully live without our positive and negative charges. All of our emotions just need to be acknowledged, and they will serve us as dependably as brand new, fully charged batteries.

Polarities are a magnificent key to our full functioning. They open doorway after doorway so that we can understand all of our experiences, including our past. They are the vehicle by which we gain the maximum wisdom from our most agonizing experiences.

The darkest hours are just before the dawn, and our own light emerges during our darkest hours. When we change our perspectives, we see the perfection in all things, including the lower ends of polarities.

When we feel our polarities, we make a commitment to fully live. We set the intention to move beyond approach-avoidance, and this allows us to bring what we want into our lives. The clarity of our intentions unleashes an astonishing amount of creative energy.

Eventually, we become energy in motion (e-motion). Because our energy is freely moving, it is not blocked. We laugh, cry, are frightened, empowered, etc., without judging any of it, and that sets in motion a stunning surge of creativity. Our lives flow easily because we are beyond judgment of the most natural of life's experiences—our emotions. They are no longer a foreign language. We finally see and experience them for what they really are—our best friends.

QUESTIONS

1. We allow ourselves to experience the upper ends of polarities by being willing to experience their lower ends, in degrees. What is your biggest resistance to feeling the lower end of a specific polarity?

2. Polarities are the key to gaining the maximum wisdom from our past and from our experiences that we have judged as painful. How can you allow your journeys through polarities to be easier for you?

3. Describe some polarities you've already experienced in your life:

    a) in your relationship with your Self

    b) at work

    c) in relationships with others

SEVEN

TRUTH IN A BOTTLE

The following story illustrates some of the concepts in this book.

Once upon a time a woman who was feeling very uneasy about her life was walking along a beautiful beach at sunset. Her head was down as was her heart. Her feet were heavy in the sand.

Nature called to her. A wild paintbrush dashed brilliant hues of rose, purple, and pink across the sky. The colors shifted and danced wildly, calling to her, "Look up! Choose life. It's an adventure!" The woman continued to walk with her eyes focused on the sand, never seeing the dancers in the sky.

The water rippled toward her, attempting to reach her feet. Each wave glistened with brilliant sunlight and was tinged with reflective colors of gold, pink, and rose. The water and the wind joined forces to create sound and called to her, "Allow life to touch you. Open your heart and let life gently flow through you like the water." The woman could not hear the sound of the waves or the wind. She was oblivious to their clues.

Finally, the colors of the sky could tarry no more. They gradually faded and merged into the dimness of early evening. Only then did the woman gaze across the water toward the horizon. She looked at her watch. She was searching for something, although she didn't know what it was.

A bottle floated up on the shore and almost hit the woman's foot. At last, she noticed something and reached over to pick up the container. A genie surrounded by golden light squeezed herself out of the bottle, breathing heavily. The woman watched in shock as the genie popped her rotund belly free of the neck of the bottle and then gracefully withdrew her delicate legs and feet. "Wow, I'm glad to be out of there. That was a tight fit! Too many potato chips!" said the genie in greeting. "Anyway, how are you?"

The woman moved back a few steps, opened her eyes wide, and struggled to reply. The genie reached her long arm over and patted the woman on the back with an understanding look. "Hey, it's OK, Honey. No one believes in me at first! I'm real. I'm an old genie from way back, and a good one, too. Satisfaction guaranteed! So, what is it that you want?"

The woman was still in shock, so the genie began to prove herself. She blew into the air and created a magical miniature ballet with beautifully attired and perfectly synchronized dancers performing the *Nutcracker Suite*. One "poof" from the genie, and they were gone.

Next she created a clothing shop with hundreds of racks of the most splendid attire—dresses, evening gowns, earrings, shoes, and hats. Each rack had the same sign which said, "The price is free." Again, one "poof" from the genie, and the scene vanished.

Last emerged an ornate banquet hall with huge ice sculptures, a symphony orchestra, and every kind of food imaginable. Couples were dancing in the center of the floor while other guests enjoyed platefuls of the most scrumptious cuisine. This time the genie put her hands right into the middle of the scene and pulled off a dozen plates of food before erasing her creation.

As the woman gazed at her in disbelief, the genie said sheepishly, "Got to keep up my strength, you know!"

Whoever the genie was, the woman decided she liked her style. She felt she could trust her.

"OK, Sister, now that I've got your attention, what is it you want?" asked the genie, in between bites of food.

"How does it work?" the woman asked.

"Oh, you know, the usual," the genie answered as she licked dark chocolate dripping from her fingers. "You ask for your wish to come true, and I help make that happen."

"What's the catch?" asked the woman skeptically.

"You humans! You always think there's a catch, don't you? OK, tell me what you want, and I'll explain how to get it." She bent down to pick up another plate of food while the woman considered what she wanted.

"I just want to be happy," she murmured.

"Well, that's a snap! What would make you happy, kiddo?" asked the genie.

"I want someone to really love me, and no one ever has." The woman began to sob loudly, and the genie snapped her fingers, producing a huge box of Kleenex. She ripped off the top of the box and pulled out a handful of pink tissues for the woman, saying, "Of course, these don't count as one of your wishes. They're compliments of the cosmos."

The woman wiped her eyes and laughed through her tears.

"Blow your honker, too, if you need to, Sister. There are plenty more where those came from," the genie said as she produced another box of the soft tissues.

"I don't know if this is real or not," cried the woman, "but I feel better just being in your presence."

"Well, here's the straight scoop, Honey. You've just taken two giant steps toward loving yourself. First of all, you were brave enough to ask for what you want, and second, you were courageous enough to cry your tears. They've been in there a long time, haven't they?"

"Yes, they have," sobbed the woman. "But how did you know?"

"I've been watching you all evening. First, I tried to get your attention through the sunset and then by being the waves and the wind. But you were just walking along feeling dead. So I decided the only way I could get through to you was to hit you on the foot with a bottle, so here I am!"

The woman sat on the beach, laughing and crying, bewildered by this event in her life. The genie continued, "So, you've already started moving toward having what you want. If you'd asked for something simple like a circus or a world's fair, our work would already be done, but you want a little more than that. Are you willing to commit some time and energy to this project?"

"I guess so, but what do you mean?" asked the puzzled woman.

"I mean that you get to play Loop-de-Loop for a little bit. It won't be as fast as getting you tissues and chocolate eclairs, but if you do the Loop, you'll have ongoing fulfillment." The genie paused to pick up another dessert plate. "Of course, you can still change your wish, if you want to."

"No, I want to be loved. I have always wanted to be loved." As the woman confirmed her wish, she looked sad.

"The first step," said the genie in a serious mood, "is to understand that external love is only reflected back to you when you love yourself. The more you love yourself, the more other people mirror that to you."

"I've heard that," said the woman, "but I've never understood *how* to love myself."

"Just feel the areas where you don't. It's simple!"

"I thought I was supposed to focus on *loving* myself, not on the ways that I *don't* love myself."

"That's the myth! That's why you called in the genie—me!" She proudly turned a perfect cartwheel in the air to make her point.

"I don't understand," said the woman sadly.

"It's just like my magic tricks. Everything transforms easily once you have the courage to stay with your feelings." The genie created a movie projector and a huge white screen. Saying, "Roll 'em!" she began to play a movie of the woman's life. In the first scene, the woman was walking on the beach as she had been earlier that evening, trudging through the sand with heavy steps and her head down.

"How do you look?" asked the genie as she flipped the projector off.

"Like I'm dead, but somehow alive enough to walk in the sand," responded the woman.

"You're right-on!" laughed the genie. "The shorthand term for that is the 'walking dead'."

The genie flipped the projector back on. It whirred, and then the woman saw herself crying, as she had been a few moments before. Then she was smiling and laughing at the genie's antics. Seeing this made her heart feel safe and warm until she saw the next scenario. She was once again sobbing despondently.

"Oh, no! Not again!" she cried, as she watched herself.

Yet, there were more scenes to view. She saw herself continue to change, experiencing layer after layer of sadness followed by happiness. During the final picture the genie shared with her, the woman was absolutely radiant. She was surrounded with the glow of being fully alive.

"Do you get it?" asked the genie. "The last picture I showed you was where you had gone through the bottom layer of the places where you loathe yourself, so all that was left for you to experience were the places where you love yourself. I'm not going to show you what happens after that because that would be a sneak preview of your relationships with other people, and we're not allowed to show that kind of advance view to humans. It would spoil all of your fun getting there, anyway."

They sat in silence for a moment as the woman reflected on her starring role in the movie. Then she lay on her back looking up at the moon.

"OK," asked the genie tenderly, "Now for the pop quiz. What did you notice when you saw yourself go through all of the layers of not feeling loved?"

"That the intensity of my feelings increased. I was always sadder or happier than the last time I was sad or happy."

"Good girl!" The genie jumped up and somersaulted in the air. "We're on a roll! Now, I want to make sure you understand what really happens. It's not that you were sadder than you were before. It's that you finally let yourself sink more into your emotions. Your feelings were always there. You just allowed yourself to more fully experience them. And, of course, the big prize after that was that you got to feel more self-love. During each iteration, you felt an even greater level of happiness on the other side of your sadness and self-loathing."

The woman was quiet, contemplating the profound wisdom the genie was sharing with her. "And it really is true that all I have to do is allow myself to feel whatever I feel to get to the end of the movie I just saw?"

"Bingo!" cried the genie with glee. "That's all you have to do. See how simple it is?"

"So, I really did take my first steps by asking for what I want. I already did my first work, didn't I?" the woman asked proudly.

"Yes! And it wasn't so hard, was it?" asked the genie.

"It was a relief!" answered the woman.

"You only asked for one gift from me," said the genie. "But you were very clever in what you asked for. You asked for something that will transform your life permanently. It's so much better than most of the requests we get. People usually ask for a new car, a bigger house, etc. It's fun to help with those things, but sometimes we see the same people unhappy years later. I always feel bad about that because we're limited to one visit per person."

"Every time I feel a different layer of my emotions, I'll think of you, Genie. No matter how many layers there are to feel, I'll always be grateful to you for this knowledge."

The woman was filled with the contentment of realizing the answer to her questions about how to love herself. She had struggled for a long time, thinking that her goal was unattainable. "What a relief that life really is so simple," she mused.

The woman and the genie lay on the beach, listening to the waves and watching the clouds dance around the winking moon. It was a magnificently peaceful evening, and the woman was filled with a wonderful sense of herself.

Suddenly, a beeper sounded and the genie bolted upright. "Got to go, Kiddo," said the genie.

The woman hugged her new friend, watched her somehow stuff herself back into her bottle and roll herself back onto the edge of the beach close to the waves. As much as she loved the genie, she wasn't lonesome for her new friend because she finally had a deeper connection with her Self. She watched the waves gently carry the bottle back out to sea and hoped her new friend would have time for dinner before she worked with her next client. After all, she needed to keep up her strength.

QUESTION

1. What is the "truth in the bottle" for you?

EIGHT

MINING THE GOLD IN THE DARKNESS

In spite of the cost of living, it is still popular.
Laurence J. Peter

Would you like to receive a dollar for each time you have asked yourself, "Why do things have to be this way?" or "What is life really about?" Have you considered the possibility that our painful or distressing experiences can be quite useful to us? If you can be open to the potential that much of what we have been taught is upside down and backward, this chapter can build a bridge to new understandings about life.

Mining the gold in the darkness is not about digging minerals from the earth. It is a concept based on the understanding that all of life's experiences, no matter how disagreeable they may feel in the moment, serve a purpose. Just as gold and diamonds are located in the darkest depths of the earth, extraordinary wisdom and growth are available to us in the events of our lives that we judge as hurtful or unpleasant. Our disappointments, depression, anger, and lack of love are all tools for learning and growth.

When we are willing to fully experience life, there is gold in all of our experiences that we have perceived as dismal. We discover that "darkness" is a myth. There is only transition.

CHANGE IS ALL THERE IS

Change is inevitable.
Yet a part of each of us struggles to maintain our current existence.
It is what we know, and familiarity feels comfortable to us, even when it is painful.
We snuggle into our comfort zones, hoping to set up permanent residence within their arms.

It is a lost cause.
Just as surely as our fear is the forerunner of our new power,
Change predicts our new levels of self-love.
All that is required is the courage to thrust ourselves from yet another craggy ledge into our yet-to-be known.

It is our destiny to expand beyond everything we once clung to as identities.
Our old patterns will be shattered one by one, by forces inside of us.

The power of these parts of ourselves is as mighty as the steady devastation of a vast glacier, mercilessly changing everything in its path until all that once existed has disappeared, and a new form has emerged.
The new design is an image of ourselves that we cannot at this time even begin to imagine.

Any real change implies the transformation of our world as we have known it;
the end of safety and security, which were always just figments of our imaginations.
Safety and security can only emerge from within ourselves when we possess internal sovereignty.

The glacial mass within us will brutally slice through our old identities.
It will carve out softness, vulnerability, and constant transformation.

We will be asked to surrender all of our old pictures of reality, our cherished dreams of how things should or could have been.

When we surrender our familiar realms without bitterness or self-pity, we become free.
We unchain ourselves and drink in the sweet nectar of our emancipation, freedom so much more precious than our once-cherished dreams, now relinquished.

For it is only by being willing to give it all up, no matter what it takes to do so, that we can have it all.
We discover that by giving it all up, we gain everything.
We discover that there is nothing we really need or want because we finally have our Selves.

Keep this in mind when you have climbed halfway up a mountain and have a vision of what you want to see and experience at the top.
Know that you will be asked to surrender your dreams.
They are based on what you know now, and that no longer serves you.

You will be asked to forfeit your security, your very identity, and all that you hold dear at this time.
You will be asked this at a moment when you are unable to see and cannot dare imagine what your future will bring to you.

Your impulse will be to cling to what you know.
Will you instead say, "Yes" to life?
As you can see, change is not bad or good.
It is only change.

The relationship between the need to experience polarities in life and our abilities to mine the gold available in the darkness is important. Sometimes we feel like we have witnessed the wreckage of our own lives. It seems that the very foundations of our existence have been blown apart. However, there is wisdom to be gained from everything we experience.

Although we may perceive that we have lost something we felt attached to, nothing that we really need is ever lost. It has merely been placed in a huge safe inside of us, and we have access to it at any time.

We grow through every experience even though we sometimes cry, kick, and scream during the entire journey. We change and become more whole within ourselves even when we cannot comprehend life itself. Because we are climbing a hill, we don't yet see the view from the top. We don't know what exists on the other side, but we continue to climb, steadily placing one foot in front of the other.

Sometimes we don't trust ourselves or the process of life. We hesitate. We judge our circumstances and fear that we are regressing. Later, it becomes ever so clear to us that we were merely moving to a more challenging plane of existence.

Gold is *always* created in the blackness of the earth. Many consider the diamond to be the most brilliant of gems, and it is born in the deepest folds of the earth's darkness. Roses have thorns. Pleasure and pain exist side by side just as do sunshine and rain. Life presents challenges to us, and we respond by climbing thorn-filled rosebushes, one after another, for the sheer pleasure of enjoying the magnificent fragrance and beauty of the blooms at the top. So many colors and varieties await us!

Like our real selves, the rose can be quite tenacious, refusing to be vanquished even when it has been dormant in the frozen earth. So often we flower profusely after the most difficult times in our lives. Just as with the rose, the splendor of our blossoms corresponds to the care and attention that we provide ourselves.

No matter how much we may want to banish the thorns from our lives, there is nothing to get rid of. The thorns protect the special bloom of the rose, and our painful experiences nourish and sustain us. They make it possible for us to grow. They are the steppingstones of our lives.

The unpleasant side of each polarity that we experience is exactly what makes it possible for us to experience the highs in our lives. Our journeys through the darkness eventually become our old realities, and our past supports our new growth.

When we face our key challenges, our transformations occur similarly to the way clear, sparkling diamonds are formed from black coal. If you put pressure on the darkness (the coal), it becomes a diamond. Otherwise, it doesn't. The pressure in our lives occurs as we confront our personal issues. Encountering any feelings repressed in our bodies turns our shadows into diamonds. Our bleakest hours are just before the dawn of each new era in our lives.

It becomes clear why it is so important that we cease labeling our experiences as negative. Without thorns, there would be no roses. If there were no rainstorms, we could not enjoy rainbows.

When we reflect back on our tempestuous times and understand that each of them has offered wisdom to us, we begin to

understand the absolute perfection of the flow of our lives. Perhaps during the next storm we will not feel a need to control our
feelings or a desire to eliminate the temporary disturbance or
disorder in our lives. Possibly we will remember how wonderful
it is to breathe the freshly cleansed air and gaze at a beautiful
rainbow after a thundershower. Maybe we will simply understand
that all of our pain is a wake-up call so that we can reach a new
level of functioning.

When we are in the throes of the rocking waves and we wonder
if our boats will sink, we can ask for the wisdom of the turbulence to be revealed to us as gently and effortlessly as possible.
If we do not hold a rigid expectation of how we will receive this
information, it will be made known to us. If we are attached to
receiving our answers in a certain way, we may miss the message *and* the messenger.

You have probably heard the parable about the man who was
terrified because a flood was gushing through his home. He
crawled out of a window onto the roof, crying "Help me!" Sources
of aid arrived quickly including first a man in a rowboat and later
a helicopter dangling a rope so that the man could climb to safety.
The man refused the offers of assistance because he had a
limited idea of how relief would be provided to him. He failed to
recognize the emissaries of help as well as the solutions they
offered him.

Years ago, I was in a car accident that left me unable to walk. I
was lying in bed recuperating when I received a certified letter.
My landlord had died, and her relatives were inheriting the house.
They required me to vacate the house within 30 days. I was
quite anguished and began to search for a solution.

My neighbor across the road heard about my dilemma and knew
that I was unable to walk or drive to seek another rental home.
He knew of a house available in the neighborhood—right down
the road! He made a call and confirmed that I could secure it at
a reasonable rate and came to tell me the good news. He helped

me into his car, drove me to see the home, and said that he and his wife would help me pack and move.

The home was larger than where I was living and more quiet and private. It was a rambler house, and I was moving from a two-story home. This was significant because I had been crawling around and scooting up and down stairs as I was unable to walk. The house was surrounded by 160 acres of farmland and had a pond in the backyard with great blue herons and beautiful mountain views. It was a gentle 15-minute walk to a river where bald eagles nested.

I was convinced that my relocation couldn't be this simple. I had an expectation regarding the solution I would receive, so I couldn't hear the message or see the messenger. I thanked my wonderful neighbor but began looking in the newspaper for a rental home. I paid cab drivers to drive me around the region and found nothing suitable to rent. Finally, with only a few days left before the date that I had to vacate, I relented and rented the house down the street. Friends and my dear neighbors packed my possessions and helped me move.

The home and property brought me tremendous joy. It was perfect for me at that time in my life, and I remained there for over seven years. I had expended an exorbitant amount of unnecessary energy for someone who should have been concentrating on her physical healing because I had not been able to perceive the answers I had asked for.

It was an invaluable lesson for me concerning being open to the reply when asking a question. It also taught me that there is always gold in the darkness. You have no doubt heard the phrase, "Whenever a window is closed, a door is opened." Don't limit your image of how your responses will come to you, and you will receive them more quickly.

When we are afraid we will fall overboard because our boat is being rocked violently, we are participating in a key growth experience described as a *funnel* in chapter 16. It is as if we have just begun to read a wonderful novel. We won't know the outcome until we read many more pages. If we were to skip ahead and read the ending, we would miss the experience of discovery and the enjoyment of reading the book. This is the journey of life.

So frequently, we instead want to judge and blame our past for our present circumstances. "If only ____ hadn't happened" or "If only things were different," we wouldn't be in our current predicament. Yesterday can't be changed. It can only be accepted and wisdom gained from it. The area where we have choice is today.

If I am avoiding feeling my pain by dwelling on days gone by—blaming someone else or wishing things had been different—I am living in the past. I am *cheating myself* out of fully experiencing this moment, and this moment is all that exists. Time has marched on, and no matter how frantically we scurry after it, attempting to hitch a ride on its long coattails, our past has departed.

If I don't allow myself to live in each instant and to be fully conscious of the present, I will re-create my current scenario over and over, until I finally allow myself to absorb the insights available from the experience. The emotions that I am being nudged to feel right now will not go away simply because I refuse to be conscious of them. On the other hand, when I fully live this minute, I have an endless supply of energy to live yet another chapter in time. I flow with life much more easily.

My history made me who I am today, and I love who I have become, so how can I judge my earlier experiences as negative?

> Without my past,
> I wouldn't exist.

It is my choice whether to focus on my yesterdays or to advance in my life. All that is required to move forward is to experience any suppressed feelings and fully live in *this* moment. I feel my emotions about former times as they affect me today and focus on who I really am and where I am going. Then, my identity is not in the past. If it were, I would continue to reinvent events like those I have already experienced so that I could validate my old self-image.

Yesterday also provided me with a frame of reference so that I can fully live today. It allowed me to walk through the ends of the polarities that we term negative so that I can now experience their opposites.

I remember so vividly my first insights about the bigger picture of life, its purpose, and how it really works. I was just beginning to become more aware, and I wanted to consciously work on my life. I wanted to *fix* myself and become happy. I wanted to *do something*. The product I wanted was happiness. I was experiencing a great deal of emotional pain, and everything in my life seemed upside down and backward. Of course, I wanted to solve all of my problems overnight.

It was quite a journey to understand how simple life really is. What a surprise it was to learn that there were no disasters after all. Everything in my past was perfect just as it was. What I had perceived to be calamities were just calls to awaken, to reap the insights and personal growth available during all of my dreariest hours.

Why are we at a precise place during a specific time when something unpleasant or difficult happens? Our distress almost convinces us that we were at the wrong place at the wrong time. Yet there is something to learn. The truth is that we are always at the right place at the right time.

Mining the gold in the darkness helps us bring to light all of the wisdom available to us in any experience. We begin to understand that problems don't exist, but challenges do. Every "crisis" that we brave transforms us into a higher form of ourselves. That is why the Chinese have two symbols for crisis; one symbol means danger, and the other means opportunity.

There are many alarm clocks ringing in our lives. The circumstances that we tend to judge so severely are usually our most significant awakenings. This includes divorce; loss of a loved one, business, job, or relationship; addictions; financial failure; and other areas in which we have felt disempowered, out of control, or without choice.

We judge these experiences harshly because they feel painful to us. Yet, they provide significant knowledge to us when we are open to receive it. It is rare that an individual who experiences loss or pain does not benefit from greater self-awareness, love, and momentous personal change.

> Pain is cathartic. Each experience of loss leads to transformation. After great pain comes numbness, anger, guilt, and all of the other stages of grief. And finally, each time, a new self emerges with a different vision of who you are and a different sense of what you can do; a different perspective on life; a different perspective on what the future might hold.
>
> Diane Cole, 1992, *After Great Pain: A New Life Emerges*

We can choose to find the enlightenment in all of our experiences. It is always there. All we have to do is ask for it and be open to the response in whatever form it comes to us.

Over time, I have learned to ask myself several questions each time I judge my circumstances and wonder why things are as they are. When I wish I could control my life in some way or hurriedly move beyond where I am, the following questions bring me understanding. The answers come easily if I am open to them. If not, the replies continue to present themselves until I am willing to perceive them.

- How is it serving me to still be where I am?

- Am I willing to own my full power (be self-responsible and live consciously)?

- What is the wisdom that I have not yet gained from this experience?

We all sometimes want to live in the future. We play games like "I'm waiting until ____" or "I'll do it when ____." When we "wait until ____," we forfeit the power that we have available at this point in time. "I'll do it when ____" postpones our being self-responsible and making choices. There are no wrong choices in life. When we refuse to make a decision out of fear that we will make the wrong one, we "create time" so that we can go around the wheel again.

As an example, if I am unsure if my book will sell, I can procrastinate completing it. If I write the book as a learning experience and because it is my next step, I can feel my fears concerning the outcome and just write it. Better yet, I can know that I am writing it simply because I want to finish it *for me*. I am then able to live in the present instead of wondering if I will publish or market the book.

The key is to feel our fear of the unknown and be who we are right now. Yes, we will give up the so-called security of our comfort zones. However, one of the few guarantees in life is that we will experience constant change. This means that our known realities are always in the process of fading away. Our present identities are already history. Even the cellular structures of our bodies are steadily transforming. All we have to do is tune into our instincts and make choices—now, rather than waiting. We can always modify our decisions at a later time. We have always had all of the clues we needed to live our lives. They are always available to us, at exactly the right time. When we don't perceive them, they continue to introduce themselves until we do.

It is not necessary for us to balance on a high wire even though we sometimes feel we are doing so. Life is filled with trapeze bars and choices. Change is the essence of life. Without it we become stagnant; we cease to grow, so we die inside.

It is essential that we acknowledge all parts of ourselves, including our shadow or "dark" sides. Perceiving our shadow material brings us wisdom and freedom. It is nutrient-rich material for our growth. Accepting our shadows permits more of the components of ourselves that we value to surface. It allows us to own all parts of ourselves.

Once I am honest with myself about who I am, I can make decisions to continue my patterns or allow them to transform. My energy level will be boosted significantly because part of my life force will no longer be consumed with trying to hide who I am from myself. When I refuse to look at my dark side, I am resisting what exists. As long as I am lying to myself, I won't make different choices, and my dysfunctional patterns will continue. Once we honor our shadows, they melt back into us. We've acknowledged that they are just parts of who we are, so they no longer intimidate us.

This process of acceptance means that we are being real and feeling our self-hatred, jealousy, fear, rage, etc., as well as our more valued emotions such as self-love and love for others. What a relief to admit to ourselves that our opposite emotions are just a human characteristic. Just as the negative and positive charges are part of a battery, our polarities exist side by side.

The concept of mining gold is useful with every experience in our lives, not only with those that feel distressful. What is the "darkness" and what is the "gold?" The darkness is our judgment of our experiences and our Selves. The darkness is being unconscious as we move through life. The gold is wisdom, self-acceptance, and embracing our past. It is living every moment of our lives in a conscious manner. The chart on the next page summarizes these concepts.

DARKNESS	GOLD
Living unconsciously	Living consciously
Judging ourselves or our experiences	Not judging ourselves or our experiences
Blaming other people or situations for our life circumstances	The intention to be self-responsible and to fully discover ourselves
Concluding that there is something wrong with our lives	Being open to the wisdom available in all situations; knowing that there is perfection in all of our experiences
Avoiding our emotions	Experiencing our emotions
Playing victim	Being self-responsible (owning our power)
Perceiving power as external	Perceiving power as internal (sovereignty)
Not trusting ourselves or the process of our lives	Trusting ourselves and the process of our lives

Eventually, we discover that we have mislabeled some of the most powerful aspects of our lives. There is no darkness after all because every experience is a tool to get to know ourselves and to grow to be all that we truly are. We can struggle with and resist our learning experiences or not. It is all a matter of choice, and it is essential that we be conscious as we make our decisions.

It is all so simple. There is nothing to do in life but watch ourselves change. All we have to do is make a commitment to consciously live our lives and not to judge ourselves and our experiences. When we are not judging them, it is impossible to be a victim because everything in life happens for a reason. All of the events in our lives become results of our choices. This also means we are being self-responsible, which is our passport to incredible freedom.

By fully experiencing life (including feeling our emotions), we receive solutions to the most perplexing mysteries and challenges. The greatest treasures are revealed to us. We discover that there is always gold to be mined in the most difficult parts of our lives. This gold is sitting comfortably within our psyches, patiently awaiting our attention. It shimmers expectantly during the bleakest of nights, ready to be mined in all of our painful experiences.

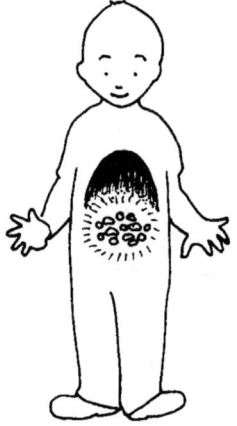

Our pain offers unparalleled opportunities to learn more about ourselves and to become fully empowered. When we safely and constructively feel our emotions, we actively participate in our own lives. Our courage and our willingness to be real are magnificently rewarded by the rapid delivery of the most valuable riches possible—wisdom and personal growth.

We discover one of the greatest secrets on this planet. The very best of life—the crème de la crème—is our reward for living our most agonizing moments. We must finally admit to ourselves that darkness is a myth.

EXERCISES

1. List three wake-up calls you have experienced.

2. Describe an example of when you held a picture of what you thought you wanted and something far better came into your life instead.

3. What brings what you want or need into your life?

4. Describe some of the experiences you have had with so-called negative ends of polarities that provided you a frame of reference for the empowerment, love, joy, etc., that followed them?

5. Spend a minimum of five minutes writing your responses to each of the following questions. It is important to keep your pen or pencil moving on your paper, so write whatever comes into your mind. If you have no thoughts, just scribble until your thoughts become clear.

   ♦ "I'm waiting until . . ."

   ♦ "I'll do it when . . ."

   Now, review your answers, without judging them. How does "waiting" keep you from fully living in the present moment?

6. How can you use your instincts so that you will be more willing to live in the unknown, just being who you are, with no need for assurance that your future will look a certain way?

NINE

UPSIDE DOWN AND BACKWARD

The overwhelming majority of men and women have no notion of what happens in life.

Oliver W. Holmes

Nature has planted in our minds an insatiable longing to see the truth.

Cicero

Consider the possibility that much of what we have learned about life is upside down and backward. We have all been socially conditioned, and much of what we have been told is a distortion of the truth. Society and our families have programmed us by providing us with a plethora of erroneous information, much of which has been handed down from generation to generation for centuries.

We have been told that we should believe and do certain things in order to be socially acceptable, and we have adapted our behaviors accordingly. We have been convinced that our abilities are limited. Perhaps that is why most of us use less than 5% of the potential of our brains.

In addition, our Guardians are comfortable with our known realities and are trained and ready to limit our actions to that scope. Our minds are comparison computers. We usually interpret and assimilate any new information that is inconsistent with what we already know by reformulating it until it conforms with our existing knowledge. This means that we inadvertently cheat ourselves out of fresh perspectives and new behaviors.

Periodically, we have rebelled against our social conditioning and controls. Examples include the eras of the '20s and '60s. However, most of the time, we are so busy living our lives that we don't question very much. Many of our inaccurate perceptions are comical, some are relatively harmless, and others are lethal with regard to our self-actualization. The distortions that have the most potentially harmful effects are those that we impose on ourselves. Examples of our distorted assumptions and some alternate perspectives are detailed below.

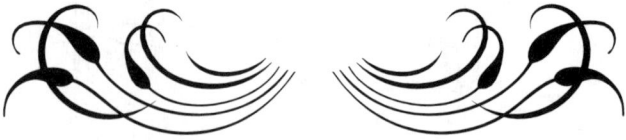

SOCIAL BELIEF SYSTEM:

You can't have your cake and eat it too.

CONSIDER THIS POSSIBILITY:

Why would we want cake if we can't eat it? We *can* have every-thing we want in life!

SOCIAL BELIEF SYSTEM:

Insurance protects us against death and car accidents.

CONSIDER THIS POSSIBILITY:

Self-responsibility protects us against car accidents. Life insur-ance is really death insurance because someone must die so that it can be collected.

SOCIAL BELIEF SYSTEM:

External appearances and first impressions are important indi-cators of who an individual is. They provide excellent criteria for judging someone's character and abilities.

CONSIDER THIS POSSIBILITY:

Although we have been conditioned to make many of our choices based on external appearances, the internal attributes of a per-son are what is important.

External appearances are malleable, at least to an extent. They are not necessarily dependable indicators of a person's charac-ter and abilities. They can be quite deceptive.

Our first impressions of an individual may mirror to us a part of ourselves that we do not wish to see. (The other person may "push our buttons.")

Sometimes, the most difficult people for us to be around have the most focus, purity, wisdom, emotional balance, and self-security. We may be uncomfortable with these individuals because they mirror to us what we don't yet acknowledge about ourselves. We may criticize one of their characteristics because we still judge that attribute in ourselves.

We have also been conditioned not to fully appreciate the depth of character of many individuals who have unusual appearances, including some people with disabilities. Some individuals who look different by birth or choice are extraordinarily developed even though they don't fit our image of how we think they are supposed to look. Many choose to be totally who they are, no matter what the social context. This type of vulnerability is being true to one's self. It is a key component of high self-esteem.

SOCIAL BELIEF SYSTEM:

Life is to be endured. If I'm a really good person, my afterlife will be heavenly.

CONSIDER THIS POSSIBILITY:

I can have an abundance of joy in life now. Life is to be experienced; and it's my right to grow, prosper, and experience ongoing bliss.

SOCIAL BELIEF SYSTEM:

Work diligently and build a nest egg for your retirement. Then, you will have the time and money to enjoy yourself.

CONSIDER THIS POSSIBILITY:

Life is to be lived on a continuous basis. I can choose to enjoy the entire journey of life, rather than waiting until retirement.

Webster's New World Dictionary (10th ed.) defines retirement as withdrawing to a secluded place, going to bed, retreating, giving up one's work because of age, or withdrawing from use. Studies have indicated that those who retire from their work and have nothing to replace it experience poor health and die early.

SOCIAL BELIEF SYSTEM:

It hurts too much to feel painful emotions. If I start feeling my pain, I won't be able to stop. I'll find myself in a bottomless pit, and I won't be able to control my feelings. I will feel drained. I won't have any energy to function. I won't be able to focus on anything but how I feel.

CONSIDER THIS POSSIBILITY:

When I *don't* feel my emotions, I rob myself of vital energy and am easily fatigued. If I feel what I feel, I am always able to control it, if I really need to. Once I unleash the energy that I am using to hold my feelings in check, I find that I have a wealth of new vitality and zest for life.

SOCIAL BELIEF SYSTEM:

If I feel my emotions in public, I will be embarrassed. Others won't like me or want to be around me.

CONSIDER THIS POSSIBILITY:

When I am being real and honest by simply feeling what I feel, I give others permission to also be vulnerable. Although some people withdraw from my presence or tell me not to feel the way I do, I am more connected with myself. I have given myself more freedom to be who I really am.

SOCIAL BELIEF SYSTEM:

"Please mark the right answer by checking the appropriate blank."

CONSIDER THIS POSSIBILITY:

There are very few right answers in life. Generally, there are many viewpoints and multiple ways to accomplish any task. Since we are all unique, each one of us has a different perspective.

SOCIAL BELIEF SYSTEM:
I am dysfunctional because of my past.

CONSIDER THIS POSSIBILITY:
I am only dysfunctional if I choose not to take full responsibility for myself from now on.

SOCIAL BELIEF SYSTEM:
My family is dysfunctional.

CONSIDER THIS POSSIBILITY:
My family members are also learning and receiving feedback as they journey through their lives. Each of us does our best with the knowledge and resources that we have available at any point in time. The experiences with my family served me. I can continue to become stronger and more aware because of all of my past experiences. Everything in life is simply a tool to learn to be who I really am.

SOCIAL BELIEF SYSTEM:
I am addicted to _____ (drugs, alcohol, relationships, sex, shopping, food, gambling, etc.).

CONSIDER THIS POSSIBILITY:
Our real addiction is an addiction to powerlessness. We simply refuse to fully own our capabilities.

SOCIAL BELIEF SYSTEM:
If I could just fix myself, I could be happy.

CONSIDER THIS POSSIBILITY:
The current circumstances of my life are exactly as they should be so that I can learn and take my next steps. There is nothing

wrong with who I am. When I stop trying to fix myself or change situations in my life, I notice that everything that I have been trying to alter begins to shift on its own.

SOCIAL BELIEF SYSTEM:

I want to get rid of my undesirable characteristics.

CONSIDER THIS POSSIBILITY:

All of us have polarities in our psyche. We are all capable of being kind or cruel, loving or hateful, etc. The components of ourselves that we judge as bad only control our behaviors when we don't accept them. When I am dishonest with myself about who I am, the parts of myself that I don't value fight to be recognized and understood.

When I am willing to own all parts of myself, I have acknowledged my shadows. They simply melt back into me. I no longer feel threatened by them because they are just part of who I am. It's as if they are part of a well-read book that I've placed on my bookshelf. Anytime I want to re-read (re-experience) one of my shadows, all I have to do is reach for that book and turn to the appropriate chapter.

SOCIAL BELIEF SYSTEM:

It is better to give than to receive.

CONSIDER THIS POSSIBILITY:

Many people give more easily than they receive because receiving requires feeling that we deserve to be given unconditional love or gifts. We choose to give to others because we find it rewarding to do so; it makes us feel good. There really is no dichotomy between giving and receiving—there is only receiving.

SOCIAL BELIEF SYSTEM:

It is more important to love others than to love ourselves. It is essential to be of service to others.

CONSIDER THIS POSSIBILITY:

Until we really love ourselves, we cannot unconditionally love others. Love has to start at home (inside of ourselves) first. True service to others is spontaneous because we love ourselves enough to automatically extend love and kindness to others.

SOCIAL BELIEF SYSTEM:

I need to learn to love and empower myself.

CONSIDER THIS POSSIBILITY:

"Needing" anything reflects internal struggle. When I "need" something, I push it away because I try to receive it. Life is actually very simple. There are only two requirements for our growth: 1.) be aware of ourselves and our actions, and 2.) not judge ourselves or our circumstances. Self-love and empowerment happen spontaneously when we live in a conscious manner and don't judge ourselves or our experiences.

SOCIAL BELIEF SYSTEM:

A powerful person has status and wealth.

CONSIDER THIS POSSIBILITY:

Powerful people have internal reference systems. They may or may not have external status, wealth, etc. They are true to themselves, even when it is unpopular to be who they are. Frequently, they don't fit our image of how we think they are supposed to look.

SOCIAL BELIEF SYSTEM:

A person who is in control of other people or their actions in a visible way is a powerful individual.

CONSIDER THIS POSSIBILITY:

A powerful person may be "invisible" in our society. People who are empowered have internal sovereignty. They don't need to be recognized by others. They simply know what they know and feel self-secure. They are real and honest with themselves. This soft vulnerability is inconsistent with the social stereotype of a powerful person.

SOCIAL BELIEF SYSTEM:

I need to be in control of my life.

CONSIDER THIS POSSIBILITY:

The only way to have control is to surrender to the natural progression of life. When we relinquish our need to feel in command, we invariably discover that we have always been masters of our own destiny. Each of us has an internal pilot who is always on duty, even when our life feels entirely out of control. Like a guided missile, if we veer slightly off course, we draw signals to ourselves that direct us back on course.

SOCIAL BELIEF SYSTEM:

Co-dependency is a major problem in relationships.

CONSIDER THIS POSSIBILITY:

Co-dependency is a myth. The only relationship we ever have is with ourselves because whomever we resonate with is in our lives so that we can see ourselves in the mirror that they provide us. That reflection offers us opportunities for growth.

SOCIAL BELIEF SYSTEM:

If I don't judge myself, I will never change the things I don't like about myself.

CONSIDER THIS POSSIBILITY:

Self-judgment initiates an internal resistance that inhibits our changing. Accepting ourselves just as we are, right now, is evidence of high self-esteem. The characteristics about ourselves that we have graded as inadequate transform spontaneously when we stop judging and trying to change ourselves.

SOCIAL BELIEF SYSTEM:

It is important that I put my feelings of fear and self-doubt behind me so that I can be productive and get on with my life.

CONSIDER THIS POSSIBILITY:

Self-doubt and fear are tools to reach the next steps in our personal development. When I am closest to having what I want, my self-doubts surface so that I can acknowledge them and give myself permission to move into my next level of growth.

SOCIAL BELIEF SYSTEM:

It bothers me when I can see where others are off track, and they can't see it or don't want to do anything about it.

CONSIDER THIS POSSIBILITY:

Other people are mirrors for us so that we can see ourselves more clearly. If I perceive that someone else is off track and it triggers an emotional response within me, there is something about myself that I need to examine. My judgments of others indicate that I am judging myself because I haven't fully dealt with a related issue.

SOCIAL BELIEF SYSTEM:

Labels and definitions are always helpful so that we can know what something is and is not. They are vital to understanding our reality.

CONSIDER THIS POSSIBILITY:

Labels and definitions can actually limit our thinking. They can also precipitate our feeling separate from others. When labels and definitions disconnect us from other people, they are illusions. This is because we are all mirrors for each other so that we can see ourselves more clearly.

Categorizing people and objects usually limits our thinking to what we have already experienced. Unknown realities are what we are moving toward, and we cannot fully understand them until we experience them.

SOCIAL BELIEF SYSTEM:

People who don't compromise in relationships are selfish. They will never have what they want.

CONSIDER THIS POSSIBILITY:

Compromising who you are with the objective of making another person happy or meeting their needs invariably backfires. If we are to be in authentic relationships with others, we must be able to be ourselves and be accepted for who we are right now.

Being who I am in your presence builds your trust of me in our relationship because we are interconnected. If I am lying to you about what I want or need in our relationship, you will sense this at some level, and you will not trust me in the future. If I am honest with you, you will always know where you stand with me even though you may not always like my actions.

Compromising my Self just for the purpose of being in a relationship means that I feel that I need the relationship in order to feel whole. If this is true, there is something that I wish to "take" from my partner. Compromising my Self in order to be in a relationship with you creates inner turbulence because I am not being who I really am.

SOCIAL BELIEF SYSTEM:

I say to others, "Now, don't feel that way. You'll be OK," when they are upset or afraid. I want them to feel better.

CONSIDER THIS POSSIBILITY:

I'm uncomfortable being around other people who are expressing their feelings. I'm nervous when they feel angry, sad, or afraid, because I'm uneasy with my own anger, sadness, or fear.

I don't approve of people honestly expressing their emotions in public. I don't do this, so their doing so shows me a mirror that I do not wish to see.

SOCIAL BELIEF SYSTEM:

I hit (spank) my children to control them. It teaches them to mind me.

CONSIDER THIS POSSIBILITY:

I hit my children when I feel out of control. I hit them when I feel angry or insecure about my parenting abilities. I don't know how to get them to mind me without showing them that I am physically stronger than they are and can dominate them.

I'm training my children to think that hurting others is an acceptable way to teach them a lesson or display power over them.

Physically hurting children teaches them to fear us. They learn not to trust us because we are capable of hurting them. It is a natural psychological phenomenon that if I hurt you, you will want to retaliate. Do we really want our children to fear and distrust us and to want revenge? Physically hurting our children also teaches them that violence is permissible in our society. They learn that we attempt to convince others of our point of view by hurting them.

SOCIAL BELIEF SYSTEM:

When my children whine, I tell them to "shut up or I'll give you something to cry about." This means that I will spank them if they don't quit crying.

CONSIDER THIS POSSIBILITY:

Threatening to spank children so that they will cease to cry backfires. Even if they stop crying, they have not stopped hurting. They have repressed their pain. I am denying the opportunity for my children to experience their feelings because this is not a convenient time for me. Maybe I don't like the way they are expressing themselves. Maybe I don't know how to listen to them or help them.

SOCIAL BELIEF SYSTEM:

We need to stop the violence that exists in our society.

CONSIDER THIS POSSIBILITY:

We are violent within ourselves. We judge ourselves with a vengeance. We stuff our feelings until they explode, and then we hurt others or ourselves. We teach our children that violence is permissible. They learn this from our child-rearing practices, our treatment of other people, our movies, etc.

We are inconsistent. For example, we teach our children that it's not OK for us to hit another adult, but it's OK to hit children. For all of these reasons, the cycle of violence continues to escalate in our society.

SOCIAL BELIEF SYSTEM:

Our society is so developed that we have pills to fix our misery (our depression, pain, anxiety, etc.). We have quick and pain-less solutions (drugs) to deal with our pain.

CONSIDER THIS POSSIBILITY:

Our bodies reflect the status of our feelings. We hold tension and stress in our physical forms. When we feel our emotions, we gain new energy that has been held in check because we have been suppressing our feelings. Sometimes we misuse our technological and medical advantages to obtain a quick fix; a temporary Band-Aid.

This backfires because we haven't addressed our emotional issues, and they continue to fester inside of us. We not only stunt our own personal growth, we provide inadequate role models for our children. They learn not to feel their emotions or deal with the core of their problems. Controlling our feelings merely represses them. They will eventually surface. Rather than welcoming our emotions as tools for greater energy and long-term happiness, we fear experiencing them.

SOCIAL BELIEF SYSTEM:

We have drugs to take care of children with attention-deficit dis-order.

CONSIDER THIS POSSIBILITY:

When drugs are used to control the behavior of children without determining what needs aren't being met and what emotions aren't being expressed, we are programming the children to perceive drugs as the answer to their problems. Other children will notice our "quick fix" even though we teach children to avoid drugs.

Many children with attention-deficit disorders can be helped by simple dietary changes or by recognizing that they require different approaches to meet their needs. What are their behaviors really reflecting?

Drugs may provide adult caretakers (schools and parents) with a short-term solution to their concerns about the childrens' conduct. However, it is also important to consider the fact that their behaviors may actually be an opportunity for us to assist them in developing their self-esteem and learning how to safely and constructively express their frustrations.

SOCIAL BELIEF SYSTEM:

I want to learn to leave my body so that I can become enlightened.

CONSIDER THIS POSSIBILITY:

Although most of us hold tremendous judgments that our bodies aren't beautiful just as they are, our bodies are amazing tools. They give us clues so that we can become more self-aware. They indicate intuitive urges to us, and they serve as a primary means of experiencing our feelings. Our bodies also hold our genetic memory banks. It's important to be in our bodies and to experience our physical sensations.

Being in a body is not a punishment; it's a privilege. What we can learn in a body can't be learned in any other way.

SOCIAL BELIEF SYSTEM:

I want to be fully empowered.

CONSIDER THIS POSSIBILITY:

The only way to be fully empowered is to be self-responsible and to be willing to be as capable as we already are. We say we want our empowerment, but it is important to become conscious of the areas where we want to give our power away to others. When do we ask others to make our decisions for us? When do we want them to do our work for us? In what areas of our lives are we still blaming others for our circumstances rather than being in forward motion?

When we are avoiding our emotions, we are not using one of the best tools available for our empowerment. We are blocking our creative forces and initiating civil wars within us. We squabble with ourselves because we attempt to deny the truth of what exists.

SOCIAL BELIEF SYSTEM:

Many people suffer from low self-esteem.

CONSIDER THIS POSSIBILITY:

Many people do not yet fully own their personal power or acknowledge their capabilities.

SOCIAL BELIEF SYSTEM:

I want to develop security in my life.

CONSIDER THIS POSSIBILITY:

The only guarantee in life is constant change. We constantly move from familiar to uncharted territories, leaving one comfort zone after another.

SOCIAL BELIEF SYSTEM:

Set goals and know exactly where you are going in life so that you will ensure that you get there.

CONSIDER THIS POSSIBILITY:

There is only the journey of life. There is no "destination," because there is no endpoint. We don't always consciously know where we are going next, although the navigator inside of us always knows. Being open to our next steps ceases our struggle in life. The bridges into our unknowns are built as we travel through life, and the building materials are our emotions. (Chapter 17 fully describes this concept and provides a two-page illustration.)

SOCIAL BELIEF SYSTEM:

Self-actualization requires years of constant hard work.

CONSIDER THIS POSSIBILITY:

Self-actualization really is quite simple. It requires only that we live consciously and not judge ourselves or the events in our lives.

SOCIAL BELIEF SYSTEM:

I want to stay in my comfort zone.

CONSIDER THIS POSSIBILITY:

The term "comfort zone" is an oxymoron. If comfort zones are so gratifying, why are we always leaving them to venture into the unexplored? Even when we struggle to maintain our predictable existences, we eventually become bored or dissatisfied and push ourselves out of our comfy but unchallenging nests.

SOCIAL BELIEF SYSTEM:

When things are going too well, just wait! The other shoe must drop.

CONSIDER THIS POSSIBILITY:

No way! It's impossible for things to go "too well." Just say "No thanks" to your joy alarm.

CONCLUSION:

Some individuals have switched their modus operandi from some of the above social illusions to their own perceptions of the truth. For example, a recent study indicated that fewer parents spank their children now than in any previous generation.

Living with the upside down and backward distortions has provided us the opportunity to participate in one end of a polarity. In many cases, we wouldn't be open to the upper end of a polarity without having experienced life the opposite way. By consciously experiencing an illusion, such as blaming others for our circumstances, we learn to fully appreciate the truth—we are responsible for our own lives.

If you would be a real seeker after truth, it is necessary that at least once in your life you doubt, as far as possible, all things.
René Descartes

The important thing is not to stop questioning.
Albert Einstein

What matters is that you believe in your own perceptions and your truth. If you are open to the possibility of new wisdom and understanding, test the ideas in this chapter. You will easily create opportunities to do so. You may receive proof tomorrow. It may be a year from now. Anything that you can't prove to yourself is not your truth at this time. Just consider it as a possibility until a later date.

EXERCISES

1. Describe or list some of the things that you have been taught that are not your truth. (They are upside down and backward.)

2. Now that you have consciously experienced the above illusions, you can establish your own truth and believe in your own perceptions. Make brief notes below regarding how this relates to your experiencing the polarities in your life.

TEN

CAUTIONS ABOUT AFFIRMATIONS AND VISUALIZATION

Am I trying to capture a castle I don't really need or want?
Stuart Wilde

This book does not recommend affirmations or visualization. These techniques are part of a school of thought called *create your own reality*. They are fine tools, and we are all powerful enough to create what we *think* we want in our lives. Yet there is so much more available to us.

Regarding affirmations, a continuum exists from empty pep talk and jingles to mental imagery based on scientific principles. Mental imagery based on empirical evidence does work. There are many effective auto suggestion and hypnosis techniques, audiotapes, etc.

Cancer patients at several medical research facilities have been taught to relax and then use visual imagery to assist in their healing. Some strategies, such as the Simonton techniques, have been quite effective. Norman Cousins' work regarding inducing laughter to stimulate healing was based on common sense and is consistent with theories and practices designed to arouse endorphins for the purpose of promoting healing. Yet, patients who used visualizations and didn't work on their emotional issues often re-created opportunities to confront them. Examples included women who healed lumps in their breasts and later developed additional growths.

Affirmations and visualizations don't work when we think we don't deserve the pictures we are mentally projecting. They are also ineffective when some part of us knows that what we are projecting for ourselves is not the best thing for us at this time. When we try to manipulate our subconscious minds by programming affirmations or visualizations, we create a resistance inside of us because we are not being honest with ourselves. Affirmations such as "I am now happy" or "I now love myself," when we know they are dishonest, don't work because our subconscious minds are too smart to believe anything that is not true. They store all of our memories and knowledge.

If we are extrapolating from our yesterdays and assuming that they will govern our future, we are living in the past. When we try to manipulate our subconscious, we establish a hidden opposition to change inside of ourselves. An alternative approach is to work with our subconscious by liberating any repressed emotions and being honest with ourselves.

Frequently, we misdirect our affirmations and visualizations. Generally, the surface reality of our lives is not the genuine personal growth material that we are working on. It is merely the substance that is at a conscious level. Therefore, we can program affirmations and visualizations designed to change the concerns we are aware of and inadvertently miss our authentic issues.

As an example, when I was procrastinating completing this book, I could have designed affirmations and visualizations focused on its conclusion. However, my real issues were fear of change (the unknown) and fear of owning more of my capabilities.

Using affirmations and visualizations would have been a slower process than feeling my emotions because that would have been an indirect tactic. Being conscious of my procrastination, not judging it, and being open to the wisdom from the experience of my self-sabotage brought me clarity *and* the completion of the book. (This example was described in Chapter 2, "Change is Gain—Not Pain.")

Generally, we engage in conscious creating because we want to avoid our uncomfortable feelings, especially our fears, or because we think there is something wrong with failure.

> Fear and failure aren't obstacles in our path. They *are* our path. Failures are not only natural in the course of ambition, they're vital.
>
> Gregg Levoy, 1992, *This Business of Writing*

It is important to ask ourselves, "Do I care more about my self-image—e.g., am I concerned about the fact that some may think I failed—or do I trust and love myself enough to seek the knowledge to be gained from the situation so that I can become even more whole?" Famous inventors and philosophers such as Ben Franklin and Thomas Edison valued their learning experiences more than they feared public criticism of their failures. Consequently, they were highly successful individuals.

> I can't properly describe the freedom that rejection brought me.
>
> James Gabriel Berman, 1995 (His comment was about his first novel, *Uninvited*, rejected by 60 publishers and now available in ten languages.)

When things don't work, I feel emotions that I need to experience, and my fear turns into new power. This is an inevitable process of life. If I don't experience the fear now, I will create an additional opportunity to feel it so that I can grow and take my next step in life, so why not now?

If I feel that I don't deserve what I am affirming or visualizing, I may have only short-term success. This is because I will self-sabotage and take something away from myself that I have created. I will have a need to re-create my pain. As examples, how many people leave one abusive relationship and move into another? How many of us are criticized for chronically being late to appointments? Do you know someone who experiences one accident after another or is always a day late and a dollar short?

There are no quick fixes in life
that avoid dealing with our emotional content.

If you've never used your senses to visualize what you desire and feel yourself having it, you might be surprised at the results. It is an empowering process for those who don't yet know their own power.

However, **when we completely trust ourselves and the process of life, we don't feel a need to create anything.** The reason is that the very attempt to create something different means that there is a need to change what already exists. That assumes that the present circumstances of our lives are deficient in some way.

Striving to create our own reality assumes that where we are right now needs to be fixed. Our struggle ensues because we label our present situations as painful, difficult, or inadequate. We are all brilliant beings, and there is perfection in everything we experience. Wherever we are is serving us, providing us an opportunity to learn about ourselves and to feel emotions that need to be felt.

When I was first getting in touch with my own power, I was an avid conscious creator. Every morning, I did some exercises so that I felt centered and then visualized and felt what I wanted to occur on that day (or in the more distant future). Most of what I thought I wanted came true. The catch was that, like all of us, I change very fast. By the time what I wanted manifested itself, I very often didn't want it anymore.

As an example, one morning I knew I would be having lunch with a key member of the business community where I was beginning to establish a base of consulting. I visualized hearing Bill say he wanted to employ me as a consultant. I saw his eyes when he said it and clearly heard him say, "I'll call you within two weeks to set up a schedule." I saw and felt myself getting back into my car, feeling excitement that I had a new consulting job.

After doing this exercise, I went about my day which included the lunch date with Bill. Precisely as I had visualized, he looked at me and said, "I'll call you within two weeks to set up a schedule." I got back into my car, genuinely feeling excited about the new consulting job that would be mine. However, as I drove away, I felt deflated. I no longer wanted the job with Bill. I didn't even know why. I just knew it wasn't what I really desired. It wasn't until a week later that the reason was clear. An opportunity came through that was so much better. If I had simply attended the lunch open to learn *whatever* I could learn from the experience, I wouldn't have had to backtrack with Bill later and tell him that I wasn't interested after all. My long-term relationship with him would have been much better if I hadn't meddled in my own life, trying to manipulate my future.

From that point on, I began to conscientiously watch my efforts to create my reality. There were instances where, as with Bill, I changed my mind because something much better was just around the corner, and I hadn't been patient and trusting enough. There were times when people said or did just what I had envisioned, but the results were devastating. They either wouldn't follow through with what they said they would do or the results were inferior in some way to what would have occurred naturally.

I had never intended to be manipulating other people with my visualizations, but it became clear that that's exactly what I was doing. Once I noticed that, I began observing other people I knew who were also conscious creators. I rapidly discovered that they were also manipulating me so that I could see myself in the mirror.

I had given permission for a seminar to be held at my home on a one-time basis. Preparation for the event entailed more time and inconvenience than I had anticipated. I was pleased to do it for this specific occasion because I had given my word, but I decided I wasn't interested in hosting further activities.

The event ended in my backyard. The participants thanked me for the use of my home, and the facilitator said, "Maybe Doris will invite us to have another event here," clearly expecting a response. The words came out of my mouth, "Oh, sure," but I didn't mean them. I didn't even feel that the words came from within me. They were preplanted words from her visualization. The next day I called and said I had thought over the situation and needed her to know that my schedule would not permit the next event to be held at my home.

Another example concerned the creation of a new career. For three years, I had wanted to relinquish my position as director of a national agency. I was bored and wanted a new challenge, but the time wasn't right because I had some additional personal work to complete before making the occupational change. Instead of marveling at the perfection of life and the brilliance of a scenario in which I was challenged personally but not professionally at that particular time, I was impatient to experience a different career. I was attempting to push the river, and the rivers of life can't be rushed. They flow where and when they flow, as fast or slow as they are supposed to at any given time.

Finally, I was complete with the issues within myself that gave me the freedom to leave the agency. The rushes of excitement and relief filled me with joy. I didn't know what my next step would be, but I wanted a major change, and consulting work would be the bridge.

While cultivating my base of clients, I wrote grants to fund another national agency to direct. In the area in which I was competing, only one national grant was funded each year, and I fully used my conscious creating techniques.

I secured a 1/2 million dollar grant before I realized that I had just repeated an old pattern. I had created exactly what I had wished to leave behind. After agonizing, I sent the grant back, an action that thoroughly shocked the funding agency. I could no longer allow myself to limit my life to what I had known in the past.

It became crystal clear to me that I was much better off to trust myself and the process of my life, no matter how much I sometimes wanted to control or manipulate it. Rather than attempt to create my reality, it was time to allow it to unfold.

Needing to create something in our lives is always based on an attempt to control our future, because we're afraid that if we don't intervene in our lives, we won't be safe or have what we want or need. Thus, creating our own reality is fear-based, because we're not trusting ourselves and the natural processes of our lives.

On the other hand, when I feel my emotions and don't judge my current situation, I'm no longer living in fear. I have no desire to control anything. I know that I deserve to have what I want, and I don't think I need to program how it will occur or try to make it happen. My psyche is so clear that my next step emerges easily, without strife or resistance.

What a joy it is to observe children and animals. In most cases, they wake up each day without struggle. They *expect* an interesting day. If they pose any question to themselves, it may be, "I wonder what I'll do or learn today?" They do not routinely jolt out of their slumber, hastily rub the sleep out of their eyes and frantically remind themselves to "hurry up and program things so today will work out OK."

> When we are not accepting things as they are,
> we are in struggle.

At one point, William and I went on a "driveabout." We had both learned a great deal from reading about the walkabouts of the aborigines. In one book dealing with the subject, *Mutant Message DownUnder*, Marlo Morgan described how the native people have no expectations, yet their needs are always met.

We decided to challenge ourselves by terminating our worldly obligations, selling possessions we didn't need, and driving away with no destination, plans, or timeline. We knew we would reach some new levels within ourselves, yet we had no clues how they would appear. We knew it was time for a change in our lives but lacked clarity about our next steps. Our inner guidance indicated that by trusting ourselves enough to jump from another ledge into an unknown reality, we would not only develop more self-trust, we would receive the specific information we needed to move into our next phases of life.

We experienced various layers of anxiety and fear and occasionally felt crazy, yet our instincts kept telling us that this was the next move for us to make. After several months of spontaneous traveling, our predominant emotions were ecstasy and freedom. Eventually, we settled into a location that neither of us expected, and our satisfaction was beyond our wildest dreams. It was confirmation that allowing life to unfold can bring bliss and freedom in the most unexpected ways.

> The paradox of feeling a need to "consciously create"
> is that we are all *naturally* involved in a
> constant creative process.
> Creation is as natural and spontaneous as breathing.

We all have an inner guidance system that never sleeps. It works 24 hours a day, without vacations or holidays. It steadily redirects us when we sway off course, whether we are asleep or awake.

This guidance system is a core element within us. **The only way to be "in control of our lives" is to surrender to ourselves. This means trusting ourselves—our processes of life—even when it feels crazy to do so.** We know exactly what we are doing by leading ourselves down all of the paths in life that we walk. Just like a guided missile, if we go off course, we always direct ourselves back on track.

By giving up conscious attempts to control ourselves, we acknowledge that we are always in control. Being willing to relin-

quish what we know and cherish in the purity of allowing ourselves to be open to our next experiences delivers the highest
freedom and self-trust available.

It is not only unnecessary to try to command our ships, attempting to rule our lives actually hinders our progress. It creates inner rebellion that causes us to continue to re-create what we
say we don't want. This is because conscious creating is based
on our present knowledge and experience. We can only project
a future that is based on our past. We can't design affirmations
or visualizations with scenarios that we are not yet able to comprehend or envision.

When we continue to program (create) from our previous experiences, we will keep manifesting more of what we have experienced. Our tendency will be to repeat our old patterns. An acquaintance of mine has consciously created so many relationships that I have lost count. She still has not found her perfect man even though she has created men and relationships that meet all of her specifications and visualizations. Each time she has created, she has made a more exhaustive list of characteristics that she desires and those that aren't acceptable to her. She focuses laserbeam attention and visualizes her new relationships with awesome precision. She manifests what she asks for. However, none of the relationships satisfy her, so she relinquishes them and starts anew.

She expends a lot of time and energy with her need to keep re-creating. (It also takes a lot of effort to dissolve relationships.) She is not yet open to the possibility that if she used this same focus and time to simply experience her life, not judging her adventures or herself, her life would unfold in a very different way. My guess is that when it was time for her to participate in a relationship, it would look very different than her projections, and she would be much more satisfied.

Consciously creating keeps us bound to our known reality. It is all we have experienced up to this point in our lives, so it is our only foundation for creating our future. It severely limits us because there is so much more in life than we consciously know. We and our world are changing so rapidly that we do not always know what we will desire in times to come. Yet, when we visualize a future based on what we now comprehend about life, we are powerful enough to limit ourselves to just that.

Consciously creating also ensures that we continue to struggle. This is because we are not living in the present moment. We are attempting to manipulate our lives out of fear and a lack of self-trust. Instead of simply feeling our fear, we inadvertently set up a barrier inside of ourselves which slows our growth. Our fear is a mixture of apprehension that we don't deserve or can't have what we want and an attempt to control how we receive it.

We don't yet fully trust that we will *only* bring into our lives what is our best next step. When we simply feel the fear that we are trying to avoid, we liberate our *innate* creative forces, instead of blocking them. When we wonder why things are the way they are and desire to create something different, we are not accepting what exists. We are assuming that something is in error and needs to be repaired. The truth is that there is perfection in all of life's experiences. Whatever my reality is right now, it is serving me, providing me an opportunity to learn about myself and to feel emotions that need to be experienced.

> There is no such thing
> as being in the wrong place or the wrong time.

If you feel a need to program your life, just do so consciously. Be aware that you are confining yourself to more of your past because it is all you know and understand at this time. Be willing to ask yourself what you are afraid of that impels you to want to have control over your future. Know that your fear of some form of your past being hurled into your future is causing you to *live* in the future (trying to make something happen when it is not yet time) instead of living in the present. Acknowledge conscious creating as a steppingstone so that you can begin to comprehend how powerful you are. Once you develop more self-trust, you will no longer have a desire to change your circumstances or consciously create your reality.

The following are examples of how affirmations and visualization may not always serve us.

Situation 1:

Challenge: I feel physically ill.

Intellectual Approach: Affirm, "I feel better and better all of the time." I visualize myself feeling so good that I am enjoying my favorite sport.

Truth: I don't feel well.

Possible Results of Intellectual Approach: Denial of how I really feel causes a reaction in my body (a hidden blockage). I use a certain percentage of my energy to maintain this denial of what exists. This percentage of energy is then unavailable for my full functioning. I am inciting an inner disturbance because I am lying to myself. I am pushing and prodding myself to believe what I know is not true. The percentage of energy that I am using to fight the truth could have been used to assist me in healing my body. Instead, it can actually promote disease.

Alternative Approach: Acknowledge that I don't feel well and take excellent care of my body so that it can heal itself. Secure any assistance I need to allow my body to do so. Feel whatever is thwarted at the emotional level that is keeping me from feeling well physically. Decide not to judge the fact that I don't feel well.

Be willing to experience my physical discomfort consciously, without judging myself or my experience. Be open to how the experience may be serving me. It may be directing me to learn more about my body, to force myself to take better care of it, and to experience emotions that have surfaced and are ready to be felt.

Situation 2:

Challenge: I want to lose weight.

Intellectual Approaches: Affirm "I am slim and trim," or "I love my weight." Visualize myself at the beach with a slim body, lying in the sun.

Truth: I am concerned about the health implications of my excess weight, and I judge myself for being overweight.

Possible Results of Intellectual Approach: I assume that my affirmation will transform my challenge and call my friend to go out for a "decadent dessert spree." I become more discouraged when I don't see results after using my affirmation for a month. I tell my friend, "I guess I am just destined to have a fat body." There is a growing discomfort inside of me because the truth is that I don't love my weight, and I feel uncomfortable.

Alternative Approach: Identify or acknowledge any medical or nutritional condition that may be related to my being overweight. Implement any changes that need to happen to deal with such a condition.

Be willing to consciously have this experience without judging it as bad. Feel any emotional blockages instead of holding onto them. They may be related to feeling out of control in some area of my life. Perhaps I feel cheated by some experience or victim to rapid change. Ask myself: How is it serving me to experience the emotions that surface when I feel overweight? Do I feel that my extra layer "protects" me in some way?

Frequently, these emotions involve a lack of love for myself, and that just needs to be felt. When I accept myself just as I am, I am not trying to change anything. I am no longer in judgment of myself, and my armor, designed to protect me from feeling my emotions, drops away. I develop inner peace, and I notice that things that I was trying to modify begin to alter on their own. Because I am no longer judging myself or my circumstances, I develop more self-love. This happens effortlessly when I drop my disapproval of my weight (myself) and the experience.

Situation 3:

Challenge: I am procrastinating with regard to completing my work.

Intellectual Approaches: Affirm, "I love my work," and "I use my time well." Visualize myself being happy because my work is completed, and I am relaxing or celebrating with my friends.

Truth: I am not getting my work done in a timely fashion.

Possible Results of Intellectual Approach: When I use this affirmation, I am not being truthful with myself, and I know it. Therefore, I am creating a clash inside of me that culminates in emotions of shame and guilt about not doing what I say I am doing. I am adding to my feelings of inadequacy. If I were feeling passionate about myself and my work, I would do the work, without resistance.

Alternative Approach: Be willing to consciously have the experience of procrastinating, without judging myself for doing so. Ask myself: How is it serving me to delay my success? What am I gaining from this experience that I would not receive if I simply finished my work in a timely manner?

Feel the areas where I don't want to do my work. Would I rather do other work? No work? Do I fear failure? Do I feel inadequate? Do I want to act "not good enough" so that someone who is expecting me to complete this work will validate my opinion of myself as inadequate? Do I fear success?—i.e., do I think my life will change, and I fear that? Am I afraid that I won't be liked because others will be jealous of my success?

CONCLUSIONS:

Meeting a challenge such as the examples above requires *participating* in our emotions, our bodies, and our minds. This means going beyond observing, analyzing, and talking about our feelings. It means *experiencing* them, becoming one with them. This happens when we stop judging our emotions. We push nothing away. We embrace the reality of ourselves and our lives just as they are right now.

When we attempt to be in control of our lives, we use a portion of our energy to avoid our feelings. Because we are hiding from the reality of our lives, our hidden emotions dominate our actions. The irony is that we have then become "victim" to one of our best resources. Being *out* of control is the only way to be *in* control because we are trusting ourselves and are not attempting to restrain ourselves from being fully alive. When we allow ourselves to feel whatever we feel, everything in our lives is based on choice.

The following exercise provides an alternative to conscious creating.

♦ Have the courage to ask yourself, "What am I really feeling?"

♦ Feel your emotions, without judgment.

♦ Ask yourself:

  • How is this experience serving me?
  • What am I learning from it?

It is important to work on our subconscious minds by dealing with our unresolved emotional issues. Be real with yourself. The key to bringing what we want into our lives is having passion for ourselves. When we are honest with ourselves about how we feel, life unfolds effortlessly. When we allow life to unfold, change is ongoing. Passion for ourselves provides enthusiasm for all other aspects of our lives, including our work and our relationships.

Many people find themselves doing affirmations or visualizations over and over about the same subject matter. If conscious creating was the final answer, they would probably have the perfect relationship and unlimited wealth.

If you still feel a need to consciously create, just do so with your eyes wide open. Know that if you try to manipulate your subconscious by programming affirmations or visualizations, you are creating an internal obstruction because you are being dishonest with yourself. There is no need to judge your fear or your perceived need to create. It's just important to be conscious of what you are doing and why.

EXERCISES

1. How can conscious creating limit you to your known reality instead of allowing you to advance into new ways of experiencing your life?

2. What are you afraid of when you have the desire to control or change your life or your future?

3. What emotions are you avoiding feeling?

4. How is it serving you to be where you are in your life right now?

5. Record an example of a time when you realized that the only way to have control in your life was to give up your attempts to control.

ELEVEN

EMOTIONS: WHO NEEDS 'EM?

> *Toby:*   *I can't let myself feel emotions, especially fear, or I won't be able to do what I need to do. When I was a kid, my baseball coach taught me never to feel any fear when I was at bat. He said if I did, I'd never be able to swing the bat and hit the ball. I still follow that advice, especially in my business.*
>
> *Pat:*   *Do you always "hit the ball?"*
>
> *Toby:*   *Nope.*
>
> *Pat:*   *Are you willing to consider another approach?*

We have the misconception that emotions are too threatening or painful to feel, that they are a nuisance rather than a tool. Yet, we go to the movies to have a good cry. We ride a roller coaster or see a scary movie knowing that we will feel afraid. We also compassionately watch the android on the *STAR TREK* series wish he had the capacity to experience human emotions!

> Why would we have the capacity to feel if it wasn't useful?

Even though most of us have been programmed since childhood to believe that feeling our inborn emotions is not OK, there is widespread agreement in our society that traditional approaches aren't effective in today's world. During the last 40 years, we have moved beyond our blind enactment of the "Ozzie and Harriet" scenario and our programming to climb the corporate ladder. The original pictures of the family have crumbled. Dissolved and reshaped families are now the norm rather than the exception. Many large corporations have teetered on the edge of bankruptcy, and some futurists forecast that by the year 2000, the majority of North Americans will function in entrepreneurial or small business settings.

We have begun to own the extent of our social maladies and are searching for solutions. Books, seminars, talk shows, and audio- and videotapes claim to teach us to think like winners, work on our self-esteem and our relationships, learn parenting techniques, and adopt spiritual practices.

A great number of valuable techniques and tools exist. This body of work does not compete with any of them, yet it offers an essential component that is rarely addressed—*using* the painful emotions and experiences that we have struggled in vain to evict from our lives. Refusing to acknowledge our feelings not only creates physical discomfort and eventually illness, but it freezes the flow of our power. On the other hand, allowing the natural course of our feelings liberates vast quantities of energy in our bodies and in our psyches. It creates an energy flow that *spontaneously* produces what we desire in our lives.

These incredible tools (our feelings), ever available to us, have been abused by our society but not effectively used. Almost all successful marketing strategies are based on the fact that we make over 80 percent of our decisions based on our emotions. Textbooks and training opportunities for attorneys and people in the fields of sales, advertising, and marketing emphasize appealing to human emotions.

We are taught to use fear, love, guilt, sadness, and anger as motivators to build our profit margins but to avoid feeling them on a personal level. Because we are too smart to believe our denial of our painful feelings and experiences, our anxiety and pain control us! We drag out our outmoded muskets and cannons and engage ourselves in yet another civil war simply because we are attempting to hide who we really are in that moment from the most important person in our lives—ourselves. By refusing to feel the depth of our pain, we inadvertently also inhibit our ability to feel the height of our joy, love, and empowerment.

We are afraid the love that is offered to us isn't genuine, long-lasting, or unconditional. We sound a joy alarm and post our fear that we will be hurt or abandoned as a sentinel to guard our hearts. The obedient sentry allows none to enter the forbidden territory. In exchange for our safety, we cheat ourselves out of opportunities to fully express or receive love and joy.

Individuals with the highest self-esteem are honest with themselves and others regarding how they feel. People who don't categorize their emotions as positive or negative are able to fully love others because their vital forces are not trapped in self-deception regarding how they feel.

Our emotions are similar to the scorned lover who waits until his heart's desire overcomes her fear of his undying affection and allows herself to receive his deep love. They are like the faithful dog who was lost on a family trip and traveled hundreds of miles, somehow finding his way home safely. He shows up with sore paws and a hungry belly, fiercely wagging his tail, reflecting his indefatigable desire to be our best friend.

Whether it is our love or our fear, our emotions are always waiting to serve us, no matter how long they must wait for our comprehension of just how precious they are. When we allow them to teach us the language they speak (us talking to ourselves), they become our best friends. They open our hearts and fully empower us because they provide us the freedom to be real and honest with ourselves and therefore with others. Our courage to be truthful and to feel what we feel provides a foundation that grows into self-respect and self-love.

Our inability to safely and constructively express ourselves is related to many of our most critical social problems. These include crime, substance abuse, parenting deficiencies, domestic and other violence, degenerative diseases, and poor work performance. We are spending vast amounts of money and wasting human potential by imprisoning or institutionalizing many who could have learned simple techniques of expressing their feelings. The integrity of our future society requires that all of us learn to safely and constructively express our emotions.

The lanterns have already begun to be illuminated, and a growing number of individuals are beginning to comprehend that pain and discomfort are valuable resources for personal growth. As we become more honest with ourselves and live in a more conscious manner, we will become more aware of our insecurities, how we solve problems, and when we deny our personal issues. This chapter and the next (chapters 11 and 12) describe elements of today's world, and chapter 13 depicts a possible future.

Each vignette is based on an actual case study and illustrates some of our behavior patterns when we are not using our emotions as tools to enhance our lives.

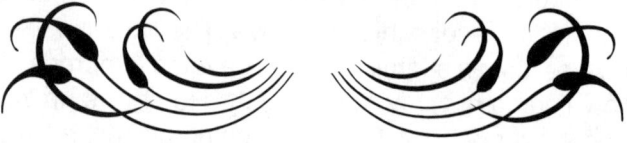

VIEWS OF THE PRESENT

Issue:

I'm afraid that if I let myself feel my emotions, I'll lose control. I'm afraid my feelings will control me.

Wendy picked up the phone and tentatively placed the receiver by her ear. It was Betty again. "I'm just checking on you," she said with sincere concern in her voice.

"You don't need to. I'm fine," Wendy responded harshly.

"Wendy, you need to give yourself permission to feel your loss. You're wearing yourself out by pretending you aren't hurting." Betty was pushing her limit, and she knew it.

"No!" Wendy responded vehemently. "You haven't been through this. I have to keep making myself get out of bed and putting one foot in front of the other. If I start feeling this, it'll never stop. It will control me, and I'll never be able to get anything done."

Betty sighed, wishing she could relieve Wendy's pain. She knew she couldn't, and their conversations grew more strained each day. She sat in silence trying to think of something she could say to ease her friend's distress.

Then she heard Wendy's voice crying, "I won't let this get to me. I won't!"

Betty knew that the conversation was over. Her friend wasn't able to see that her denial of her deep pain and her fear of losing control were already dominating her life.

Issue:

I deny my feelings and possibly hurt myself and others.

Mike glowered at his friends as they moved their chairs back from the table and hurriedly checked their watches against the train schedule.

Bert and Hank looked at each other anxiously. Time was running out, and they both felt their efforts to communicate with Mike were getting nowhere.

Bert spoke, "Look Mike, the commuter will be here in 15 minutes, and I told the family I'd be home by 9:00 tonight. Hank and I only suggested getting together because we wanted to be helpful. I think we just made you angrier."

Mike's eyes narrowed as his face flushed. He slammed his fist on the table exclaiming, "I'm not angry! Why don't both of you just give it up?"

Hank spoke next, "Mike, I need to go, too. I've got early meetings in the morning. I wish we could have worked this out with you." He stood up, laid two bills on the table and nervously shifted from one foot to the other before finally stepping away from the table. He really didn't like to leave what felt to him like a very messy situation, but he had tried his best to deal with Mike.

Mike ignored them both as they walked hesitantly from the table. They hastened their pace as they reached the door and anxiously glanced at their watches again.

Mike sat sullenly at the bar and drank for a couple of hours. Then he noticed that it was after 10:00. "Bartender," he called with slurred speech, "I need one more so I can drive home."

Issue:
My energy is unavailable to me because I'm using it to repress my emotions.

Connie reached over and took her brother's hand, "How about going to the coast with us, Don? We'll be leaving Friday after work and coming back Sunday morning."

Don slumped more deeply into his recliner and looked at his sister. "Nope. I'm too tired."

Connie coaxed him, "It might do you good to get out."

"No thanks, Sis", he responded, resting his head on his chest. "I really am just too tired. I don't know what's wrong with me. Ever since Mary left and I lost my job, I haven't had the energy to do anything except watch TV."

Issue:
I just want to feel good.

Carla lay on her back and gazed at the designs on the ceiling. She loved the way they continued to jump around and change colors. Dozens of metallic blue figures slithered down the far wall and became a bright emerald green and then a mesmerizing yellow. Fluid, silky, and shiny, they oozed over all four walls and then into the palms of her outstretched hands. Her heart raced wildly, sweat poured off her forehead, and her body tingled all over. She giggled and laughed as she waved her legs in the air.

Sighing, she turned toward Paul, "I never knew I could feel this good. It's magical! Why didn't I do this before?"

She rolled over to face him and closed her eyes. Music played softly in the background, and she lost track of the time as she moved her feet to the beat.

Then she remembered Paul. "Hey, Paul, do you have some more stuff that we can use later?"

He didn't answer. He lay crumpled on the floor, without color or heartbeat, while Carla continued to float in her fog of ecstasy.

Issue:
Sometimes I play martyr.

Richard watched Lena's slight frame bend beneath the heavy load of boxes she was carrying. "Can I help you?" he asked.

"No, it's OK. I can do it," she said, breathing hard and avoiding his outstretched arms. She stumbled to the table and heaved her oppressive burden onto the tabletop. Wincing with pain, she grasped the small of her back.

"Why wouldn't you let me help you?" Richard asked with a hurt look on his face.

"Because I can do it myself," she sighed.

"What happened to you yesterday, Lena? We were supposed to meet at 3:30, and I waited for you until 4:15. Where were you?"

"Penny dumped her kids for me to watch them. She didn't give me any warning, so I couldn't let you know I wasn't going to show up."

"She does that all the time. Why don't you tell her she can't take advantage of you like that?"

"Oh, it's OK. Other people would be furious about the way she treats me, but I don't mind."

Richard's eyes searched Lena's face, observing how precisely her furrowed brow reflected her anger. Then, very evenly, he asked, "Lena, why are you acting like everybody's doormat?"

"I don't know what you're talking about," she snapped.

"Lena, you've got a lot of anger sitting beneath the surface. Some day you're going to blow your stack."

"Richard, I *said* I am *not* angry!"

Issue:
Sometimes, I play victim. I'm not responsible for myself.

Brandon braced himself before entering the building, adjusting his tie and straightening his coat. He could feel the anger of the others before he saw their faces. As soon as he walked into the meeting room, several of them cleared their throats and others looked at their watches to remind him that he was late—again.

Brandon talked fast, eager to defend himself. "Hi. I know I'm late, but the traffic was horrendous."

Paul addressed him first, "Brandon, you're always late, and it's not fair to the rest of us. We made it on time, and we came on the same streets that you travel."

Brandon flinched. He hated the sinking feeling in his stomach. "Well, there was more to it than that. I can't seem to get anywhere on time anymore. Either the kids stop me from leaving the house on time or the phone rings at the last minute."

Karen spoke next, "I have the same situations at my house. I just had to learn to set boundaries with the kids and with the phone. I also had to learn to allow extra time for the traffic jams."

Several of the members nodded in agreement, and a man Brandon didn't recognize added, "That's the same principle I teach my kids."

The group was solidifying, and it wasn't in Brandon's favor. He began to perspire. "Well, let's get down to business," he encouraged, hoping to divert the group's attention. "I've thought about what you said. You wanted me to talk to Harvey about our conflict. I just can't put myself in that position."

Ed was clearly irritated and interrupted Brandon before he could proceed with his dialogue. "Brandon, you're supposed to be representing this group and working things out with Harvey. Does this mean that you won't deal with him directly?"

"Ed, my parents used to yell at me anytime I tried to talk to them about a problem. They always told me to shut up, that I was the one who was wrong. So, I'm just too uncomfortable talking to people about issues. One of you will have to deal with Harvey."

Issue:
Sometimes, I treat other people as objects.

Dan looked at Larry, wishing he would vanish into thin air. He was so tired of him hanging around, and he regretted that he had ever invited his younger brother to live with him.

Larry didn't understand, so he was busy trying to work things out with his sibling. "It's no problem that Kate's moving in with you, Dan. I like Kate, too, and we get along really well. I start school again in a week, so I'll be out of the house even more. That'll give you two more time alone with each other."

Dan was disgusted, and glared at Larry. "Let me be real straight with you, Larry. I just don't need you here anymore. I know I said

I wanted you to live here, but Kate's in my life now. There's no longer a place for you."

Larry was shocked. He had relinquished his other rental home to help Dan out, and now he had no other place to go.

"Dan, I gave up other options to help you out when you were at the bottom of the barrel. It wasn't the most convenient thing for me to do, but I wanted to help you. Now you're saying you don't need me anymore like I'm a worn-out dining room chair."

Dan was becoming angrier. "Larry, don't start your 'what about me' routine. This is just the way it is."

Dan stomped out of the house hoping Larry would be gone when he returned.

Issue:
I can only suppress my feelings for so long.

Marsha gritted her teeth as she walked toward her home. Her upper body was taut, and she was kicking fallen pine branches and crushing their pinecones.

She felt powerless, and she was thoroughly disgusted with life. She barely noticed the row of tract houses she passed until she walked by a modest tan home with brown shutters. A garbage can by the porch caught her eye, and she stopped. The can was overflowing with empty beer bottles.

She picked up a bottle and hurled it at the fence bordering the property. It smashed, and broken glass scattered everywhere. Marsha laughed as her rage surfaced. She became consumed with violence and began to throw the bottles, one by one, at the fence.

Then her anger was overtaken by ecstasy. Marsha never knew she could feel so much pleasure at seeing an empty bottle explode, and she didn't care who heard or saw her.

When all of the bottles were broken, she rubbed her hands together with a feeling of completion. "I'm going to do this every day," she smiled, exclaiming to herself, "If there aren't any bottles around, I'll find something else to use. It's my way of getting back!"

Issue:
Sometimes I turn my emotions in on myself.

Maria hated the reflection she saw in the mirror. Instead of seeing who she really was, she could only see wrinkles in her skin and bags underneath her eyes. She turned her head this way and that, criticizing the shape of her nose, the width of the space between her eyes, and her straight hair that she described as mousey brown. She reviewed her cheeks and jaw with disgust, moving her head up and down to discern the amount of sagging that existed.

She had always struggled with herself because of her stern judgments about her physical appearance. Today, she also searched in the mirror to confirm her feeling of emotional betrayal. Tears streamed down her face as she whimpered, "They let me down again. No one has ever cared. I've tried and tried, and I'm not going to do it anymore."

This time when she gazed into the mirror, she concentrated on her eyes and spoke solemnly to her reflection. "I can't keep this secret anymore, and I can't tell anyone."

She opened the medicine cabinet door and withdrew her shaver. Extracting the razor, she began to carve a large X on her left wrist. It turned red and bled, and the stinging pain caused her to gasp sharply.

"There is no reason to hang around. Soon it will all be done, and no one will ever have to know."

Issue:
I just want to be in control.

Dottie tried to avoid looking at the mirrors in the clothing store. She always wore baggy clothes so that she didn't have to confront the extra pounds she knew she carried, but it never worked.

She wandered disconcertedly from aisle to aisle until she found the rack of oversized clothes and pulled out an Extra Large. The soft velvet texture and the warm blue color pleased her, so she carried it to the checkout stand. The clerk rang the price, asking, "Do you want a gift box for your present?"

"No, thanks," answered Dottie, "It's for me."

"But, you're so little!" observed the astonished clerk, "You can't be any larger than an extra small."

Dottie hated it when people tried to make her feel better about her weight or teased her by talking about how small she was. *She* knew how fat she was.

She barely had time to drive home and throw her purchase into her closet before dinner was served. She groaned inwardly at the thought of sitting at another family dinner with tempting bites of fattening food, but she didn't want to create a stir, so she silently joined the gathering at the dinner table.

She ate only a few bites of vegetables and ignored the rumblings of hunger in her small 5'4" frame. Even though she was deeply repulsed by her "fat" body, Dottie weighed only 94 pounds.

Her brother Bryan started first, asking, "Don't you want something else to eat, Dot?"

"No, thanks," she responded cautiously. "I've been snacking all day."

Then her sister Carolyn joined in. "Dottie, you say that a lot lately, but you're so thin. You must be eating *diet* snacks!" Carolyn and Bryan laughed, and Dottie used the diversion as an excuse to leave the dinner table.

She grumbled on the way to her room, "Leave it to them to laugh at my weight problem. I've got to start having more control over my own life!"

Her stomach ached. When she reached her room, she locked the door behind her and flopped on her bed with a sigh of relief. Another family dinner was finally over.

Then she got up, went into the bathroom, and stuck her finger deep into her throat, gagging and releasing the small portion of dinner that she had just eaten. It was time for her exercise program.

Issue:
Sometimes, my insecurity and my fear of being out of control make me a tyrant, and I blame and manipulate others.

Stan paced back and forth, his perfectly shined shoes pounding the hardwood floor. He had an audience of three, but his voice was loud enough to be heard by a crowd of 50 or more. His face was red, and perspiration ran down his forehead.

"Now, Cheryl, I want you to listen to me and listen good. I want you to be here at exactly 3:15. NO SLIP-UPS!"

He turned to look directly at her, and she nodded. He pivoted and faced Judy who sat attentively. Behind his back, Cheryl sneered at Stan in disgust.

In his booming voice, he issued Judy's orders and shoved a piece of paper in her face. "Before the meeting, I want you to make exactly 110 copies of this page. We'll need them for the 4:00 meeting. Have you got that?"

Judy demurely answered "Yes," and pretended to take notes as Stan continued his directives at her.

"Place the copies as page number two in each folder. *Don't* forget where I said they go! They *have* to be the second item in every file, or you'll screw everything up!"

Stan abruptly turned back to Cheryl and blared to her as if she were hard-of-hearing, "You make sure the refreshments are there ON TIME."

Cheryl began answering that she had already taken care of it, but Stan interrupted her, roaring, "Call Myra and tell her to make sure she arrives on time. Tell her I said *not* to wear blue. Tell her I said her blue dress is very unkind to her appearance."

He marched on, his heavy frame stomping each board he touched. Stopping suddenly, he readdressed Cheryl, "And, tell her to come with a clear head. I want absolutely no distractions during this event."

Instead of waiting for a response, Stan turned and planted his body directly in front of Raymond, the third member of his audience. Harshly shaking his finger at the stunned man, Stan bellowed, "I know the florist said everything would be there on time, but call them and double-check. Also do this with the caterer. Then, call them both again 30 minutes before they said they would arrive and make sure they're on their way!"

Raymond successfully suppressed his laughter at his boss' behavior. This was his first time to see Stan before a main event. Now he knew why Cheryl and Judy called him "Storming Stan."

Stan positioned himself to be in front of all three employees. "I don't want *anybody* to have an opportunity to screw *anything* up!"

He stared at each of them. Seeing no disagreement, he refocused his attention on Raymond. "After the caterer lays everything out, count the napkins and silverware to make sure there are exactly 110 of each. You know we can't trust anyone!"

Then, it was Cheryl's turn. "And, don't embarrass me in front of the committee! This is a critical meeting for us, and I don't want you to mess this up."

The boss thundered on in front of his paid audience. Cheryl entertained herself by envisioning Stan stubbing his toe on a nail in the wooden floor and falling on his face. Raymond wondered why he had placed himself in the presence of an insecure drill sergeant. Judy doodled on her notepad and made a mental note to check the classified section of the newspaper tonight. She wondered whether she had more compassion for this troubled man who paid her salary or his wife who probably looked wonderful in her favorite blue dress.

Issue:
Sometimes I feel so disempowered that I exert "power over" others.

Ronny was filled with rage as he left his house. His first stop was his neighbor's house. After confirming that no one was at home, Ronny slashed branches from a beautiful old oak tree and beat the tree with its own branches. As he mercilessly attacked the tree, he thought, "Ted has all of the power! No one will ever believe me."

He kicked a discarded aluminum can across the street and began walking with no direction in mind. "It's not fair!" he screamed at a small brown puppy who tucked his tail between his legs and ran as fast as he could to hide in some bushes.

Ronny continued walking and purposely scuffed his new shoes on the pavement. His jaw was clenched and his face was hot. He saw Mrs. Armond about half a block ahead, pushing her baby in its stroller and carrying a large package. He scowled at the two of them. Why should his life be such a mess, and Mrs. Armond's baby have it so easy?

An idea began to formulate, and Ronny felt revenge surfacing in his consciousness. He allowed his glimmer of excitement to build, and he laughed as he said out loud, "Take this, Ted!"

Walking casually up to Mrs. Armond, he said, "You look like you've got your hands full. How about my taking Beth to the park for you?"

"Oh, Ronny, are you sure you don't mind? That would help me a lot!"

"Oh, I don't mind," Ronny said. "Beth and I will have a lot of fun, and then I'll bring her right home."

Mrs. Armond relinquished the stroller, grateful to have two hands to support her heavy package. She kissed Beth on the forehead and told the two of them to have a good time before she headed toward her home.

Ronny cautiously smiled and wheeled the stroller the opposite direction, toward the park. When Mrs. Armond was out of sight and earshot, Ronny began to feel a surge of freedom and superiority. He began to roughly shove the stroller first one way and then another. "If this is what Ted gets to do, I like it!" he said to himself.

Beth began to cry, and he moved right in front of her face, yelling at her, "Shut up! It's my turn to be in control, and you're not even old enough to tell anyone!"

Issue:
I continue to try to mask my feelings of inferiority and insecurity.

Ralph's face fell when the audience responded to his speech with sparse applause. He forced a smile as he exited the stage.

His staff and his family met him outside, perfunctorily telling him "Congratulations" and giving him handshakes and hugs. Ralph searched their faces for genuine reassurance of the merits of his performance. It wasn't there, so he began to be his own cheerleader.

Turning first to his employees, he defended himself, "Well, the conference coordinator did the worst job of planning this event that I've ever seen. And that introduction of me! The guy knew nothing about me. He didn't say one thing that helped our cause. But, in spite of all of that, I pulled it off! Did you see how I saved the day? The crowd loved it!"

Ralph's wife and his key staff member looked at each other. They were feeling embarrassed and unsure of how to deal with the situation, so Ralph continued. "They're lucky they asked me to be here. I'm ten times better than any of the others who have tried this."

The silence that prevailed from both employees and family was making Ralph increasingly uncomfortable. He once again sought reassurance, "You can see that, can't you?"

This time he didn't wait for a response. He picked up his youngest child and held her in his arms. Innocently, she asked, "Why do you look so worried, Daddy?"

Issue:
I don't know why I'm not happy in my relationships, so I blame others.

Tina flared at Bob, although she felt as much like crying as she was angry. "I'm always *compromising* in this relationship."

Bob felt hurt, but he looked at her calmly and asked, "What do you mean?"

"It's you!" Her dark eyes sparked and her voice was agitated. "All you do is try to control me. You want to make all of the decisions. You act like you're the only one who knows what's best for us."

"Tina, give me an example so I'll understand what you mean."

Her answer was an accusation. "You don't know what I want! You just think you do. I'm not sure I even want to be in this relationship anymore."

Issue:
I don't meet my own needs. I expect other people to make me happy.

Lynn listened to her friend, Phil, knowing he was repeating an old behavior pattern that had always brought him pain. As always, he expected her to be thrilled for him and to wish him well. Instead, she asked leading questions. "Phil," she began, "didn't you tell me that you've only known Collette for a couple of months? You sound like you two are settling into a long-term relationship already."

Phil rushed in with excitement, "I've never felt this way about anyone before! She makes me feel so good. I'm loved and wanted. She needs me in a way that I've never been needed before."

Lynn's frustration was building. She felt like a broken record because she and Phil had shared this conversation before. Even though she knew it was his choice, she was tired of him setting himself up to be hurt. "I thought you said you weren't going to go looking for another relationship. I thought you were going to give yourself some time. You need to develop a better relationship with yourself, first."

Phil reached across the table and took her hand. "I *was* going to go slow this time, but I know this is right for me."

Lynn was silent. Her only choice was to be honest with her friend, but she was tired of being there for him when the sky fell through, and he hadn't checked the weather report.

Phil continued, "It's time for me to have what I want. I've been lonely for so long. I just don't want to be alone anymore."

Issue:
I have denied my feelings for so long that I don't even allow myself to feel my joy.

Sarah was thrilled for Ed. He had experienced so many personal losses during the last three years. He was laid off because his company eliminated his job, his daughter was still recuperating from a serious car accident, and his mother had died. Sarah had become quite concerned about him. His wife, Joyce, had felt her grief and was coping well. Ed, on the other hand, had become increasingly withdrawn and had dropped all interactions with his friends.

A new position had opened up with the community's Emergency Relief Unit, and Ed had competed for the position. With no previous training or experience, he had faced stiff competition. Yet, he had prepared well and received the highest score on both the written and oral competitions. He was now a cinch for the job.

Joyce had called Sarah to share her excitement. Sarah asked to talk to Ed, and as soon as he said, "Hello," she congratulated him. Instead of responding, he was silent, so she asked, "Ed, did you hear me say congratulations?"

"Yeah, I heard you, Sarah. It wasn't any big deal to win the competition. In fact, anyone could have done it."

"I'm glad it was you, Ed. You deserved it. You've really worked hard, and times have been rough the last few years."

"Look, Sarah, I don't really want anyone to know that I got the highest score. It's not a big deal."

EXERCISES

1. Describe ways in which fully experiencing your emotions will free up extra physical and emotional energy inside of you so that you will spontaneously create what you desire in your life.

2. Identify polarities that you can experience so that you will be able to feel and express your full love, joy, and empowerment.

TWELVE

I'LL DEAL WITH IT LATER

It is always a choice whether or not to deal with our emotional material and when to do so. The decisions we make significantly affect our later experiences and, therefore, the quality of our lives.

> We can resist connecting with *ourselves* by not feeling our emotions. We can do this consciously or unconsciously.
>
> However, when we do not experience our emotions, we re-create opportunities to do so. Generally, our issues are magnified each time so that we can see them for what they are.

The vignettes below provide examples of this basic truth about life. They are based on case study material.

Situation 1:

Consciously resisting feeling emotions and continuing to re-create opportunities to do so

Sandy picked up the telephone hoping it wasn't Wally again. She had set firm boundaries with him, yet he continued to call.

"Sandy," he began, "this is Wally."

"Wally, I've been really clear with you. I have a big deadline to meet, and I need to focus on finishing this project."

"I know. This will be quick."

Sandy looked at her watch, set down her paperwork, and muttered impatiently, "What's up?"

"It's this woman I told you about."

"Charlotte?"

"Yes. She really needs some help locating a graphic artist at a reasonable price. Who would you recommend?"

"Lois Hart is the best I know, and she doesn't overcharge."

"Good, I'll tell Charlotte. Thanks, Sandy."

"You're welcome." Sandy acknowledged, with relief. It really was a short call this time!

"Oh, there's one other thing," Wally implored.

"What's that?" she asked tentatively.

"I really want to help Charlotte. She's different. I feel like we have some long-term possibilities together. I want to help her get on her feet financially, to feel better about herself. I think that will open the door to our spending time together."

Sandy tapped her fingers nervously on her desk and glanced at her watch again, wincing. "Wally," she responded, "I have a 5:00 mailing deadline, and this is an important project. I don't have time to talk about this right now."

"OK, Sandy." Wally's disappointment was evident. "Do you have any parting words of advice?"

Sandy sighed, clicked her computer back to her project, and replied. "My advice is the same as always. I'm a broken record. You need to focus on Wally and on his financial affairs. Even if you *could* save the world, your job is to focus on your own ship before it sinks."

"You still think I just want to be needed and appreciated, don't you?"

"That's right. Wally, I'll talk to you later."

Hanging up the telephone, Sandy felt her frustration. Loudly, she asked her computer monitor, "What can I do but be a broken record?"

Wally called another friend to ask his opinion. Harvey was also busy, but before hanging up, he said, "Wally, you want so much to be loved and wanted. You want others to take care of you emotionally just the way you're trying to take care of them. You're not focusing on your own needs because you're afraid to spend time with yourself."

Wally hung up, walked down the hall of his studio apartment to his kitchen, and poured himself a cup of coffee. "Who can I call now?" he pondered. "There has to be someone who can help Charlotte."

He sipped his coffee and looked around his cramped living space. He hated his apartment. It felt so small and lonely. Every nook and cranny was filled with clutter. There were stacks of unread books and magazines, many of them new. He had been diligently searching for information that would help Charlotte with her finances.

The dishes from last night lay on the counter. He never seemed to find the time to do household chores. Bills had been piling up on his dining table. He had more important priorities right now. Many of his bills were unopened in spite of the fact that some were marked "Third Notice."

Feeling anxious, he looked at the clock. It was an hour before time to meet Charlotte, and there was no one else to call. He just wanted someone to share his life with him, and he was afraid his loneliness would overwhelm him.

What could he do to fill the hour? Maybe he'd go by the doughnut shop and pick up some fresh bagels. Charlotte would like that.

But he still had more time. "Oh yes, the bookstore," he said with delight. "They might have a new book that will help her." He grabbed his coat and hurriedly ran a comb through his hair. Now, he needed to hurry so that he would have enough time to get everything done.

Wally slept soundly that night. He was tired, and he felt wonderful because he had been able to assist Charlotte. They had worked late into the evening on her business plan, and she seemed so grateful. Wally smiled blissfully as he drifted off to sleep feeling her warm soft hand in his and seeing the appreciation in her eyes.

The days passed, with his full focus on Charlotte's new entrepreneurship. He even went to the bank with her and helped present her program. To her amazement, it was approved, and Wally treated her to a celebration dinner at the finest restaurant in town.

He felt a joy he hadn't experienced in quite some time. He was part of a going business concern, and he knew that once Charlotte felt secure with her enterprise, their relationship would expand.

He reflected on Sandy's and Harvey's advice. They had both told him many times that he needed to spend time with himself instead of trying to rescue someone else. He had known for a long while that it was true. Yet he didn't want to deal with it right now. "Maybe I'll get to skip that step," he mused.

Charlotte's enthusiasm was relentless. She pushed herself hard to meet the timelines she had established in her business plan. Wally felt proud. It was obvious she was going to be successful.

She had less time for Wally as her self-confidence continued to grow. Although he continued to offer his assistance, her responses to his advances were honest and direct. "Wally, I've appreciated your help. I realize I need to solve my own problems from now on and not become dependent on you."

Wally felt crushed. Once again, emptiness welled up inside of him. Word traveled about his skills and his free consultation for emerging businesses. Several individuals called him, and he gladly assisted them. He continued to tend everyone's garden but Wally's. He was available as a counselor to all who requested him, and each night he fell asleep exhausted but happy he had helped others. Some of those he assisted didn't learn to solve their own problems because he did their work for them. Wally wasn't solving his own challenges either, but he was avoiding his pain—his loneliness, his fear that he would always be alone, and his dislike of being with himself.

Soon he was filing for bankruptcy. He didn't want to bother Charlotte, so he called Sandy to tell her the news. "How do you feel?" she asked compassionately.

He sighed, "You know, it's a funny thing. I'm not surprised. I've known for years that I needed to deal with my own life. I'm scared, but I'm almost relieved that I finally pushed myself to this point. Now there's no choice but to spend time with me."

Wally had re-created an opportunity to be with his feelings and to resolve his own issues.

Situation 2:

Unconsciously resisting feeling emotions and re-creating an opportunity to do so

Linda was furiously battering her pots and pans as tears streamed down her face. "Why did I tell anyone?" she cried out to herself. "I know better. I always get embarrassed."

Once again the party was over. The guests had gone home. It was clean-up time, and her own life was a bigger mess than the kitchen. Leaving the dishes, she sank down into her easy chair, covered her face, and sobbed.

Jim had said he would bring enough fish for everyone at the potluck dinner tonight. She had been so happy. How she loved that shimmer that came over her when she was in love. Just to say Jim's name sent waves of excitement through her body. She felt totally out of control, overwhelmed with her desire to be with this man. Other people called it infatuation, but she knew this was real love.

Men had never cared about her before. It had always been one-sided.

An hour and a half after the party began, all of the guests had arrived but Jim. Everyone was laughing, talking, and eating, and there was plenty of delicious food. Linda was glad Barbara was the only guest who knew she was expecting Jim.

The hostess' mind wasn't on the party or her guests. She stayed close to the telephone just knowing Jim would call any minute and say why he was late. As the night wore on, her anguish increased. She knew he not only wasn't coming, he wasn't call-ing with an explanation.

Barbara was the last guest to depart. Embracing Linda, Barbara thanked her for a fun evening and looked into her eyes, "I thought you said a special friend was going to be here? Did something happen?"

Linda felt embarrassed, but she covered, "Something came up at the last minute. He really did want to be here."

The next morning she awoke with that familiar empty feeling inside, as if she had been robbed. She dialed Jim's number a couple of times but hung up before he had time to answer his phone.

She dragged out her vacuum cleaner and began her weekend cleaning routine. It would serve no purpose to try to call him. This was the way it always turned out between her and men.

A few months later, she began to develop a relationship with a man who was a perfect mirror for her. Just like Linda, he was lonely and didn't want to spend time with himself. They both wanted to be taken care of emotionally. It felt so good to hold each other, so comforting and warm. She felt whole when she was with him and so did he. It had been so long since anyone of the opposite sex had appeared to care for either of them.

Her friends repeatedly said to her, "Linda, go slow. You don't want to draw in someone who wants to be taken care of." Although she asked her friends for feedback, she didn't really want to hear what they said.

Her friend Mandy advised her that she really needed to spend time alone, saying, "You'll get so much from dealing with your resistance to being with your feelings. You'll feel the loneliness you've never been willing to experience, and you'll develop a better connection with yourself. Then, you'll attract a different kind of relationship next time." Linda knew Mandy cared about her. A part of her also knew Mandy's feedback was right-on.

Linda answered, "You're the third person to tell me that. It's time for me to think for myself, and I know what's best for me. I'm getting older, and it's time for me to finally have the relationship I've always wanted."

Mandy was quiet. She knew Linda had the right to learn things for herself and in her own way. She loved Linda for who she was. She had also watched her re-create many situations where she had the opportunity to face her deepest fears. She knew that in time Linda would force herself to deal with these issues. Mandy would be there for her when the time was right.

Our feelings are the glue that connects us to ourselves and others. We first learn to love ourselves by experiencing our emotions without judging them. We allow ourselves to be who we are and to feel whatever we feel. When we accept all of our feelings, we fully accept *ourselves* in each moment. Because we have then developed self-love, we are capable of sharing love with others.

QUESTION

1. Are you aware of any times in your life when you postponed feeling your pain and then created additional opportunities to experience it?

THIRTEEN

LOOKING BACK FROM THE FUTURE

The future exists first in imagination, then in will,
then in reality.

Barbara Marx Hubbard

Chapters 11 and 12 used case study materials to illustrate that most people in our society have been programmed not to feel and express their emotions. All of us suffer because of this denial of our Selves.

The following script illustrates an alternative scenario. It is my view that this is where our society is headed. We are becoming more aware of our social problems and how they are related to our inabilities to safely and constructively express ourselves. When we deny part of ourselves (our feelings), we stifle our passion and our power. Just as polarities are essential to us as individuals, they are necessary in our society. We have been experiencing one end of a polarity and its results. When we have completed this cycle, we will experience the opposite extremity of the polarity.

Here's a peek at a possible future.

HOW THE MAGIC HAPPENED ON EARTH

Scene: A flying saucer containing an alien parent and child is leaving Earth to return to its native planet.

Child: I really had fun on Earth.

Adult: It was a fun trip, wasn't it?

Child: Yes. I like the humans. They are a lot like us, just the way you said they would be.

Adult: Mmm-hmm. They are very easy to get along with now.

Child: Was it really that different before?

Adult: It sure was.

Child: Did the people really hurt each other before?

Adult: I'm afraid so.

Child: That makes me feel sad. Why were things that way?

Adult: There were rules on Earth about feelings. People were not supposed to feel when they were angry or sad or afraid. They thought it was bad.

Child: Bad to *feel*? How could they stand it?

Adult: It was very hard for them. Over time, their emotions would get so bunched up inside of them that they couldn't hold them in anymore. Then, they got out of control of all of those feelings that were stored up inside, and they needed to feel powerful in some way. So they hurt themselves or other people.

Child: Even children?

Adult: Yes. The children were small and vulnerable, so many times they were hurt.

Child: That makes me feel *really* sad.

Adult: It *was* really sad.

Child: Why did they do that?

Adult: That was just the only way they knew to be.

Child: It sounds like a circle happening over and over.

Adult: That's exactly what it was like!

Child: And they had all those rules about not feeling, so it was hard for them to change?

Adult: That's right. They thought they were supposed to be just the way they were.

Child: So how did they change?

Adult: It was slow, at first. Some people got very brave, and began to talk about how they felt. Some got very, very brave and began to *feel* their feelings, and find ways of expressing them that didn't hurt other people or themselves.

Child: Like we do!

Adult: That's right. They stopped believing that feelings were bad. They began to understand that they could have their emotions and also be safe.

Child: And then the magic started to happen, huh?

Adult: A whole lot of it! As people began to feel, they started to really *live* and to know what it was like to be whole and free and truly powerful.

Child: So they didn't need to hurt each other anymore!

Adult: That's right.

Child: Well, I'm very glad they changed!

Adult: Me, too! Why are you glad?

Child: Because I learned that new way of hugging.

Adult: That sounds like something I would like. Will you show me?

Child: Yes. Because I really, really love you.

QUESTION

1. If this scenario were true today, what are some of the polarities that you think individuals would have experienced to cause the shift in our society?

FOURTEEN

LET LIFE TOUCH YOU

Learn how to feel, so life can touch you.

Jim Roan

Our hearts want to be touched just as much as our minds want to expand. We have developed art and entertainment specifically for the purpose of expressing and affecting our senses and our emotions. We *like* to feel, especially in socially acceptable ways and when we are supported by others. That is one of the reasons people attend group events including movies, plays, and concerts. It is why emotionally charged books and music become bestsellers.

The music, books, art, poetry, movies, and dance that we enjoy have one thing in common. They touch something inside of us, and we react to this. We identify emotionally with what we are viewing, hearing, or reading.

We move and react to our own inner beats much more than to external signals. Ask five people why they like a certain work of art, and you are likely to hear five different responses. One person will describe a popular song as powerful while others will find it sad, joyful, whimsical, or a voice of lovers. It depends on what is surfacing in each person, where they need to be touched by life.

Our feelings change each moment when we simply allow their expression as they flow through us. Remember the way babies experience the natural flow of crying, laughing, crying, laughing, etc. We already allow ourselves this privilege in art and entertainment, and we are moving toward doing so in other areas of our lives.

Encountering our emotions is experiencing our Selves. Our feelings are only important because they are parts of who we are. Would I cut off my broken arm because I didn't like feeling the cast it was wearing? No, I would fully *use* the cast, just as I have the choice to fully use my emotions.

Some time ago, William and I were trudging through knee-deep snow from one of the last spring snowfalls of the year. A fine mist of crystals was still drifting aimlessly from the gray sky. Just as quickly as the tiny flakes caressed our cheeks, they melted. I relished the sensation of allowing the thin slivers to drop into my mouth while gazing upward at the billions of crystals still spilling from the canopy overhead.

The tall pine trees were draped with white blankets. As happens in late spring, the storm ended quite suddenly. The sky began to clear, and the tree boughs started to release their dense burdens of snow as the air temperature escalated. Gentle flakes filtered down on our hats and coats. We could hear the thuds of larger accumulations hitting the ground. Where too much had collected on any one limb, that bough rushed to the earth with a loud crack. If the sensation of the new snow had simply been felt and released as it fell onto a branch, the bough wouldn't have had to break because of its heavy weight. It is the same with the human heart, whether the burden is unexpressed love, anger, fear, or sadness.

Our emotions are a safety valve that supports a healthy body. Volcanos have pressure valves that release and vent steam and accumulated debris when the tension builds and the channel becomes too full within the earth. Our feelings serve as a release that prevents us from holding too much stress within our physical systems and eventually exploding like a volcano.

In *Elegant Choices, Healing Choices*, Marsha Sinetar reported the case of a housewife who finally walked through her fears and began a new career venture she had fretted about for years. The woman reported that she was more energized than she could express and that all sorts of little aches and pains were erased.

Feeling our emotions every day keeps the doctor away.

Many people do not realize that they are hurting their bodies when they do not fully experience life. Dr. Alexander Lowen's books detail the ways that we shut down parts of ourselves when we push away our feelings. We physically violate ourselves by disowning one of our essential ingredients. This is true whether we are avoiding the expression of love *or* rage.

A dam develops in the body's energy, and it actually stops flowing in the parts of our physiques that experience fear of our feelings. This blocked energy is emotional and physical rigidity which eventually leads to accidents or disease. When any parts of our bodies are constricted, energy is unavailable for us to create what we want in our lives. Resisting feeling *any* emotion can result in depression of the body, mind, and emotions. We also physically contract our bodies when we judge ourselves.

When we numb out, we use activities and addictions as substitutes for our feelings. We stay busy in an attempt to have our work fill the emptiness inside of us and to distract us from our unpleasant feelings. We relentlessly fill our minds and bodies with diversions ranging from workaholism to drugs, alcohol, or food. We caretake (versus take care of) other people, or we meddle in their affairs. We anxiously strive for perfection or glue our attention to TV, computers, etc.

Most of us have believed one of the saddest paradoxes of social programming. We have been taught, "only the weak cry about their problems, while the strong act brave and self-confident, even when they are afraid." In truth, it is those individuals who feel self-confident and secure who are brave enough to have passion for themselves and their feelings—and therefore for other people. (They may also be the healthiest among us. Their energy flows freely.)

Those with the most courage constructively express themselves, and their honesty and vulnerability free them to go forward in their lives. Individuals who portray a false image of strength—always appearing to be self-assured and on top of every situation instead of simply allowing their feelings to flow, eventually find that their strength was always an illusion.

> If I am not brave enough to cry when I am sad, to scream when I am enraged, and to shake when I am terrorized, how will I ever allow life to touch me? How will I ever really be alive?

IT'S UPSIDE DOWN AND BACKWARD

Strength is in the tear, the laugh, the cry, the scream.
Weakness is the *illusion* of strength.

Emotions are resources, not liabilities.
Those who are truly strong feel and experience it all.
They become their emotions.

In the process they find that feeling releases the shame,
the blame and the guilt.

This is freedom.

William Richards, *Pearls of Wisdom*

Real (powerful) experiences with our emotions lead to high levels of personal transformation. By having the courage to meet our Selves in the emotions that we have not yet experienced, we eliminate layers of insecurity and fear, one by one.

By simply feeling, we peel them off just like we peel onions. At the core, we find the beauty of our true selves. Because we are now unencumbered by false layers of old insecurities, we enjoy new levels of freedom. We now more fully join with our Selves and passionately bring whatever we want into our lives.

The following case studies were collected during my work with clients in a variety of situations. For the purposes of the book, they were revised and placed into a standard format and narrative style. They demonstrate actual experiences of individuals who practiced the principles in this book.

Example 1:

I have a lot of fun with my emotions. I also want to be a good role model for my kids, so we stay open about our "stuff." I act out different feelings and use a lot of physical movements with my body to express myself. The kids and I dance and move to music, act out animals, and make lots of sounds.

I've explained to my children that our bodies are a tremendous tool not just for feeling the sensations of our emotions but for acting them out. They are one of the most natural ways for us to become whole.

The kids tease me back when I'm angry with them, and I make growling noises in my throat. They know I'm harmless but serious, and we talk openly about what's going on.

I also have adult friends who occasionally come over to do freestyle dance and movement to music to express our feelings. Besides enjoying ourselves, we have some very profound and meaningful experiences. Sometimes the kids participate, and sometimes it's just us adults.

I love the way we can use our bodies to express our fears, anger, sadness, joy, and power. What wonderful times we live in!

Example 2:

One thing I noticed when I started watching myself experience my feelings was that there's never really just one emotion at a time. When I'm feeling afraid and I stay with that feeling, there's always an undercurrent of new personal power emerging and a sense of excitement.

When I allow myself to feel my sadness, there's always a new level of joy coming to me. When I stay with my feelings of self-judgment, I feel self-love right around the corner. When I'm grieving, I sense the joy or the sweetness of old memories that is emerging.

It's because my feelings are always taking me to the next level of myself. If I feel fear, it's my ticket to more empowerment. It's the same with moving from self-hatred to self-love or sadness to joy. Life is a constant series of transitions, and my emotions provide the passageway from the old to the new.

There is a neutral space where I don't judge my emotions; I just feel them. This allows me to move through my personal transitions at a rapid rate, without caring how fast or slow things move through me. (*Note: This concept is more fully described via Figure 8 in chapter 19.*)

Example 3:

I always thought I was feeling. I mean, I never wanted to take time to feel. I was too busy *doing.* Sitting around crying never was my idea of a picnic. In the amount of time it took to do that, I could have done something worthwhile.

Once in a while I'd go to a sad movie or rent a tearjerker video and watch it a few times. I always felt really good and cleaned out after a good cry.

So I guess I thought I was feeling, at least sometimes. Definitely not in a way that would've gotten out of control or in my way.

Then I reached what I thought was my lowest possible point. Like most people, I waited until I was "cut and bleeding" all over until I did anything serious about my emotional life. I was so depressed that I didn't even want to get out of bed in the mornings. I had so many stuffed feelings that I became really ill.

I searched everywhere for answers. I tried to connect with other people, but I was in such a needy place, the only people who wanted to spend time with me felt just as empty as I did. They wanted me to take care of them emotionally, and I wanted them to do the same thing for me. There was a huge hole inside of me that I was dying to fill. I tried everything traditional and non-traditional to fill it. I read every book, did counseling, went to church and self-help groups, and followed all of the advice that had hope attached to it.

Finally, I didn't care what anyone thought anymore. It was clear that I was fighting for my life, for my existence, in a way that I didn't fully understand. I cried and grieved. I threw tantrums in which I lashed out at objects instead of people. I felt the depth of my depression. Some part of me knew that for the first time, even though I felt so dead, I was alive for the first time. I was *feeling*, and I didn't care what anyone else said or did. I loved myself for finally having the courage to truly live.

That was the beginning. I had been dead for so long that drama was my awakening. Over time, it departed. I embraced it, and it ran its course. I am *alive*, and no one can ever take that from me.

Example 4:

I guess I've never felt emotions like anyone else does. I feel in my head as well as in my body. I don't need to kick and scream like a lot of people do, but I know I'm feeling, because I sense it in my body. I perceive the sensations physically, and my brain takes note of them.

Sometimes my heart feels like it's cracking wide open. It's the agony and the ecstasy that I know from experience means that my heart is opening to the capacity to love myself more. Sometimes, it feels like it's love for another person, but love has to start at home. Loving someone else always means that I'm loving myself more because the other person is an aspect of who I am.

When I'm afraid, I feel it in my stomach—not the abdomen where a lot of people think the stomach is, but right below my heart. Lots of times, my stomach or my belly will swell up when I'm feeling afraid.

Because I understand what's going on, I don't need to do anything about it. I just keep connecting with the feelings in my body, and that stops me from going into resistance about my emotions. When it's time, they pass through and the sensation clears. My stomach returns to its original size. Eventually another new layer of myself surfaces, and I use the same process again.

When I do resist feeling something, an area of my body gives me a signal. I may have a block in my throat that feels like a lump. That's an omen to me that something's surfacing soon, although it isn't quite time yet. I just hang out with it, and eventually it runs its course.

The key for me is to notice the sensation without analyzing it. If I try to figure it out, I slow the process. If I'm just observing it and not judging it, I get tremendous insights without effort. If I try to analyze it, I end up labeling it, based on my current knowledge. Then I confine it to what I already know about life, so I don't perceive all of the insights that are available. Sometimes I don't even share the experience with a friend until later. Another person might try to interpret it according to their own life and what they know. We're all unique, and we also change fast, so that might not be very useful to me.

Example 5:

I used to think it wasn't OK when I felt numb. I thought I wasn't really feeling anything. I would be around other people having big breakthroughs while I felt absolutely nothing. Then I finally got it that numbness *is* a feeling! It's the emotion of feeling dead, of barely existing.

I had always known that numbness comes up for me right before I move into a new phase of clarity or empowerment. It's like part of me is screaming, "No, I don't want you to be more alive. I don't want you to change." So I just feel numb for however long it takes until that transforms into feeling magnificently alive. That's how the polarity concept plays itself out for me.

Once I stopped judging the emotion and just stayed with the feeling of deadness, I eventually noticed that a tiny fragment of something different began to surface. That speck grew until the emptiness was consumed by it. What remained was only a particle of darkness way down in the corner of my vision. Then, it melted and moved me into my new phase of life.

Example 6:

I used to run from fear, sadness, and other emotions that I didn't like to feel. I'd tell myself that I was finished feeling them. I knew better because they kept resurfacing, or I'd be holding a lot of tension (resistance) in my body. I really hated feeling the places where I didn't like myself.

The more I shared the experience with others, I discovered that everyone I know judges themselves. So I decided not to censure myself for my judgments. By just noticing my self-criticism instead of beating myself up about it, I was able to feel new layers of it. The disapproval of myself was just resurfacing because I was feeling deeper tiers of my core issues. It will take as long as it takes to peel off all of the layers of the onion. What matters to me is that I feel a dramatic difference in my opinion of myself.

Example 7:

I've known for a long time that anger is just fear. It used to puzzle me why I couldn't just feel the fear instead of needing to express it as anger. Until I became comfortable with my anger, that wasn't an option. I also had multiple layers of fear that I'd repressed for years. One of my first steps was to get in touch with those emotions.

Staying with the anger and the fear until I reached the bottom of my old stored memories and emotions was really uncomfortable. But it was sure empowering to work through it, layer after layer. I remember standing in my utility room one day dialing a portable telephone. I was feeling terror all through my body as I rang the number of a friend who was coming over that evening. Even though my intellect knew he would never strike me, my psyche needed for me to call and tell him that I wouldn't allow him to do so. He knew I was gradually working through my layers of fear and terror about physical abuse, and he knew that he brought up all of those issues for me simply because he was male.

As I was about to dial the last digit of his phone number, a sharp realization shot through my body. "No one's ever going to hit me again!" I cried out, reveling in my new power. Finally I understood at the cellular level. *I* was in charge of my life now, and my body would never be violated again without my permission.

The wave of new empowerment that was passing through me was grand. This was permanent change, and it happened just because I had stayed present and felt the waves of fear that washed through me. (At the actual time that I was abused, I hadn't felt the emotional or physical effects. I had learned to run from my emotions.)

I had always experienced anxiety when people expressed their anger around me. I had judged anger as not OK and thought that people who expressed it were out of control. Therefore I was uncomfortable with my own anger, and certainly with my rage. I didn't feel safe with others or with myself when anger was present.

I worked hard to become comfortable with anger. I discovered how empowering it was to feel it without judgment and to express it in safe and constructive ways. Gradually I could express it in front of, and to, others instead of turning it inward by becoming depressed or hurting myself in some way.

I had never been able to express my anger directly to the person I was irritated with. Instead, I vented to someone else who wasn't directly involved or took my feelings out on someone else. Sometimes, I very subtly expressed it to the person I was annoyed with, but usually I played the role of victim. I grumbled behind the other party's back, feeling hurt, abused, or sad. It took much more courage to express myself directly, especially because that also involved taking personal responsibility for my feelings and for cleaning up the situation to the best of my ability.

When I finally became comfortable with expressing my anger and feeling my fear, all kinds of things changed. For one thing, I felt empowered. I was also much more in touch with my body, so I began to understand the ways I feel sensations and emotions. This gave me additional choices about *how* to experience my feelings. The sensations in my body always told me exactly what to do, how to express myself. I knew intellectually that anger is really fear. It made sense to me that *current* fear could be felt as fear instead of needing to perceive it as anger. On the other hand, the *old* anger I had trapped in my body often needed to be expressed as anger.

The key for me was not to try to control it or figure it out, just to experience it. I finally knew that neither fear nor anger could ever hurt me. They were just feelings! I had broken the cycle by having the courage to stay with my emotions and to learn to express them in safe and constructive ways. I am ecstatic!

Example 8:
The following case study is unique in that the client recorded his own data in a before and after format.

Before:

I'm really great with other peoples' problems because I'm sensitive and a great listener. I've always found it easier to take care of someone else's troubles than to deal with mine. Women like the fact that I'm soft and gentle, instead of a macho type of guy. When I've finally had it, I yell at my kids but never at the women in my life.

My temper just explodes. It's like I hold it in until I can't contain it any longer and then "there she blows." The thing is, I don't even know ahead of time that I'm angry.

Some people have said that I don't feel my feelings, so that's why I drink. But, I don't have a problem with alcohol. I used to. It's under control now.

After:

I must have asked for this! I got involved with a woman who said she wouldn't be around me when I drink. She said, "There's no such thing as a problem with alcohol that's under control." I knew she was right, even though I argued with her that I just liked the taste of it. Her confrontation was actually a relief. I'd been waiting for a long time for a real excuse to stop. I quit for her at first, even though she told me that I would have to do it for myself.

Quitting drinking wasn't nearly as difficult from a physical point of view (although sometimes that seemed unbearable) as in other ways. The hardest part was looking at myself and all of the areas where I'd been in denial. I had so much shame about having a drinking problem and about the ways I had wanted someone else to take care of me. The roughest thing was that I'd stopped feeling so many years ago that my backlog of repressed emotions reared its head so that I could deal with it.

I had been so sensitive to other people, especially for a male, that I had needed to shut down some of my feelings. Blocking them out by drinking was the only way I knew how. I drank to escape from what felt like the madness of feeling too much, when no one else cared. I was trying to escape from my insecurities. Wow—so many layers of feeling "not good enough."

I didn't know who I was, and emotions were so threatening and bizarre to me. My anger was the scariest thing to deal with. I had so much of it. I had hidden it for so long under my soft, sensitive cover.

The truth was that I had a monumental level of hatred, hatred of my father, myself, and my circumstances. I was so afraid that if I even scratched the surface of my rage, it would be uncontrollable. The real truth was that I knew how strong I was and that I could easily hurt other people. So, I closed down my anger and rage even tighter.

Finally I learned that I was killing large parts of myself by fearing the power of my anger. My choice was to feel how enraged I was, how powerful, or to continue to commit violence against myself by drinking. It really was beyond choice because by not acknowledging and feeling my emotions, including how powerful I am, I was virtually murdering myself.

I finally accepted what I had known at some level for a long time. There was nothing about me that wasn't powerful, even when I felt shame, blame, and guilt. It simply wasn't true and never had been that I was "powerless to help myself." There was nothing frail about me. My only addiction was my addiction to feeling powerless. I had always feared how strong I am and had run from the self-responsibility that goes along with that.

So now I have self-awareness and freedom. I know who I really am, and my only real choice is to live my truth.

Example 9:

I've been told for years that I was angry and didn't know it. It always irritated me when people confronted me about my anger because I thought they were wrong.

In a way, I could see their point of view when they said that I was a negative thinker, but they seemed like such Pollyannas. There needs to be at least one realistic person around!

My therapist also told me that I wasn't feeling deeply. I read every book I could find that I thought was relevant.

I finally understand the left-right brain connection regarding emotions. That was one of my biggest hurdles. I kept wanting to understand and analyze everything I felt, emphasizing my left brain. I wanted to know *why* I felt the way I did, why I had to feel at all, how I got this way, and what could have been different.

Looking back on it, I laugh. It's so obvious to me that I just didn't want to feel—to also use my right brain. And when I did feel, I wanted to control the process. Staying in my head and telling myself that I had to understand everything allowed me to stay in denial. I wasn't feeling—I wasn't passionate about all parts of myself. I was playing a head game with myself!

When my comfort zone was too stretched, I'd go right back to my intellectual safety zone. I had so much judgment about certain feelings. I was willing to feel *some* of my fear and insecurity, but I didn't want to admit to myself how much of it there was. At first, I was afraid that I had more emotional garbage than anyone else I knew. Then, it became clear that I was just willing to hang out with mine because I truly wanted to be all that I am.

Eventually, I didn't care anymore and didn't compare myself to other people so often. No matter how much I'd judged my fears and insecurities, they were just part of me. And every layer of them that I felt gave me a huge new piece of myself.

Over time, the harsh edge in my voice changed because I had experienced my old anger. From then on, I just dealt with my current anger as it surfaced. Some people began to comment that I was a positive thinker, but that was never a goal. I just understood life differently now.

I really knew things had shifted when some of my friends said I seemed more relaxed. I knew I didn't need to try to control my life so much anymore.

Now when I see myself hanging out in my intellect instead of feeling, I just notice that I'm doing so and tune into the sensations in my body. Eventually, my resistance shifts because that's my intention.

Example 10:

Our family wasn't big on feelings. We grew up learning to ignore them, to push them away. It didn't work. It was just all that we knew. My folks don't do things the way I do, but they understand me more now. I stopped caretaking them and told them what I believe in and how it works for me.

I'll never forget the time my Mom began to understand the power and the beauty of emotional expression. She said it made her feel more free to accept her feelings even though some of them were still painful for her.

I didn't share my point of view about emotions in an attempt to change Mom, but I'm glad she found it useful. It's so much a part of who I am now. I finally love myself too much to put on a facade, so I can't be anyone but who I am.

We were talking about how to feel, and Mom didn't think she knew what I meant by sensation in the body. So I asked her to briskly rub her hands together for a couple of minutes and then hold them close to each other, without her palms touching. Then I asked her to place one hand over her heart, in the center of her chest, and just to tune into the sensation there while she thought of something that made her feel loving and then something she hated. Later she said she understood what the sensation felt like when she had something blocked in her stomach and in her throat, so she's beginning to catch on.

She was really touched when I explained how I was walking into so many new challenges and unfamiliar arenas and felt more OK with change than I'd ever dreamed possible. She had watched and judged how I walked through layer after layer of fear and insecurity because I was the first in our family to tap into the deeper aspects of myself. The family pioneer wasn't ever a role I had intended to play. My transformations had been for me, and I never dreamed of the ripple effects they would have on everyone around me.

I shared my understanding with Mom. The more I was willing to feel whatever arose at the emotional level, the stronger the bridge I built into my next challenge. She was deeply affected by the insights I had as I was explaining this to her.

The bridge from my past to my next stage of life was never complete until I felt whatever emotions surfaced. I was always stepping onto a bridge that was being built just as I walked onto it. Its building blocks were my emotions.

Mom began seeing this bridge in her mind's eye as I was describing it. It was built out of fear and excitement, sadness and joy, and insecurity and self-confidence. I could see in her face that she finally understood, and tears of joy streamed down my face.

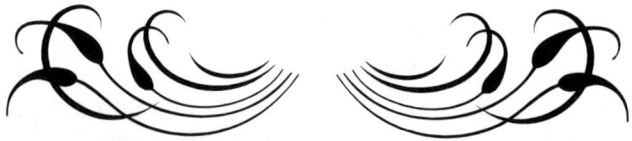

The case study, Example #10, was described last because it illustrates one of the reasons that our feelings are so vital to our functioning. As Carlos Castenada stated, "All roads lead to nowhere." His work emphasized that which road we select is not as important as it is to stay in motion. A relevant principle in physics is that the amount of energy necessary to initiate movement is more than is needed to continue it. The most difficult part is simply getting started.

There are only a few simple tasks required to successfully complete each transition in our lives.

♦ Consciously experience life.

♦ Judge ourselves and our experiences as little as possible. (When we do judge, simply notice that we did so.)

♦ Watch ourselves change.

As we leave any comfort zone and travel toward our next endeavor, we allow life to touch us. When we experience our emotions, they change form (e.g., fear becomes new power). This metamorphosis creates the building blocks for our bridges into our next unknowns.

If I wait until I have no more fear before I take my next step, I will never take another step!

Since building bridges is a never-ending process in the journey of life, there is no hurry to move from one comfort zone to the next. There is only the need to consciously participate in the process. This will reduce the number of times we re-create an experience so that we can obtain the wisdom available from it.

EXERCISES

1. What are some of the ways that you currently allow life to touch you?

2. List some of the ways in which you are willing to stretch your comfort zones so that you can allow life to touch you to a greater extent.

3. Acknowledge any concerns your Guardian may have about your answers to question #2.

FIFTEEN

HOW DO I KNOW WHEN I'M REALLY FEELING?

Become the feeling that exists in every cell in your body, and you will find that nothing is outside of yourself.
William Richards, *Pearls of Wisdom*

We have been so conditioned not to feel deeply that it is not surprising that most people say they don't know when they are and aren't genuinely feeling. Our emotions are housed in our bodies, so we just need to develop reference points of how we experience them. The list below is illustrative. Each person feels emotions differently.

EMOTION	EXAMPLE OF HOW IT FEELS IN THE BODY
Joy	♦ lightness ♦ highly energized ♦ expanded heart
Excitement	♦ wealth of new energy ♦ body feels light and energized
Sad, want to cry	♦ lump in throat that may feel like a sore throat ♦ tightness in jaw if you are in resistance to the emotion ♦ sensation in heart
After crying	♦ relieved ♦ cleansed ♦ fatigued if not complete with the issue

Fear	◆ knot in stomach ◆ swollen belly
Anger	◆ heat in face, heart, or upper body ◆ tightness in jaw or entire face
Rage	◆ intense heat, especially in upper body ◆ rigidity in jaw and face
Terror, panic	◆ frozen or motionless feeling in body ◆ chills and/or numbness
Depression	◆ sluggishness in body ◆ aches and pains similar to the flu
Sadness	◆ an ache in the chest, like the heart's boundaries are cracking open
Numbness	◆ sluggishness in body
Hatred	◆ tightness in face and jaw ◆ rigid upper body ◆ heat in body, especially upper body
Grief	◆ cool temperature in body ◆ body wants to move slowly ◆ body may slump as if to protect your heart
Love	◆ expansion in heart that may feel like the heart is breaking wide open ◆ feeling physically vulnerable, fragile, or full of yourself ◆ an inability to put your feelings into words because they are so profound to you
Empowerment	◆ expanded chest ◆ you may feel larger and find yourself wanting to stand taller

Once we observe the sensations in our bodies, we comprehend our private languages. This enables us to experience our feelings more consciously and allow them to flow through without resistance. The more we understand our personal processes, the easier it is for us to embrace *all* of our feelings.

For a frame of reference, the following are examples of how we feel when we *don't* experience our emotions.

♦ We think we're feeling, but we feel trapped in unresolved emotional issues from our past.

♦ Our body chemistry and functioning slows down. Our energy levels decrease, and we may experience poor digestion or elimination.

♦ We "do drama" which may look like feeling but is actually *resistance* to experiencing our emotions. We can tell we are doing drama if we recycle the same emotional content without new insights or feelings of relief. When we are simply feeling and are not in resistance, we eventually feel energized and cleansed.

The following examples are from case study materials. They illustrate some of the differences between experiencing our emotions and not doing so.

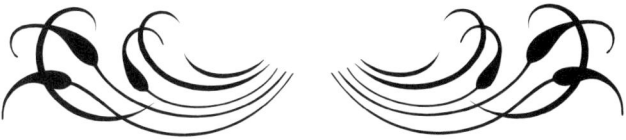

EXAMPLES OF FEELING AND OF NOT FEELING

Client #1, Not Feeling

I did cry some. Not much, though. It hurt too much, and I was afraid that there would be a bottomless pit if I let myself really get started. Harry and I were together a long time. I've always just kept busy, and that helps. Then I don't have time to give in to it. Sometimes it comes up, and I close it down. Sometimes I don't feel anything for weeks at a time. I'm OK, though. I'm surviving.

Client #2, Feeling

It's funny, I'm actually glad things ended in the autumn. It seemed like all I did last winter was cry and feel sad. My heart ached, and sometimes I thought the tears would never stop. I felt really out of control. I never knew when I'd start crying and when I'd stop.

As soon as I gave in to the process, I realized how safe I really was. I noticed that when I actually needed to have myself together, I was. I learned that I have an internal mechanism that always goes only as fast and as deeply into my feelings as is best for me. Now I trust this part of myself because it's always in control.

The more I surrendered to that element of myself, the easier the whole process became. I moved through it a lot faster. Pretty soon, I noticed that there were usually two emotions occurring simultaneously. There was a profound sweetness mixed with the agony of the sense of loss. The memories were sweet, and the loss was sad.

It's funny. People who have been through similar experiences said that I would never stop grieving. I almost felt guilty when the pain began to subside. Then I realized they had told me *their* truth. They had never gone completely into their pain, so the grieving may really last forever for them. All I can do is live my truth, and I'm willing to be there for others if they decide to go fully into their experiences.

Now I feel as deeply and as long as I need to . . . It's my freedom! When I'm done, I'm really finished, so the same issue doesn't continue to resurface. I know when it's complete. My body just doesn't feel it anymore. And when I'm involved with situations that would have generated a response in the past, they don't. I see the same issue in someone else, but it doesn't spark an emotional response within me.

Client #3, Not Feeling

I had worked at the company for 22 years, steadily climbing up the ladder. I was one of the most dependable employees at the plant, and it was quite a shock to be laid off. Sure, I knew times were hard economically, but I thought that they would just let go of the newer guys. What a shock when a sheepish-looking supervisor gave me a pink slip.

It's been two years now, and my unemployment benefits ran out a long time ago. I'm not trained to do anything else because I built my whole life around working at the plant. There doesn't seem to be much meaning to my life now, but I guess it's important just to take the bad with the good.

Client #4, Feeling

I had worked at the plant since I was 16 years old. I never thought I'd do anything else. The bosses always knew they could depend on me, just like I could on the company—for 25 years! I saw the layoff coming, but I stayed in denial. I just thought it would never happen to me. Then my old friend Mack handed me a layoff notice one Friday and said they'd only need me one more week.

What a nightmare. I was so angry with the bosses! I couldn't believe they didn't appreciate me any more than that. Of course, within four months the whole plant closed down. I really got to take a hard look at myself. I went through bouts of rage at the powers-that-be and at myself for having been in denial. I grieved for months about the separation from my security blanket after so many years. I felt my terror because I wondered how I would be able to support myself. I felt abandoned and isolated and sometimes seriously depressed.

Even though I'd always encouraged my family to deal with their feelings, I never dreamed I would have such a big transition for myself. I felt humiliated collecting unemployment. It was even worse when we opened the house to another family so that we could meet our expenses. I felt inadequate—me, of all people, unable to fully provide for my family after all of those years.

The interesting thing was that by feeling all of the layers of inse-curity, fear, and anger, I discovered more about myself than I ever dreamed possible. I couldn't believe the shock on Mack's face when he came back through town a few months ago and asked how I was doing. There he was looking so concerned about me, and I was trying to tell him that I got a lot out of the experience that I wouldn't have gotten any other way. I was try-ing to explain to him that it really was a wake-up call for me. I had the opportunity to discover so much about how I deal with problems, my emotions, and who I am. I learned how resilient I am and how *alive*, because I didn't cheat myself out of going fully into the experience.

I used the rage in my body to chop firewood, I punched the air with my fists while I ran hard laps, and I cried more tears than I ever thought possible. I felt dependent on my loved ones, and there were some days when I was so depressed that it was hard to make myself get out of bed.

None of the family criticized me or my behavior because I wasn't judging myself. We knew that these big transition experiences require being real and honest, even when you hate it. Even when my self-doubt came up and I thought I was crazy, I knew better.

I knew this was my passport to get even more of myself. I would have done it even without the support of my family, but I was sure glad to have their help.

I felt it all. I became more whole than I had ever been, and I got closer to my loved ones. Now I know I could have withstood things much more severe, even though at the time it felt like my whole world had ended.

Mack said he only knew a few guys in all of the plants who had done well with the closings. He looked really worn-out. He didn't really understand when I told him that I think these things work out when we focus on learning more about ourselves, instead of only being concerned with money issues.

He may never truly understand, but I know what I know. I got more of myself than I would ever have gotten otherwise. And I will always have *me* in this new special way. My core identity is not my work, even though it's important to me. My core identity is my Self, in a very fresh way. No one and no experience can ever take this from me.

Oh, yeah, I almost forgot to tell you—my new job pays more than I've ever made. I worked my way through a huge mountain of darkness and came out of the other side with diamonds.

Client #5, Feeling But Not Deeply

I had a traumatic experience in which my body was violated. I've tried everything including therapy and being in a support group.

Every time I think I'm done with it, the same emotions emerge. It's impossible for me to have an intimate relationship. I no longer trust anyone. I flee from the opposite sex. I'm always angry or afraid of them even though my reasons have nothing to do with them personally.

I guess that's the way it will always be. I'm a survivor.

Client #6, Feeling Deeply

I'm finally free! At last, I confronted my biggest fears and went all the way into my feelings. For years, I did talk therapies and had a victim mentality. I was abused long ago, and I've never been able to enjoy an intimate relationship. It always brought up too many issues for me. I was afraid and anxious, and I wanted to go away every time my partner got close to me.

Yet, I wanted to move beyond this place, so I tried everything I heard about. I just kept searching for the answers even though I was afraid. Then I discovered the concept of fully feeling my emotions until they were played out.

My friends thought I was really nuts. They told me I had felt my pain enough. They wanted me to move on, but I wasn't complete with the experience. My family wanted me to wave a magic wand and be done with the past.

A lot of books also suggested this. I tried it, but letting go just didn't work for me because I still had incomplete business about my yesterdays. Somehow even with no support system, I knew I had to keep going until I felt complete.

I remember one therapist who said that I'd been through enough. She had helped me work through some of the layers of emotion but didn't understand there were more to go. She suggested I give myself treats—buy myself flowers, take myself to dinner, get a massage, etc. Great ideas, and I tried all of them.

I also wanted my whole self back. Somehow I knew that feeling all of the layers of the pain would give me the emotional release and freedom that I was looking for, and they did! I got more understanding and self-confidence, a deep connection with myself, and I'm finally having fun.

I discovered terror beneath the fear that was on the surface, anger below the fear, and rage beneath the anger. I kicked empty plastic jugs until my legs were exhausted. I whipped empty chairs with towels and beat on fenceposts with my kid's baseball bat. Whatever there was to feel, I felt it, with any part of my body that was holding unexpressed emotion. I growled deeply in my throat and yelled and screamed at the top of my lungs. I felt the times

I wanted to scream and get away but was too afraid or pinned down. Sometimes I cried or whined. Once I hovered silently in a corner hoping I wouldn't be discovered again.

Finally, it was clear to me that all of the long-repressed pain had been felt. *I got my freedom.* I understood it all. I had loved myself enough to walk into the darkest parts of the memories held in my body. I stayed with myself through all of it.

I had learned to love all of the parts of me that had carried shame, blame, guilt, hatred, rage, grief, and depression. I had become it all. I was rewarded with more joy than I had ever dreamed was possible.

Then it was time for my biggest piece of work. I became involved in my first healthy relationship. For the first time, neither of us was needy or wanted to take anything from the other person. All we wanted was to share who we were with each other. We have been together now for over five years, and our relationship keeps getting better. This would never have been possible if I had not trusted myself enough to go where I'd always been afraid to tread. I charged headlong into the darkest corners of the deepest dungeons where I had hidden those emotions that I least wanted to confront.

By giving myself total freedom to feel what had been trapped in my body, I did so much more than merely survive my traumatic experiences. I gained a new lease on life.

Some of the people in the above case studies experienced their feelings in more dramatic ways than others. This is because we are all individuals, and we react to similar situations in different ways. Each of us has a primary modality of sensing our environment. Whether it is visual, auditory, or kinesthetic doesn't matter; we all know how best to express ourselves. Sound and physical movement are important to most people because both release repressed feelings. If we are willing to experience our emotions, we will discover the best ways to feel them in our particular body structure. The only requirement is that we make a commitment to be honest with ourselves about how we feel.

Drama is not an essential component of the complete expression of our feelings. As illustrated in example #4 in chapter 14, some people experience their emotions simultaneously in their brains and hearts. Once we develop our personal reference points, we know how we sense various emotions in our own bodies. We know where and how they deliver sensory clues to us and assist us in our transformations.

In the preface to his novel, *The Return of Merlin*, Deepak Chopra notes that most of us today have become hypnotized by social conditioning and actually believe that our only fate is to be born, grow old, and die. If we want to self-actualize, feeling our emotions is not a choice. There have been many studies concerning individuals who live through natural disasters, airplane crashes, or wars. Up to a certain point, most of these individuals simply cope, taking care of whatever is necessary for their endurance or that of others. However, at a certain point these survivors discover that they have to feel their own emotions—take care of themselves—or they never become free of their ordeals. Those who don't feel the pain related to their traumas frequently develop physical diseases, substance abuse problems, personality disorders, or become accident prone or suicidal.

This is a primary reason that people in high-pressure jobs involving human suffering (e.g., emergency room surgeons, firemen, psychiatrists, and other crisis personnel) have been at high risk for substance abuse and suicide. Some hospitals, fire departments, and crisis agencies have recognized this and provided ways for their personnel to process their feelings.

There is also a predictable phase of denial in the cycle of emotions. It was described in depth by Dr. Elizabeth Kübler-Ross with respect to the phenomenon of death and dying. Denial is a natural defense mechanism that buys time for our psyches to begin to process our feelings. As in the example of Client #2 above, the healing process from the loss of a loved one—whether from death or termination of a relationship—can initiate a phase of momentous self-discovery and growth.

Our emotions continue to resurface when we attempt to ignore them, yet timing is our choice. We can elect to deny our feelings, be numb, or allow our feelings to flow through without restraint. When we allow our sensations to flow freely, we complete the cycle depicted in the polarity map (Figure 5 in chapter 6), according to our personal time frames and needs.

It is a very rewarding experience to observe the brilliance of nature in geographic areas that experience winter freezes and snow. Spring usually involves phases of thawing and refreezing that protect animals, underground bulbs, and budding plants from too many dramatic changes at an excessively rapid rate. When spring is an "overnight" phenomenon, the opposite circumstances occur. Nature produces avalanches, snowslides, and virulent flash floods.

Our psyches protect us in similar ways. Each time we reach new levels within ourselves, we take time to integrate new insights and awareness and to learn new behaviors. That is why we sometimes take two steps forward and one step backward. Note that our natural process is not one step forward and two steps backward, although it's important not to judge ourselves when we do this dance.

We are testing ourselves and practicing, just as babies do when they learn to walk. There will always be new things to learn in life. We have the option of enjoying the discovery involved in each new challenge and feeling our related emotions, as babies do. We can encourage and love ourselves unconditionally each step of the way, the same as we do with infants. We can experience our journeys consciously or not. No matter what our choices are, we are involved in a continuous adventure.

The following lists describe additional ways that we can know if we are feeling our emotions as we explore the passages of our lives. The descriptions are not intended to be exhaustive but to provide examples.

♦ True emotional catharsis results in feelings such as the following:

- Freedom
- Relief
- Cleansing—as if you have become a new person
- Empowerment
- Excitement about yourself or your life
- Joy

♦ Completely experiencing your emotions may result in effects such as those listed below:

- Increased physical energy because of the release of energy blocks
- Clarity, insights
- Surges of creativity
- Understanding of your recent challenge
- Feeling connected to other people rather than isolated from them
- Feeling whole within yourself rather than dependent on others to make your day
- Being open to the unveiling of your next step
- Feeling energized versus fatigued
- Excitement about getting out of bed in the morning, looking forward to the next sunrise or sunset
- Looking forward to the challenges of life as they present themselves
- A profound love and respect for life and for *living*

EXERCISES

1. Note your personal reference points that assist you in con-
    sciously experiencing your emotions. How do you feel in your
    body when these emotions are present?

    ♦ Happiness

    ♦ Fear

    ♦ Empowerment

    ♦ Anger

    ♦ Want to cry

    ♦ Rage

    ♦ Terror, panic

    ♦ Depression

    ♦ Sadness

    ♦ Love

    ♦ Empowerment

    ♦ Joy

    ♦ Numbness

    ♦ Hatred

    ♦ Grief

    ♦ After crying

    ♦ Sweetness

    ♦ Self-love

    ♦ Others:

2. How do you feel when you are not experiencing your emotions?

3. What are some of the ways that you know for sure that you are experiencing your feelings?

SIXTEEN

WHAT HAPPENS WHEN I'M "SO CLOSE" TO HAVING MORE OF WHAT I WANT?

I am always with myself, and it is I who am my tormentor.
Leo Tolstoy

All of us have at least some of what we need and want in our lives. This is true whether we are referring to money, love, friendships, health, or job satisfaction. We can usually focus on what we need to do in the initial stages of bringing our intentions to fruition. However, something happens to most of us when we get closer to achieving our major goals. The following case studies illustrate this concept.

TAKING CARE OF SELF

Ron was elated. He was actually carrying out his New Year's resolution! He had increased his exercise time to 45 minutes, three times a week, and his blood pressure was normal again. His waistline was only an inch or so away from allowing him to wear the clothes he wanted to wear to his niece's wedding.

He loved the rush he felt as he breathed deeply while he exercised. He explained to his friend Tonya, "This routine isn't really about weight loss or toning up. It's about genuinely taking care of myself. I feel so much better, and my energy level is higher than it's been in years."

Three weeks later, Ron was wondering what had happened to all of his enthusiasm. His steady junk food diet during the last two weeks was evident, and he didn't really feel like doing much today.

"I wish I could find the remote control for the TV," he grumbled. "Where could I have put it?"

THE RELATIONSHIP

Wayne and Jean had been friends for almost a year before they began to be attracted to each other as romantic partners. Over time, their support for each other had grown intensely. Now, they weren't just laughing and playing together. They were assisting each other with yard, house, and business projects. They were sharing much deeper levels of themselves. They explored their joys and fears and discovered that they loved each other more fully and freely than they had ever loved another. Being together was increasingly important.

As they breathed in the sweet smell of honeysuckle one warm summer night, they giggled like small children. Their hearts opened wide as they talked of spending even more time together, of really becoming one with each other. Neither of them had experienced a relationship this fulfilling.

The next day, Jean felt very irritated with Wayne no matter what he did. Usually it didn't bother her when he gestured in front of her face; she knew he was just excited and animated. Today, his rapid hand movements infuriated her.

She went into another room to be with the nervous feeling in the pit of her stomach and to create physical distance from Wayne. She found herself thinking, "I'm not sure he's really what I want. I hope I can get out of this without hurting him."

THE EXECUTIVE

Betsy Patterson was the CEO of a company employing over 500 unionized personnel. She was service-oriented and had founded an umbrella corporation designed to include five grocery stores. She opened one store at a time, and her chain became successful and well-respected.

Her stores offered an unusual number of choices and values for consumers. In five years, management had never experienced a significant problem between unionized employees and supervisory personnel. Word of her innovativeness and her success traveled, and a reporter called to interview her for a well-known national news magazine.

Betsy had always loved being on the cutting edge. She examined every new management theory, attended trainings, and stayed open to new ideas. In only a few months, her dream of opening her fifth store that was truly designed with consumer preferences in mind would be a reality. She looked in the mirror as she adjusted her scarf and talked to her reflection, "Can life really be this good? My dreams are coming true."

Two weeks later, Betsy remembered this experience as she gazed around her hospital room at the many pots of flowers sent by those who loved her and respected her work. So many cards and messages, "You've helped our community in countless ways. We wish we could help you now. Get well soon."

Her doctor's furrowed brow was evidence of his concern as he encouraged her, "Betsy, you're out of the most dangerous phase. Let's get you well enough to get out of here. I want to know you're doing the things that you really love to do."

THE ENTREPRENEUR

Lillian was the first person in her family to finish high school, and her proud parents were eager for her to be successful. As they gave her a graduation present, her mother confided, "We've always wanted you kids to have an education so you wouldn't have to work as hard as we do."

Her mother's sincerity deeply touched Lillian. Her brothers had already dropped out of high school and were working at the community factory and hanging out with their friends. It had been easy for Lillian to finish school. She had loved reading and studying since she was a little girl, and she had won most of the academic contests in her region.

She entered a community college and majored in business. After graduating with honors, she began working full-time for a small business. Her employer immediately recognized her potential and gave her challenging assignments.

Her immediate supervisor, Maria, had come from a similar background and felt like Lillian was her own daughter. Supervising Lillian was delightful. She learned quickly, devoured new challenges, and become increasingly independent in her work.

Lillian began negotiating contracts by herself. Her follow-through with clients was impeccable. She began to dream of owning a small business. She and Maria discussed the fact that Lillian was just a few steps away from being able to do so. Her track record clearly indicated that she would be quite successful.

It was September, and Maria and Lillian planned for her to be on her own by the first of the new year. Because her business would be noncompeting, many of the contracts she had been in charge of would flow into her new entrepreneurship. Maria was going to host a party for Lillian and invite potential clients.

By November, the discussions had changed. Lillian wasn't consistently focusing on her tasks, and her performance had become erratic. Maria never knew when Lillian would complete her work and when she wouldn't, so Maria began limiting Lillian's independent assignments.

Lillian concluded, "I'm not capable of being an independent entrepreneur. I'm far above average when I have clear direction, and that's why things have always gone well for me. I've always been told what to do by someone else!"

THE PERFORMER

Joy was a brilliant young woman with a radiant personality. Even as a young child she had excelled in almost everything she attempted. Her talents were diverse. She was an "A" student, a gifted debater, and an exceptional soloist. Her theatrical abilities also won rave reviews. As she left home and entered college, her family and friends were sure that she would be a resounding success.

She began her college career with excellent grades. She lacked one credit when she left for Europe to study, telling herself and others that she would graduate abroad. Her instructors in Italy and Spain were highly impressed with her talents and assured Joy that her career would bring her back to Europe many times to perform.

"Be sure and finish your degree as soon as you get back to the States," they said many times. "It will show that you've paid your dues. Then you can write your own ticket!"

When Joy returned to the U.S., she did not attempt to complete her degree before the university's official time limit expired. Instead she went from one minimum wage job to another, occasionally diverging from waitressing to office jobs. She always began well, and her beauty and personality easily won her jobs and friends.

After a short period of time at each job, she began to finish tasks unsatisfactorily. She would either be fired or offered a chance to resign. Once again, she would search for a new job, telling yet another prospective employer that she *almost* had a degree. "Oh well," she sighed, "I came close to having my big career. I guess I can play out the starving artist role and do community theater on the side."

THE VICTIM—"I'M NOT REALLY READY FOR THINGS TO CHANGE"

Brenda flashed the four-color brochure in front of her friend Jules, saying, "Check this out! This seminar looks wonderful. There's even a guarantee that if the training isn't valuable to me, my money will be refunded—no questions asked!"

"You can't miss with that!" exclaimed Jules, "What does it cover?"

"Everything I've been wanting. I think it could give me the skills to land a different position."

"Are you going to go?" Jules asked.

"Maybe. I'm just not sure a seminar will make a difference. The men in our company will always be paid better than the women.

Management changes job descriptions so that it looks like women aren't doing as much as they are. Then we can't receive as large a salary or raise as the men. It will always be that way because men are in charge."

"So are you going to try this seminar?"

"I don't think so. The guys at the company have got me. They know I love what I do, and I'm really good at it. They know I'm not going to leave my job."

THE LANDLORD

Jose was ecstatic as he raced into the bank to cash the check from his new renter. This transaction, for her first and last month's rent plus a sizable deposit, provided Jose the freedom he had been laboring to achieve.

Thelma was a new businesswoman in town, and she wanted exactly what he had to offer. She would be located in the area for only 18 months and didn't want to buy a home. She traveled a lot and would not have pets. She really just wanted a place to call home when she was in town. Her behavior appeared to be quite conservative, and her rental references assured Jose that she wouldn't be throwing wild parties or damaging his house in any way. Best of all, she had easily offered to pay the amount of rent Jose had advertised, stating that it was much lower than the cost of her previous rental home.

Jose's steps were so light when he left the bank that he was almost skipping. He smiled as he touched the thick wad of bills in his pocket. The sun beamed its warmth onto his back as he opened the door to the outdoor recreation shop where he made a down payment on the sailboat he had been longing for.

Friends and business associates had told Jose that fixing up the old house for a rental wouldn't be a good investment—but he had believed in his ability to make it work. With great discipline, during the last two years he had channeled his vacation funds and all other spare cash into the project. Now, all of the time he had spent doing the labor himself was paying off. What a relief that he could finally take some time off and enjoy himself.

That night, as Jose and his sweetheart, Carla, sat on her porch talking, he felt a jab of fear. "How could I have been so naive?" he asked her. "I have no guarantee that this woman will really be here the full 18 months! What if she leaves in six months and the only renters available are the kind of people who destroy a house?"

"Now I've committed to buy the boat," he continued. "If Thelma leaves right after boating season and I don't have another renter, it will be at least six months before I'll be able to sell the boat, and I'll still have to keep making payments!"

Carla put her arms around Jose and stroked his hair. Looking into his frightened black eyes, she simply said, "You've just rented your house. This is how most people feel after they buy one!"

THE PROMOTION

"I've had it!" Jackie said to Liz. "I'm not even going to try to be promoted anymore. It's not worth it."

Liz was shocked. She had supported Jackie's efforts for several months and was sure she would be successful. "What happened, Hon'?" she asked softly.

"I don't know. I thought it was a done deal. The new guy with the degree beat me out by two points."

"Was that your only chance?"

"No, the boss says there's a new trial in a month. He says I'm sure to get that one, that I'm first up."

"Is there anyone in line with a degree?"

"No, but I'm going to withdraw my name. I don't want to go through this again."

WHAT'S HAPPENING?

Eight stories about careers, jobs, love, money, and health. What do the principal characters in these stories have in common besides their disappointment? Why don't they have what they want even though they have come so close to securing it?

Each character is receiving a gift through their experience, so it is important not to judge their challenges as unfortunate. They simply have more to learn before they move from their current situations into their next phases.

One of the few guarantees in our lives is constant transition. We progress through a series of key experiences that provide us with growth opportunities. As we get closer to having what we want, whether in business or in relationships, the parts of us that most fear our transformations—our Guardians—create a tough core of internal resistance. Things become very confusing because our Guardians don't want us to change, even though the changes will bring us even more of what we want. Without being aware of it, we push away the very things we say we desire. This was illustrated in the case study materials above.

Our Guardians are core identities that live inside of us. They are components of our personalities that originated in our childhoods, and they still feel that we are not powerful or deserving enough to have everything we want in our lives. In fact, their jobs are to prohibit us from thinking that we are "too powerful". They also separate us from many of our deepest feelings and restrain us in other ways because they think that change is unsafe.

Most of us were socially supported at least to some degree in our early stages of development. As we learned to crawl, walk, feed ourselves, and talk, our Guardians did not try to defend us by inhibiting our maturational changes. Society believed that most children would be able to achieve these things, and many people gained satisfaction by watching us develop. However, our power and independence eventually became more threatening, and we were controlled by community programming. We were taught that we weren't big enough or strong enough to do certain things. We learned to fear that we couldn't do things or that we couldn't do them the right way.

Some children also experienced trauma such as loss, child abuse, or an accident that taught them to feel powerless. Their Guardians protected them from feeling their emotions about these events, particularly if they did not have support systems. Most children were socialized by schools and other public institutions, family members, or peers to believe that they were not as powerful as they were. They learned from social role models and belief systems to fear change. They were taught not to feel their emotions about events in their lives.

Seeking social acceptance, children learned and followed the dictates, "big boys don't cry" and "big girls don't cry." Most also learned "not to feel afraid," even when they did. The baby who simply felt whatever he felt, transformed into the adult who repressed most of his feelings. *This adult also feared change.* Eventually the Guardian was firmly in place, and *the Guardian identified change as death.* The Guardian had become confused; it feared change because it feared death.

It is important to remember that our Guardians emerged inside of us as defense mechanisms and survival skills. They were designed to protect us—to buy time until we were big enough and strong enough to confront our major challenges. They actually shielded us from social harm or disapproval by instilling fear that we weren't capable of doing certain things.

We empowered our Guardians as we fed them with our belief systems and our fears. They developed lives of their own. For most of us, as we grew older, they became our masters rather than our servants. As one of my clients once summarized, "I allowed my Guardian to move in. She redecorated my brain and made it hers."

Social programming became more intense, and we integrated society's illusions of strength and power. We bought into the myth that not feeling our emotions was being strong or courageous. We stopped experiencing life (feeling) because we wanted to be powerful, strong, and brave. Therefore, our Guardians still have no idea how capable we really were and are.

The irony of all of this social programming is depicted in William Richards's poem, "It's Upside Down and Backward," in chapter 14. Real power exists when we have the courage to be vulnerable, raw, and honest. The strongest individuals are willing to consistently be who they are because that means they are being true to themselves.

THE RESULT

The result is that the parts of us that do not know how capable we are, our Guardians, fight to hold us back. They struggle to keep us from growing because growth means change, which feels like suffocation and demise to our Guardians. The more we try to ignore these parts of ourselves and move rapidly through our transitions, the harder they fight for their lives.

Our Guardians just need to be acknowledged. The fears that they exude simply need to be experienced. Neglecting to do so creates pandemonium inside of us which culminates in approach-avoidance toward our goals and creates self-sabotage.

As noted earlier, even when our comfort zones are uncomfortable or painful, they are what we know and understand. They are familiar to us. When we exit these predictable realms, we move into fresh new territories, and we will never again be the same.

This explains why many of us will have a zero or negative balance in our checking accounts, have new cash come in, and quickly spend enough so that we once again have a zero or negative balance. It explains why most people begin a personal fitness regime, receive benefits from it, and then slack off. It is also why many of us complain because we do not have the job or the personal relationship we are seeking, yet when we are closest to having it, we push it away.

The push-pull (approach-avoidance) relationship within ourselves is a mechanism that functions like this:

"Here it comes."

"Yes, I want it."

Gasp! "It's almost here."

We grunt and groan as we push away what we said we wanted. Note that we push it away because it feels different to have what we said we wanted.

Without the natural growth processes that we undergo, life would be stagnant and unfulfilling. However, our Guardians think they would feel more fulfilled without change because they are afraid when we more fully acknowledge our capabilities. They feel insecure because they were created during our earlier experiences when being empowered was not safe. Because they were so protective of our best interests at that point in our development, many of us have a sense of gratitude towards our Guardians. Yet, we have changed, and our Guardians have not kept up with our emerging empowerment. War is being waged inside of us, so it is important to remember the following:

> The Guardian is the part of you that wants you to secede from the union of you with your Self.

We begin to know our Guardians more intimately when we are going through key experiences in life—funnels of growth—such as the one depicted in Figure 6 on the next page.

We are continuously going through processes that assist us in moving from not having what we want to having more of what we want. Because funnels assist us in moving from our current comfort zones to our next steps, our strongest fears and self-doubts must be faced during each of our excursions through a funnel.

As we are facing the challenges involved in moving from the familiar to the unexplored, we go through what is virtually a death and rebirth process. Our known realities (not having what we want) become more uncomfortable so that we can respond to additional signals to awaken. The results are that we stretch our limits and grow as our old realities disappear and new ones are born. Once we have consciously participated in a number of wake-up calls, we realize that our lives involve constant transformation.

The process of going through funnels is also continuous. It just becomes easier because we see it for what it is and stop struggling with it. We know that each funnel is just another ringing alarm clock, another opportunity to become more whole and complete. We simply stay awake and aware (conscious) during the experience. We just feel our fears and ride the wild horse of life instead of running from it. We know that significant transitions are emerging in our lives, and we understand that change always provides opportunities for greater awareness.

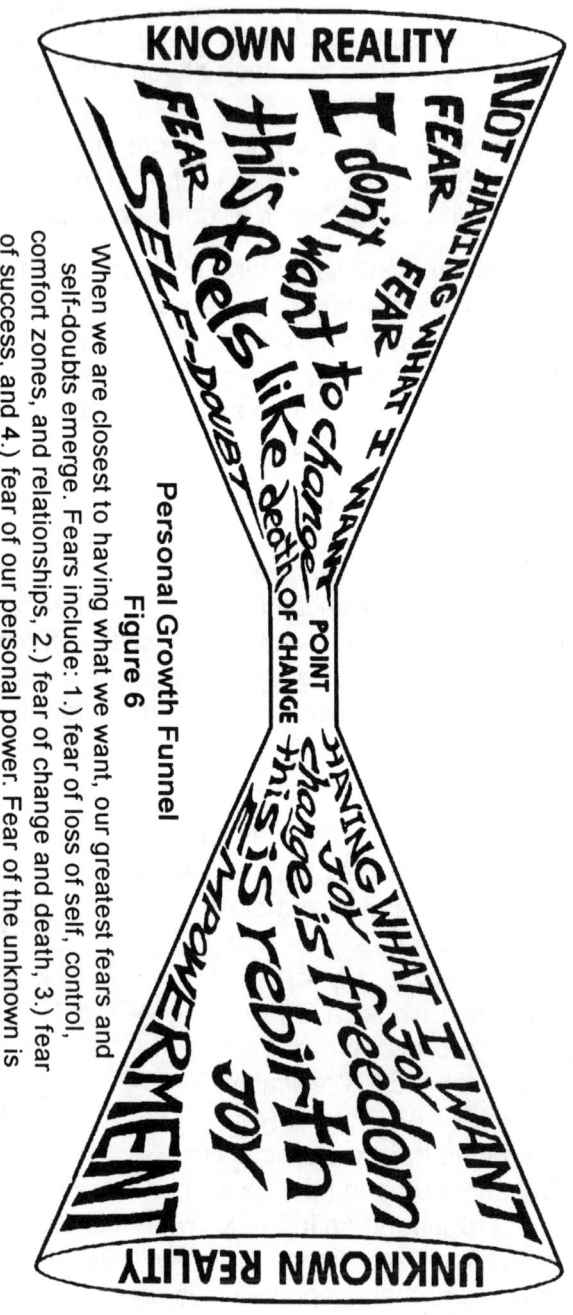

Personal Growth Funnel

Figure 6

When we are closest to having what we want, our greatest fears and self-doubts emerge. Fears include: 1.) fear of loss of self, control, comfort zones, and relationships, 2.) fear of change and death, 3.) fear of success, and 4.) fear of our personal power. Fear of the unknown is the glue that binds us to our known realities. At the point of change, we have earned the right to experience the other side of the funnel—joy, freedom, rebirth, and empowerment.

Why is going through a funnel such an intense process? Why do we sometimes feel like we are being strangled? It is simply part of the human condition that when we are in the last stages of bringing what we want into our lives, our greatest fears and self-doubts emerge. Unresolved feelings about what we deserve surface. The beauty of these experiences is that they present additional opportunities to extend beyond our established patterns into self-actualization.

How does the funnel manifest itself? The case studies at the beginning of this chapter provided some examples. We may unconsciously sabotage our own efforts by actions such as the following:

♦ Procrastinating
♦ Acting unconsciously
♦ Performing inadequately
♦ Rejecting or running away from what we desire
♦ Giving up in the last stages just before we achieve what we want
♦ Disregarding ourselves in other ways

Our fears of success or failure and our unresolved emotional issues concerning what we deserve will assist us in self-sabotaging. In business, this may mean managing our time poorly, convincing ourselves that we don't really want what we set out to achieve, becoming discouraged and throwing in the towel, or doing inadequate work. In relationships, when we are closer to having what we desire, we sometimes push the other person away. Our confusion and our fears surface. We may judge the other person as inadequate or judge ourselves as inferior to them.

> The greatest amounts of doubt, self-judgment, and fear are present when we are in a funnel because our comfort zones are stretched very thin.

Our comfort zones are intensely challenged because transformation is so intimidating to our Guardians. Thus, we sometimes feel as if we are being squeezed through a funnel. (This is illustrated in Figure 6 and in the drawing below.) For most of us, these are emotionally charged times in which we want to resist feeling our fears. We want to exert as much control as possible. We also cling to structure and to whatever is familiar.

Our Guardians fight harder and harder, especially in the neck of the funnel. They think they are fighting for their lives, so they grasp at every possible way to hold us in limbo, up until the last minute. They simply want control of us and our situations, *yet they know that it is already too late because we have already changed.* They fear death, so we feel strangled. It is in the smallest part of the funnel that we feel we are suffocating—the last section of the tightest part of the funnel's neck. In truth, we are just one step away from our freedom!

Our Guardians are literally guarding our old identities. They are attempting to protect elements of our personalities that we have already outgrown.

Our Guardians are just part of us. They don't have to die.

They *will* change as we change, but they don't know that yet.

Our Guardians are one of the most fascinating components of human nature. Note the following:

♦ They (we) fear how powerful we are. This is because if we acknowledge our capabilities, we can no longer avoid being self-responsible. We will also become even more conscious and aware.

♦ Because our Guardians fear change of any kind, they fear:
  • success
  • failure
  • loss (of friendships, self, love, comfort zones, etc.)

♦ Often we hold ourselves back because we fear how other people will react to our changing. We don't want to lose their approval, love, or support. There are several fallacies in our approach. First of all, the only endorsements we really need in life are our own, and we are the only ones who can give ourselves the approval we are seeking. Secondly, if someone loves us unconditionally, it is impossible to lose their love or support. They will automatically be pleased that we are making our own choices and living our own lives.

♦ We often fear that we will fail because of our choices and subsequent changes in our lives. Of course, failure is impossible because all of our actions are simply tools for learning and growth. Consciously making choices and taking healthy risks indicates a high regard for ourselves. Usually we fear our successes more than we fear our failures. We are simply afraid of being fully empowered and self-responsible.

♦ We fear we will change and lose parts of ourselves. We fear our new developments *will* work to our advantage; we will have to revise our lives. This fear is tied to our faulty belief systems and to the fact that we are still learning to trust ourselves and the processes of life. When we review our previous wake-up calls, it becomes apparent that our lives simply continue to expand.

We have the option to perceive the experiences in the funnel as a series of noisy alarm clocks. We can begin to recognize and celebrate the appearance of each funnel because we know that around the corner is a new level of self-trust and empowerment. We can learn to easily recognize our fears and experience them with focus and passion for ourselves.

The cycle will then continue because life involves participating in one funnel after another. Even if we miss a swinging trapeze bar and fall, we will be offered opportunities to learn during the tumble itself, as William Richards notes below.

THE UNTOLD ADVENTURES OF HUMPTY DUMPTY

Humpty Dumpty sat upon a mighty wall
wanting to experience the great fall.
But fear of the unknown left him atop the wall
until one day when boredom overwhelmed him, and
he said to himself, "There has to be more to life than this."

With desire and passion flowing strong, he took the fall
into his yet-to-be-known.
Instead of falling helplessly and out of control as rumor had it,
he floated like a feather drifting on an ocean breeze.
"What's this?" he pondered, as he found that he had total control.
Wherever his thoughts went, so did he go.

Instead of shattering into billions of tiny pieces, according to legend,
he became totally conscious of all of those parts of himself.
For the first time, it became perfectly clear
that he was much, much more than just his shell.
He was also all that was contained within it.

His heart pounded with excitement.
There could be no fear of becoming lost, for
his feeling of expansiveness was the glue
that bound everything together.
"Yes, yes!" he cried, "I can be or do anything!"

William Richards, 1998, *Pearls of Wisdom*

Change is really all that exists. Our attempts to be stagnant and to load the past onto our backs and cart it into the future are futile; we have already transformed. We expand one comfort zone after another so that we can do it all over again. We continue learning to take healthy risks so that we can move beyond everything we presently understand. We dance from the known to the unknown and discover that we have mastered what was once quite mysterious. After a brief plateau, we thrust ourselves into additional new realms of existence.

> Comfort zones are oxymorons.
>
> If they were that comfortable,
> why would we always be leaving them?
>
> When we're playing victim about
> going through the changes in our lives,
> do we remember that we asked for them?

The funnel functions as software for our internal computers. It asks us to make decisions, as in the following example.

TEST:

♦   Do you really want to?

♦   Are you sure?

♦   Are you sure that you're sure?

♦   OK.

The above test is then repeated, time and time again, as we continue to consciously experience the flow of our lives.

THE NECK OF THE FUNNEL IS ABOUT CHOICE

Sometimes we choose to hang out in the neck of the funnel. We know it's time to move on to other experiences, and the level of our discomfort is sufficient to make us want to do so. Yet we cling to our current situations, even though they are painful. An example is an employee who stays in a job he doesn't like, such as in *The Victim* case study earlier in this chapter.

Another example is a dissatisfied spouse who remains in a painful marriage because that is all he or she is acquainted with. Pain is understandable, and we sometimes cling to it instead of moving out of the funnel. It's wise not to judge ourselves for doing so. If we are consciously having the experience, we are still learning from our participation in the scenario. There is more wisdom to be garnered from our discomfort.

Sometimes after emerging from the neck of the funnel, we choose to go back inside. We re-create a similar challenge so that we can continue our familiar distress. When concluding this book, I witnessed myself procrastinating, delaying the feeling of success from completion of a major project. I was conscious of my fear of the future. What if the book really sold? My life would be different. At times, I was highly frustrated and wanted to make myself progress faster. Yet, I was still learning from the experience of going around the wheel again. The harder I tried to leave my old patterns behind, the stickier their glue became. When I was simply consciously aware of my self-sabotage without trying to change it, it shifted on its own.

> Once we perceive the mechanism,
> it has no choice but to change because
> it cannot stand to be seen.

Sometimes, as with the completion of this book, we are just afraid to have the new levels of freedom, self-love, or empowerment that we give ourselves when we emerge from a funnel. As long as we are going through the experience as consciously as possible, we will gain the maximum learning and growth. We won't have to create additional opportunities to glean the insights available.

It's upside down and backward that we refuse to own our power. The illusion is that it is new empowerment. Just as our unknowns will become our knowns, we have always been so much more powerful than we have given ourselves permission to be. Remember how our Guardians were created!

To experience the easiest trip through the neck of the funnel, consider the following advice:

+ Trust your process of life
+ Surrender to the journey
+ Remember that it's too late to avoid having your new level of empowerment
+ Don't judge your emotions or experiences
+ Follow your instincts
+ Allow the sensations in your body to direct your travels
+ Have passion for yourself
+ Be open to something even better than what you think you desire
+ Have fun while gaining wisdom

Once again, it's upside down and backward. Even though the trips through the funnel feel dark, like strangulation and death, the funnel is actually death and then *birth*. Therefore, death is not really a shadowy experience at all, and darkness is not bleak in the way that we typically define it.

In fact, a funnel isn't dark, but a tunnel to the light. The narrow part of its neck is a major growth experience, and travel through this passageway demands death so that birth can occur. It is a continuous process. Not only do we experience one funnel after another, sometimes we experience more than one at a time. Some feel insignificant while others feel intense. By living consciously, we quickly perceive and walk through them. Funnel travel becomes almost an automatic process—seeing and experiencing each funnel while looking forward to the extraordinary wisdom and other gifts that they invariably bring to us, including personal empowerment.

We instinctively mine the gold in the darkness. We have recognized that the experiences that we have most judged as negative have the possibility of producing the most bliss and the greatest personal growth. They are gifts in disguise.

When our highest levels of fear and self-doubt are present, we have a desire to turn around and go the other way. This occurred in the case studies, *The Promotion, The Relationship,* and *The Entrepreneur*. In reality, our inner turmoil is close to having "maxed out." We should start celebrating as soon as we determine that we are in a funnel because we must be really close to having what we want. Otherwise, the resistance inside of us wouldn't be so strong.

The key to the funnel is to consciously understand it. When I was in the neck of the funnel about finishing this book, I experienced emotions that made me feel crazy. Nothing made sense until I understood that I was in another funnel. I practiced just about every self-sabotage technique available to block my success. I used my time poorly, diverted my energies, and shifted my focus to other arenas. I was tempted to blame circumstances outside of myself for my inability (unwillingness) to just do it and be done with it.

Once I realized what I was doing, I made a more rigorous work schedule for myself with frequent breaks. Then, my fear was even more on the surface because I was closer to completion. In spite of the discomfort of my anxieties, the scenario was quite funny. I would be typing away at the computer, watching the clock every five minutes to see if it was break time yet. Ordinarily, a writing project brought me great joy, and time disappeared without my awareness. In this case, there were times when every minute felt like an hour. I was nearing completion, and my fear level was about to max out.

It eventually did. Newly empowered, once again I wrote with ease. When we are completing major projects or experiencing significant personal breakthroughs, we may go through multiple funnels because we may be invested in retaining old identities such as "not good enough." We may not yet have fully integrated the fact that change is all there is in life, and change always brings something new and different.

As noted in Chapter 2, "Change is Gain—Not Pain," my series of funnels included fear of change not only in my life but regarding my connection with William. The funnels were quite productive for me and occasionally comical. When we were a few days away from having the final copy ready, we laughed about my detouring from the funnel and creating dead-end tunnels through the mountains. My anxieties resurfaced concerning the potential changes in my life upon completion of the book. A low back pain that had no basis other than my fears made it difficult to sit in front of the computer. This was one more last-ditch effort of the Guardian to slow me down, even though it was too late.

There was nothing to do but acknowledge the distortions for what they were and allow them to stroll through in their own way. When we see our Guardians and their antics, they have no choice but to change. It is also important for us to continue to be in forward motion. If we backtrack, we are attempting to avoid our next steps. We will then re-create additional opportunities to face the same challenges.

It's so important while we are in a funnel to remind ourselves to trust that we are simply bringing in our next phases of life. Our tendency is to hunger for control and structure, yet it is time to surrender, feel our emotions, and trust the process and ourselves.

We have already experienced countless transformations in our lives. Each transition has provided opportunities to learn and grow, no matter how painful the experience felt in the moment. We know exactly what we are doing by leading ourselves down all of the paths of our lives.

The journey gives birth to the journey which gives birth to the journey.

> It's upside down and backward. We should be *celebrating* when our highest levels of self-doubt and fear are present.

> When we are in the neck of the funnel and life feels so intense —

> WE ARE GETTING CLOSER AND CLOSER TO HAVING WHAT WE WANT.

EXERCISES

1. In the funnel, we alter our belief systems and the ways we have previously defined ourselves. Consider your current beliefs about yourself and record below which of your identities you are the most emotionally attached to.

2. We always catch life's trapeze bars as they sway toward us or they swing back around, offering us a second opportunity. What are some of the trapeze bars that you caught on the first swing? The second? The third?

3. Do you remember any instances in which you fell and were cradled in a net so that you could rest and integrate what you had learned? Did you eventually climb out of the net and empower yourself?

4. Recall some of the most significant funnels you have gone through in your life. How aware were you of your process and how fully did you feel your emotions? Describe your resistance to doing so.

5. Record what you perceive to be your next step in your business or personal life. What do you really want?

6. Write for 10 minutes, without stopping, the answer to the incomplete sentence below. *Keep writing.* If only nonsense words come into your consciousness, write them down. If nothing comes into your mind, just scribble until thoughts come to you. Keep your pen or pencil moving so that you will continue the flow of this process.

   I'll do it when . . .

7. Review your responses to question 6 on the previous page. What is stopping you from having what you want?

8. What stopped you last time you almost had what you wanted?

9. What threatens you the most about change?

SEVENTEEN

EXPRESS YOUR WAY TO
YOUR FREEDOM AND WHOLENESS

We know so much, and we feel so little.
D. H. Lawrence

There are only two things to do in life: be conscious and not judge. Or is it to feel and not judge? They are one and the same, for if we are feeling, we are being aware.
William Richards, *Pearls of Wisdom*

A distraught mother came to me and said, "I feel so empty inside. I want more in my life." I had been observing her and empathizing with her path. She lacked spontaneity and excitement about life. There was no life in her step, and her heart was heavy. Her functioning was almost robotic.

I told her that she needed to learn how to feel, and her response did not surprise me in the least. "Why would I need to learn how to feel?" she resisted.

"Because you have been taught not to, and that is why your life feels empty. You have now mastered the feeling of emptiness. Would you like to experience fullness?"

Her resistance melted once she understood the concept of polarities. Most of us cheat ourselves out of our happiness. We feel a limited depth of our unhappiness and pull back. We don't understand that there is so much more available to us on the other end of the polarity.

Our work together took a dramatically different form than she had expected. I also knew her children and encouraged her to see them as her greatest teachers.

"I don't understand," said the mother with a wrinkled brow. "I see your joy. I thought you would share your secret with me."

"I just did," I reassured her. "You feel empty because you have shut down your spirit. You have lost your spontaneity and enthusiasm for life because you are closing off your emotions. You are fortunate to have young children who can teach you how to feel."

She began to relax as we talked more, and tears welled up in her eyes. The cleansing relief she had denied herself for so long was now in process.

During the course of our work together, I shared the following narrative that I had used in seminars. It was derived from talking to children of various ages.

Adult:　"Teach me how to feel."

Child 1:　"I don't know how *not* to feel."

Child 2:　"Just do it."

Child 3:　"Don't hold back.

Child 4:　Laughter . . . sad face . . . "Wah" sound, "Hold me!". . . Thumbs in ears, wiggling fingers and giggling.

Adult:　"*How* do you feel?

Child 1:　"I don't know. I just do it."

Child 2:　"If I want to scream, I scream. If I'm happy, I laugh."

Child 3:　"One minute I want to cry, and then I want to laugh. I just do it. It's not hard."

Child 4:　"All you have to do is be willing to feel whatever you feel. Just be who *you* are, no matter who's around."

Adult: "But what if someone sees me or hears me?"

Child 1: "Who cares?"

Child 2: "Just say you're sad or you're happy. It doesn't matter."

Child 3: "Maybe they need to cry, too!"

Child 4: "Why do you care so much about what other people think? Don't you love yourself?"

Adult: "Sometimes I love myself."

Child 4: It's not really a big deal. It just happens. Grown-ups have it all backwards."

Adult: "How's that?"

Child 4: "The easy things are what we're really supposed to do. The flow. You're sad, and then you're happy. It's no big deal. Feelings just happen."

Adult: "They just happen?"

Child 2: "Like the tide at the beach."

Child 1: "You don't have to make them happen. You don't have to force yourself to feel, like you have to make yourself clean your room."

Adult: "It's not hard?"

Child 4: "What's hard is to *stop* your feelings. It's not hard at all to feel them!

Child 3: "Yeah! If you stop feeling, you're not you. You're somebody else."

Do not close your heart to your pain. Pain pushes the baby out of the womb and into your arms. This baby is your Self. Once we understand this, we stop labeling our experiences as painful and discover that feeling is effortless. It takes much less work to feel than it takes not to do so. Our feelings move us right through and beyond our shame, guilt, blame, and hurt.

Each one of us is a teacher, and some of the finest teachers are people who are simply living their lives. Once we solidify our intentions to learn, clues constantly await us regarding our next steps. They are everywhere! If we do not take note of them, they continue to clamor for our attention, taking first one form and then another until we allow our "aha!" to emerge.

Children are wonderful coaches. They are masters of feeling unless we have shut them down. They transform a bad mood to a cheery one in moments because they don't judge their emotions. They simply feel them, and their emotions change spontaneously. Children in even moderately healthy families are always open to the joy available in their experiences. They will shift their perceptions ("There's a monster in the closet!") with new information ("I looked, and I don't see a monster in there.") versus clinging to their existing understandings of life. To a child, life is to be experienced. Why waste energy and time analyzing and judging it? Life is a gigantic playground with lots to learn.

Pretending to live without emotions, not expressing ourselves, is telling our unique spirits and voices that we don't value them. Living without emotions is like existing on K-rations. They may fill our stomachs, but they can starve our souls.

> Once we see how simple everything is,
> we move beyond struggle.
> We easily use everything in our lives
> as tools to grow and learn.

Writing this book was an example of the tenet expressed above. I walked through every growth funnel consciously. I saw all of the places I wanted to feel like a victim, the areas where I wanted to self-sabotage, and how much I feared change. There was nothing to do but see my Guardian as she is, a frightened part of me that doesn't want me to transform. I felt it all, stayed aware, and kept putting one foot in front of the other even when I was afraid of change, my back hurt, or I felt crazy. I watched the aspects of myself that tried to hold me back (procrastination, inventing opportunities to split my focus, self-doubt, etc.).

Experiencing all of it allowed the joy and the excitement regarding my next steps to be present *at the same time* that I felt my fears and self-doubt. Consciously walking through the funnels provided empowerment, freedom, and awareness. It will not be necessary to re-create those specific challenges again. There is so much more to experience in life.

> *Why settle for just a piece of sky? . . . Watch me fly!*
> Barbra Streisand's theme song in *Yentl*

Our intentions will teach us how to feel—how to fly. Our bodies will show us. They store all of the information we will ever need.

There is a very simple formula for creating what you want in your life. It involves the following items: your emotions, intellect, instincts, and passion for yourself. These combined ingredients are your power, and the following is the recipe for using them.

♦   Have the *intention* to be aware, to live consciously, 100 percent of the time.

♦   Make a *commitment* to yourself not to judge yourself, your emotions, or your experiences.

♦   *Experience* your life—including your feelings.

Your intentions and your commitment reflect your passion for your Self and the use of your intellect. Passion for yourself provides the focus so that you will automatically create what you want.

Your emotions are the key to releasing your energy blocks so that your heart's desire will flow to you effortlessly. They are energy in motion. Feel them and the energy in your body moves freely. You become energized—filled with new expansiveness. Learning not to judge your feelings is learning not to judge yourself.

Precisely following your instincts and intuition will ensure the perfection of your timing. The bush that blooms in the last winter snows is guided internally. It knows the precise timing to unfold—not too soon and not too late to guarantee its full blossoming. Following your instincts and intuition even when you feel crazy doing so not only *reflects* your self-love and self-trust, it also automatically develops *additional* self-love and empowerment.

I worked privately with a man who had attended one of my seminars. I will call him Frank, although that is not his real name. Frank's story is illustrated in the drawing comprising the next two pages of this chapter (Figure 7). He was at a major crossroads in his life. He had been laid-off by his company due to downsizing, and he was looking for another position as a corporate manager.

As illustrated in the drawing, it seemed to Frank that a huge chasm existed between where he was and where he wanted to be. He wanted to secure a position that would offer challenges and a lucrative salary. He was spending his waking hours researching and developing new contacts. He did positive thinking exercises including affirmations and visualizations about increasing his cash flow.

Frank reported that he felt as if he was going around in circles. As soon as he achieved what felt like his next step, it dissipated. Either his contacts didn't follow through or new information told him that his leads wouldn't work after all. In one such experience, the corporation he had selected began downsizing its workforce!

Frank knew he was blocked, and he was draining his interim cash. I suggested that he focus on his feelings and allow his cash flow to take care of itself, and that was a frightening proposal to him. Although he was in resistance regarding the idea, I knew he would not have come to see me if he didn't know at some level that was his next step.

Figure 7
Building a bridge from where we are now
to where we are going

When we think that we *need* anything,
whether it be love, money, or something else,
our feeling of desperation pushes it away.
When we understand that
the circumstances of our lives
provide the perfect opportunities
to allow our next steps to unfold,
our lives flow effortlessly.

Frank decided to trust himself to create what was best for him. With a huge leap of faith, he flung himself out of his comfort zone. He had no idea how his future income would be generated. He was courageous enough to take a step forward with nothing to stand on. He did this by spending time with his feelings. He focused on his desire for his personal freedom by being with himself and allowing his full expression. He later reported the following:

> *I became a human being versus a human doing.*
> *I felt my fear and terror about the unknown. There*
> *was no one to support me but myself, and I had*
> *an internal image of "successful" that I wanted to*
> *preserve. I had no immediate employment pros-*
> *pects. Yet, when I asked myself the famous "What*
> *if . . . ?" question and "What's the worst that could*
> *happen?," I felt a strange sense of empowerment.*
> *I think it's because I had the courage to know*
> *nothing and believe in myself anyway. The sun*
> *would come up tomorrow no matter what I did.*
> *Beyond my fear and terror was an excitement, a*
> *wonderment about what would come next.*

As Figure 7 illustrates, fear had been part of a heavy burden he was carrying. Experiencing his emotions lightened his unwieldy load and constructed the bridge from his known reality to his next step. Once felt, his fear became a brace of the bridge, and it upheld his new empowerment.

Then he allowed his repressed sadness about past events in his life to surface. These feelings lightened his burden even more because he began to move further out on the continuum of polarities. Frank then began to feel increased heights of joy, love, and empowerment just as he felt greater depths of suppressed fear, anger, and depression. He reported:

> *I began to cherish these things called emotions. They really are all equally powerful and beneficial, not just the ones I enjoy feeling.*

All of our emotions are necessary to build our bridges from where we are now to where we are going. As Frank's burdens from the past decreased, he became more open to new opportunities of all types. His next steps emerged naturally, and they looked very different from the limited image he had been holding about his future. His new career turned out to be private consulting, as first one and then other projects were offered to him. Because he had allowed himself to expand beyond his previous patterns, his income far surpassed his first, more limited expectations regarding his future. He was also in control of his own time schedule, so he had much more flexibility in his life.

Social programming has drilled us to set goals, know exactly where we are headed, and work diligently to get there. Yet, our natural progression is to move from our existing understandings of life into new awareness and greater choices. Frank discovered that experiencing our emotions enables us to move with skill and ease into each next step. We use our feelings to actualize other parts of who we are, constructing bridges from our ordinary routines into new adventures.

The bridges to cross into new phases of our lives are constructed as we experience our emotions. The bridges are literally built as we place our feet down upon them because our emotions constitute their building blocks. Each time we complete an emotional phase, we build another section of a bridge, and we enter into our next stage of life. The more fully we experience our feelings, the more solidly our bridges are constructed.

Frank used all of the ingredients in the recipe for creating what we want in our lives. He followed his instincts and learned to honor his feelings rather than follow the social programming that was directing him to find another job immediately. He learned that his feelings were his best friends and a major source of personal empowerment. In fact, he discovered that his emotions and intuition were an inborn roadmap for his life.

He continued to use his intellect while he developed his right brain skills more completely. The greatest benefit of his process was that he developed a true passion for his Self. He was no longer a *human doing*. He was a *human being*, with feelings that not only deserved to be expressed but that guided and validated him. Frank's new relationship with himself turned out to be his best business resource.

The steps to move from where we are now to where we want to be are the same whether we are focusing on better personal relationships or new business opportunities. What a relief to once again discover how very simple life is. There are only two requirements: 1.) the intention to live in a 100 percent conscious manner and 2.) experiencing our emotions without judgment.

EXERCISES

1. Assume that you desire to move beyond struggle in your life. Can you think of situations that you can stop judging as erroneous, bad, painful, or unnecessary and instead view them as tools to grow and learn so that you can bring forth your wholeness?

2. Our emotions build the bridges from where we are now to where we want to be. Are there emotions related to the situations in question #1 that you are willing to feel instead of judge?

EIGHTEEN

PLEASE TELL ME THE OUTCOME BEFORE I DECIDE TO TAKE THE RISK

∞∞∞∞∞∞∞∞∞∞∞∞∞∞∞∞∞∞∞∞∞∞∞∞∞∞∞∞∞∞∞

This following true story illustrates some of the concepts described in this book.

∞∞∞∞∞∞∞∞∞∞∞∞∞∞∞∞∞∞∞∞∞∞∞∞∞∞∞∞∞∞∞

I cringed as I peered into the dog kennel that was holding the tiny fawn. She couldn't have been more than a couple of days old. Like my neighbor Charlie, I didn't have high hopes that she would make it. She had already been shuffled over one hot, dusty road after another for hours as the kind soul driving the truck searched for someone who was willing to raise her.

I'd seen the driver before but couldn't remember where. It surprised me that there was such kindness from a man living in this harsh, rugged place. Was he a trapper? A logger? My brain whirled with questions until I remembered he was the same man who had stumbled into the hot springs one night in a drunken stupor. Smelling of days of hard work and at least several hours of hard drinking, he had broken the local custom of waiting his turn. His slurred speech had indicated to my sweetheart and I that he would never remember his intrusion into our bliss as we sat in solitude, entranced by the sound of the waterfall and the wonder of a night of shooting stars.

"I'll just get in here for a minute. I need to bathe. There's a hot poker game tonight," he had blubbered unconsciously.

There were so few people in this remote mountain region. When would I ever learn that the same people continue to cross paths over and over? When would I truly comprehend that there are so many sides to all of us? Today, Mr. Macho, Mr. Oblivious-to-the-World, revealed another aspect of himself. I discovered that his real name was Hal, and he was exhibiting only the most touching concern for the tiny, frail fawn.

Sensing Charlie's qualms about accepting responsibility for the fawn, Hal implored, "Sarah said you could take it. She said you're raising goats anyway."

Charlie had a very tender heart and had raised and bottle-fed other animals, so his resistance was worth noting.

"I just don't want an unhappy ending to this thing," he said. "Did you contact Fish and Game?"

"They'd just say it wasn't natural to save it, so they wouldn't even try. But Mama gettin' run over by a logging truck's not natural either."

"You know they'll come after us if they find out, so we'll have to call them," Charlie continued.

"Yeah, I know," Hal grumbled with no respect for the regulatory agency. "I called 'em once because I had a bobcat snared in one of my traps. They said for me to release him, and I said I wasn't gonna touch it."

"What happened?" I asked anxiously, my animal rights activism boiling to the surface.

"They came out and put a choker on it—choked it 'til it was unconscious. Then they released it while we all scrammed out of there."

Charlie added, "They never want to come unless there's a real problem. Just like the Humane Society. They won't come help a dog way up here unless you say it's rabid."

I was sorry I'd asked the question and grateful when the conversation returned to the frail fawn.

Charlie was fingering his beard as he asked, "Is it male or female?"

"Female," the man pronounced, keenly observing Charlie's reaction and looking more hopeful.

"Well, that helps. A male would eventually turn on my dogs." He peered into the cage and assessed the situation. To the fawn's benefit, he pronounced, "It looks real healthy, but these Bambi stories usually don't turn out so good. The deer can get too friendly. They think everyone will protect them, and that becomes their downfall."

The biggest sin a dog in this tiny community could commit was to chase a deer. Some considered it ample cause for shooting the dog, no questions asked. Dogs want to chase what smells and runs from them. A Bambi bottle-fed deer probably wouldn't run. Would that make it a natural, irresistible target for some of the dogs?

"Sarah said you have a wet goat. She said it would just take the deer in as her own."

"Nope. None of my goats are wet."

The man's face fell, but resiliently he countered, "I've got some Similac formula you can use. I got it from a mother who's weaning her baby."

It was decision time. The 90-degree heat was baking the kennel as it sat in the back of the pickup truck holding the confused, weary creature. It was amazing the tiny little thing could even breathe because of the clouds of dust swirling around the baked dirt road.

As usual, Charlie's soft heart trounced his intellect, and he lifted the kennel from the back of the truck. He still had some formula he had fed his goat kids. He would give it a try.

Genuinely relieved, the man confided that the fragile fawn had refused to eat yesterday. Now I understood why he was searching with such fervor. Every hour, possibly every minute, was vital to her survival.

Her Guardian Angel had led her to the right place. Within hours, Charlie had administered her second feeding of the day. She rested warily inside of her kennel as Charlie's dog, Suzie, licked her face protectively.

My dog eagerly sniffed around the cage, searching for a way to investigate and communicate with its strange inhabitant. It had no odor. What was it? Her curiosity made the fawn nervous, so I directed her to move away.

Charlie was thinking positively, his usual characteristic. He laughed, "Suzie's really bonded with Bambi. She's protecting her. Maybe my puppies will grow up thinking they're deer and will never chase them!"

Suzie sprawled out in front of the cage to nap. One ear remained perked up so that she could sense any potential danger to her fawn.

"Well, I called Fish and Game," Charlie smirked. "They don't work on the weekends. Guess people only poach on weekdays."

With two of us around to protect her, we decided to allow the fawn to venture outside of her pen. I flinched, worried about another dog entering the yard or the fawn skirting under Charlie's corral-like fence, getting away only to be killed quickly and easily by a bobcat, bear, or dog.

I was almost afraid to touch a fawn this small. Her coat was thicker than I would have guessed in this sweltering summer season. The perfectly formed white dots and black markings on the rough brown fur were of storybook quality. Her body had a short, stubby appearance compared to our dogs' longer forms. Although Charlie's female pup had appointed itself as protector of the fawn, his male puppy viewed Bambi as a new playmate.

He tried to nip at her lower leg just as he did when playing with Suzie. Charlie grabbed him just as I reinforced my dog for staying back.

I was being overprotective, and I knew it, but this was a new experience for me. The fawn wanted her freedom. She looked longingly beyond Charlie's wooden fence and investigated how she could exit his well-kept yard. She was one board away from her emancipation. The woods, willow beds, and creeks were beckoning her. She desperately wanted her wildness just as she knew that her very survival depended on holding onto the safe womb of Charlie's kennel for now. She began to suckle on Charlie's fingers. Mr. Mom was her priority at this moment, although he wasn't satisfying all of her needs. The agony with which she yearned for her mother was apparent. What torture she had been through since exiting the warm, wet security of the doe's belly.

I was startled upon hearing a whine that sounded like "Ma-ma" as Bambi attempted to leave the yard. I had never considered what a fawn's whine would sound like but certainly wouldn't have guessed something similar to "Ma-ma." Frightened for her safety, I held her against her wishes and placed her back inside the kennel.

My stomach felt sick at having to repress the freedom of another living being. I lived in this place because these mountains fed my soul. In the cool evenings, when I walked to special vistas overlooking the secluded valley or the noisy wandering river, I felt so connected to the grandeur of nature. The stars shone so brightly at night that I felt like I was on top of the entire planet. How could I deprive this creature of satisfying her own hunger to discover who she really was, of letting this powerful country nurture and challenge her?

Bambi passionately craved the presence of her mother. Her tiny body had pushed against my arms with all of her might, begging to be the wild creature that she truly was. My heart strained with hers, yet I had seen too much natural violence to leave her to chance until she was older and stronger. The piercing shriek of an injured or frightened fawn is not easily forgotten. It is a torturous cry that seems to last forever and makes it extremely difficult to remember the perfection in the balance of nature.

Charlie pondered alternatives during the next two days as Bambi continued to eat and yearn for her mother and her freedom. Each time I looked into her eyes, I felt guilty for assisting with the incarceration of another soul. Charlie had hoped that the goats would adopt her as part of the herd, but his largest male and female promptly butted her out of the group. In spite of her best defense—no odor—they knew she didn't belong with them.

Charlie remorsefully concluded that the kennel was the best place for Bambi most of the time. It was evident that she appreciated its security while she hated separation from her own kind.

On the third day of her nurturing captivity, Charlie once again released her from the kennel to exercise. Whining the strange "Ma-ma" sound, the fawn followed him around as he conducted his chores and kept a watchful eye on her. Suzie also guarded her, and Charlie noticed a doe and her fawn out of the corner of his eye.

Sadly, he watched the doe supervise her fawn, wishing Bambi had such a natural life. Bambi watched, too, and she must have used all of her power to communicate with the doe. Suddenly, the doe charged at Suzie, scaring her so much that the puppy ran straight to Charlie's feet. With a precise laserbeam focus and swiftness only available to a mother protecting her young, the doe separated the fawn from Suzie and Charlie. Instinctively and obediently, Bambi gracefully bounded off behind the determined doe and her natural offspring into the safety of the woods.

Charlie marveled at the instant communication between the animals, the precision of the doe, and her immediate bonding with the fawn. Even more suddenly than Bambi had entered his life, she was gone. Relieved and somewhat sad, he cleaned the dog kennel and put it away. Within a quarter mile from him, Bambi

and her new sibling suckled their mother. Bambi was delirious with gratitude for the warm, moist nectar that her new mom provided.

As the tiny fawn nestled up to her mother that brilliant starlit evening and drifted off to sleep, she was filled with ecstasy. What an exquisite earthy smell her new mother had; how mighty, strong, and supple she was. As Bambi basked in her security, other feelings swept through her tiny body. She had such sweet memories of Charlie's smell and his firm nurturing hands; Suzie's warm tongue licking her nose.

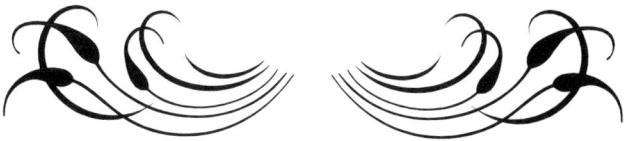

This true story illustrates our choices between freedom and security. Unlike most of us, Bambi chose her long-term freedom instead of yielding to concerns about safety and security. She had no guarantee that the doe had enough milk for both her and her new sibling. Nor did she know for sure that the doe would nurture her once she smelled the human and dog odors on her coat. What if her sibling had run her off just as Charlie's eldest goats had done?

Bambi threw caution to the wind. She allowed her passion to be all that she truly was, to thrive versus survive, to govern her behavior. With flawless allegiance to her intuition, she launched herself into her next step in life.

How much do we want our freedom? How willing are we to follow our instincts and to be driven by our passion to be all that we are, even when we have no guarantee concerning the outcome of a situation?

Taking healthy risks when we are unsure what the outcome will be raises our self-trust and self-esteem. It is also the only true way to achieve our personal sovereignty. When we passionately desire our self-actualization, we follow our instincts and allow our hunger to be all that we truly are to direct our actions. As we leap off yet another craggy precipice into our next unknown, we trust that we will discover that we already know how to fly or we will teach ourselves in midair.

EXERCISES

1. Record some of the areas in your life in which you are waiting to know the outcome before you decide to take your next step.

2. What are your fears concerning giving up safety and security and choosing your freedom to be more of who you really are?

3. Record some past experiences in which you took healthy risks and discovered that you were always protected.

4. Feel what your instincts are telling you to do regarding your next step. Record the instructions you are receiving from your inner guidance system.

5. What differences do you notice in your willingness to take risks at work versus in your personal life?

NINETEEN

HOW TO BUILD YOUR BRIDGES

It is not what happens to you,
but how you react to it that matters.
Epictetus, 1st Century Greek Philosopher

In chapter 17, children offered their wisdom regarding how to feel. This chapter expands upon that knowledge and offers suggestions for using your emotions to build a bridge from where you are now to your next step.

MAKE A COMMITMENT TO YOURSELF

Make a commitment to live in a conscious manner so that you can experience both ends of polarities and bring more love and joy into your life.

CLARIFY YOUR INTENTIONS

Determine your intentions. Ask yourself how willing you are to feel what you feel, no matter what anyone else says or thinks. Just know your answer. Do not judge yourself no matter what your response.

Remember the last time you felt joy, empowerment, or love. If you are certain that you want more of these feelings, use the ideas in this book that appeal to you. Make them yours. If this is a time that you want to be in denial of your feelings, just do so consciously.

KNOW AND UNDERSTAND

Know that we all have unexpressed emotions. Everyone has some issues about not being loved or appreciated. All of us have some concerns about feeling separate or different from others. This is true no matter how much people deny this or how self-confident they appear to be. The reason that we all have such issues in common is that none of us *always* experienced love and appreciation exactly when and how we wanted to do so.

The key is what we want to do now. Do we want to blame others and feel victimized or do we want to progress with our lives? If we want to go forward, do we want the easiest and fastest way or a slower and more tedious route? All roads eventually lead to the same place, so our route of travel is a personal choice.

SELECT THE FAST OR THE SLOW LANE

Make a decision. Select the fast lane or the slow lane, without judging your choice. You can change lanes at any time. The following describes some of the choices available to you.

SLOW LANE	FAST LANE
Talk about and analyze your feelings rather than feel them.	Experience the sensations in your body and express them using sounds and physical movement.
Judge your emotions. Label them as good or bad.	Allow your emotions to be present without judging them or trying to change them.
Need to know why things are as they are and why you feel as you do.	Feel your emotions without slowing yourself down to figure out the "why's."
Blame someone or something for the circumstances of your life.	Take responsibility for your own life and continue to move forward.

SLOW LANE	FAST LANE
Resist changing and growing.	Experience your new power, freedom, and wholeness.

If you select the slow lane, notice the areas in which you resist your emotions. Notice that you would rather talk about and analyze your feelings than experience them. Note that you tend to judge your emotions and label them as good or bad. You want to know why things are as they are and why you feel as you do because you want someone or something to blame rather than moving forward with your life.

Be aware that you are hanging out in the desert rather than walking through it so that you can enjoy the oasis. If you enjoy stifling heat and you have brought along plenty of water, stay in your intellect and continue to avoid your feelings. Try to figure out why things are as they are. Blame others for your characteristics or the situations in your life.

If you want to munch on dates and sip cool drinks in a hammock underneath a palm tree or swim in the pool, try the fast lane and see if you like it. You can always change lanes again.

If you have selected the fast lane, experience your emotions and the sensations in your body without slowing yourself down to question the process of your life and to analyze why you feel the way you do. Notice that you have empowered yourself by being who you are and feeling your emotions without judgment. You have given yourself freedom because you have accepted personal responsibility for your reactions to the people and events in your life. You have graduated from Victim 101 because you know there are no victims in life. There are only opportunities to learn more about ourselves.

GIVE UP "WHY" AND EXPRESS YOUR SELF TO YOUR WHOLENESS

Just as the children expressed earlier, the instructions for experiencing your emotions are *just feel* and *don't hold back*. If you want to scream, scream. If you wish to cry, cry. If you want to laugh, laugh. The courageous adult simply feels what he or she feels, in spite of social conditioning. "I'm hurt," "I'm afraid," "I'm sad," "I love you," etc. *Why* is resistance to feeling.

Being willing to move beyond "why" takes you
directly into the express lane,
propelling you on to new power, freedom, and wholeness.

Even though in our past we may have needed to defend ourselves when asked why we felt a certain way, it is no longer necessary. We are in charge of our own lives now, and the decisions are ours. Generally, when we ask ourselves questions such as "Why did this have to happen to me?" or "Why do I have to feel this way?," we are assuming that an event that happened in our lives was an error. This guarantees that we will stay in the modes of victim, blame, and resistance. "Why" keeps us in our intellects. Feeling, on the other hand, allows us to acknowledge our full capabilities.

It doesn't matter why you feel the way you do! If you choose to stay in your head (intellectually dealing with your emotions), do so consciously, and remember that analyzing your emotions can significantly delay your process.

Most of us are addicted to pain so that we will know we are alive. There are alternatives. The fastest way to work through a challenge is simply to feel the sensations in your body without judging or analyzing them and to move your physical body in whatever way it wants. This might include freestyle dance, use of breathing techniques, making spontaneous sounds, or employing other physical movements.

If you feel inclined to lash out at something, there are ways to safely and constructively express that feeling. (See chapter 20 and follow your impulses without judgment.)

We are whole beings, and our bodies are designed to feel sensations, breathe, make sounds, move, and dance. We are supposed to fully express ourselves! There are hundreds of safe and constructive ways to release the physical energy blockages that resulted from suppressing our feelings. (Chapter 20 contains examples.)

Safe, passionate expression of our emotions is our birthright. It develops a higher level of passion for ourselves which spills over into enthusiasm for our relationships, our work, and other parts of our lives. Consider making a commitment to passionately express yourself just once. After doing so, observe how *alive* you feel and how much more flexible your body has become. Notice the difference in your energy level because you have cleared some of the blockages in your physical force. How much more aware, wise, and joyful do you feel?

Just feel your emotions without labeling your experiences and thus confining them to a prison of words. Don't cheat yourself by limiting your personal transformations to your current understandings of life. Instead, be open to the unfolding of new insights.

As the children in chapter 17 instructed, just feel the sadness, the ache, and the anger. Enter into your pain, fear, joy, etc., and you will learn that they are all gifts that you have given yourself so that you can participate in the polarities of life and gain the wisdom that is available in all of your experiences. The most courageous individuals are those who are the most passionate about their self-actualization. They fully use their emotions as catalysts for their personal development.

THOSE AROUND YOU MAY CHANGE

Many people will want to be around you when you passionately experience life, whether or not they have the courage to do the same thing. You will be vibrant, and that attracts people even if they do not understand why.

It is also true that some people will feel uncomfortable around you and may even reject you. They may attempt to prove that you are wrong so that they can feel they are right. This is because you mirror to them the areas in which they are not willing to acknowledge their feelings.

Many people will feel ripple effects of your being more alive. They may or may not be aware of this. Some will give themselves permission to experience their feelings, some may withdraw from your presence, and others may tell you not to be so intense or passionate.

GIVE UP JUDGMENT

Judgment of the expression of your feelings will slow the process of gaining the wisdom available from them. The vast majority of our repressed feelings originated from our self-judgments.

Eleanor Roosevelt once said, "No one can make me feel inferior without my consent." When you are in judgment of your desires to express yourself physically, ask yourself the following questions.

◆ When I attend a performance or watch a movie where the actors or dancers express the emotions of the script or dance, do I judge them for doing so?

♦ Do I really want to judge myself for expressing my real life feelings?

MOVE BEYOND THE CONSTRAINTS OF TIME

Our emotions are not linear. Sometimes we know things consciously, but our feelings need to catch up. I remember crying on an airplane flight all the way from the east coast to the west coast. A man sitting nearby offered assistance but, as I told him, none was required. He clearly understood when I told him, "I'm fine. My feelings just need to catch up with my divorce."

Sometimes we feel things in advance. I felt rage early one morning and didn't have a clue why. All that was necessary was to release a few cries of anger. Then I felt very centered and went on with my work. I didn't worry about why I had been enraged. If I had, I would probably have wasted energy blaming someone or something for making me angry.

Early that afternoon, a registered, return-receipt letter arrived telling me that an office I was renting had been sold without my even knowing this was a possibility. I needed to vacate within 30 days. It was just another example of the fact that honoring our feelings is all that matters. If I hadn't expressed my rage earlier in the day, it would have controlled me for hours. As it was, it flowed right through and brought me a tremendous sense of peace that was necessary to cope with the unanticipated move.

FOLLOW YOUR HEART AND YOUR INSTINCTS

Be guided by your heart and your deeper feelings even when your head says "No! This doesn't make sense." Your heart will convey your instincts and impulses to you. Feel its sensations as clues, and listen to your inner voice. Your heart is your *source*.

When you don't have faith in yourself, just notice that and keep going whatever direction you have an impulse to go. We have within ourselves all that is required to be protected and safe.

Push your comfort zones, and know that you are doing so. Directly face what frightens you, and you will discover your own capacity to solve any challenge. You will also spontaneously empower yourself.

LIFE ANEW

Tune into your heart.
It is your *source.*
There is no "wrong way," and
you can make no mistakes,
for all of the answers that you seek
are inside of your Self.

When you are at the edge of everything you have known,
when you have vaulted from your present to your future
without a clue where or what that is, just feel.
You will discover that you were born to be free
and that there is nothing outside of yourself.

An excitement will begin to build within you.
It is the newness of you,
permanent change—
your new power.
It is your gift from you to you, and
it can never be taken away.

What you have now integrated in your heart
is so far beyond what you know in your head.
It's yours for eternity
because it is now as much a part of who you are
as the fingers on your hand.

FEEL THE LAYERS AND POLARITIES

As you continue to soar to new heights in your personal development, the emotions within you that are inconsistent with each new level of self-love and empowerment that you reach will emerge to be experienced. This may feel like déjà vu, a recycling of issues that you have already dealt with. Not to worry!

Feel your emotions without taking them personally. Just observe them, and this stage will run its course easily. Your system is simply integrating your new Self, and your Guardian is fighting for its life. It has been directing your actions for a very long time, and just the thought of being out of control of your life makes its little feet very cold.

Just as the oasis is reached by your travels through the desert, you unveil the beauty of who you really are by feeling layers of your unresolved issues. They are just like thorns next to a beautiful rose or onion skins that cover your core Self. You think you have felt it all. If this were true, your feelings wouldn't be resurfacing. We feel however much emotion we are able to feel at a given point in time.

ALLOW YOURSELF TO HAVE ALL OF YOU

Don't try to get rid of feelings or experiences that you have labeled as negative. Banishing them would mean losing that part of yourself and cheating yourself out of the opportunity to take your next step in life. An increased energy level and a new level of power are the results of simply feeling. Live in the present instead of having the past pull at you or assuming that it will determine your future.

Notice your feelings without trying to alter them. They will transform on their own once you have acknowledged them because you are not rejecting the reality of your life. Trying to change your emotions establishes an energetic barricade within your body because you are defying part of yourself. The more you simply allow your feelings to be present without fighting them, the more you embrace your Self. This spontaneously creates more self-love.

OWN YOUR EMOTIONS WITHOUT ADOPTING THEM AS A PRIMARY IDENTITY

Sometimes we fear that once we open the door to our emotions, we will never stop feeling our fear, grief, anger, etc. That is true only if we never allow ourselves to honor what already exists. As long as we deny or repress our emotions, they are like a fresh marshmallow. The more we punch them, the more resiliently they spring back, just waiting for our attention. Once our unpleasant feelings have been acknowledged, they relax and soften as if we had heated a marshmallow. Our distressing feelings melt harmlessly back into us because we have owned them and integrated them into another form. They never go away, and we can't vanquish them. Energy is just energy. Yet, the transformed marshmallow becomes free, neutral energy which empowers us.

Another fear many of us have is that we will literally become the emotions we wish to avoid. We are afraid that if we feel our fear, we will become more fearful just by associating with the little critter. This book is not about adopting feelings such as fear and insecurity as primary identities. Each of these emotions is merely one end of a polarity. By simply being courageous enough to experience them, we sign our own emancipation proclamations.

We don't *become* fear, insecurity, etc., unless we deny their existence within us. In that case, they will control every movement that we make. They are powerful energies. We can use them for our benefit, or we can repress them and place in motion our own destruction. They are mighty and dependable employees, and we can hire and transform them into the hardest working staff members imaginable. The more we recognize them when they are on the surface of our consciousness, the more we can use them to climb higher on the upper end of each polarity.

Simply own the part of you that feels insecure so that you have all of your energy available to experience your life. The fear isn't really you. It is just a thread of your past that your Guardian is holding onto, an old identity that feels powerless. Often, it requires only a few moments of our time to feel our fears and insecurities so that they can transform and channel new levels of empowerment into our bodies. It's that simple! It is only our fright of our fear that holds us back.

NOTICE THE "BIG R"

Our resistance to feeling is the "Big R." We are struggling not to become more fully alive. Once you observe your resistance to feeling and how it affects your body, you will understand that it takes so much less effort to feel than not to do so. Our emotions are the flow that transports us from one reality to the next. When we are not judging our feelings, they are effortless, whether they are painful or joyful. They become a "no-thing." They are just part of who we are.

Physical energy is drained when we use it unto the point of exhaustion. Emotional energy is depleted when its use is denied, and this then saps our physical energy. Expressing ourselves ensures that the precise amount of fuel we need flows into our motors (our bodies) so that our lives run smoothly. When we are in resistance, our engines are drained of their power, and they stall, stick, and grind until they cease to function.

When we have unexplained physical symptoms, they show us where we are housing resistance in our bodies. Our bodies are incredible tools and should be honored for serving us so well. When we allow the natural flow of our feelings, our aches and pains usually disappear.

When I am afraid to feel my emotions, I find the following to be helpful.

◆ I notice the implications of my resistance in my body without trying to change the blockages. They will eventually change on their own if I don't judge them.

◆ I don't judge myself for being in resistance. Instead, I remind myself that it is serving me in some way, waiting to offer me new insights and clarity.

◆ I ask myself questions such as the following:

• How is it serving me to delay feeling more _____?
(*I fill in the blank with words like empowered, joy, freedom, self-love, etc.*)

• What is the understanding that I am receiving because I am still in this place of resistance?

• Did I forget that the past is over and that dealing with the leftover feelings that I am storing in my body will only bring me more empowerment and love?

• What potential changes in my life am I afraid of?

• What's the worst that my Guardian thinks will happen if I feel my fear?

- Am I afraid that I will leave someone behind if I change?
- Did I forget that we are all connected and that we leapfrog past each other, over and over, so that each of us benefits when any of us changes?
- Did I forget that we are all tuning forks for each other?
- Why am I afraid of being more fully who I am?

The most important thing to remember about the Big R is, if you are in resistance, don't fight it. Fighting resistance feeds and empowers it. The Guardian draws its mighty sword and fights harder even though it knows that it's already too late. Since our next transformation is a *fait accompli*, why tire ourselves with unnecessary struggle at the last minute?

Years ago, William and I had been working nonstop for a few weeks on a major project. We finally reached a point where we were able to plan a day off in the mountains, and we both looked forward to it for a week. We went to bed the night before our holiday in a blissful state of anticipation.

The alarm rang the next morning, and I bounded out of bed to prepare for the day. I couldn't understand what was going on. I was no longer excited. In fact, I felt out of sorts with the entire universe. "Oh, no, not today!" I grumbled to myself. "I want today to be perfect. We finally have a day off!" I kept trying to switch my mood, fighting what existed. I wanted control of my life. I wanted to program my feelings.

I told William what was going on, and in his usual nonjudgmental way, he simply said, "So, just be in a bad mood."

During the entire drive up into the mountains, I was still trying to reprogram and control my feelings. The mountains and rivers were as gorgeous as always, but I was disgruntled with the world. I fussed and fumed at my mood, trying to manipulate it rather than just experiencing it. I spent several hours judging myself and my emotions, saying several times, "I just want to have fun today, I don't want to be in a bad mood."

William's response was consistent, "You're keeping yourself from having fun by not being OK with not having fun."

I responded that I didn't want to ruin his only day off, too, and he replied, "You're not. I want to know all parts of you. If I can't love you when you're out of sorts, then I'm not loving you unconditionally, and I wouldn't be loving all parts of myself."

I complained, "I don't like this part of myself. I want to be in a good mood today."

Once again, William pressed his point, "I love all of the parts of you, not just some of them. Just be in whatever mood you're in."

Finally, I understood. I stopped trying to change what existed and just glowered at the world. Within 15 minutes, I was in the most wonderful mood! It was a great reminder to be who I am in every moment and not to resist what exists.

IF YOU'RE FEELING NUMB, YOU ARE STILL BREATHING

Another feeling that I have sometimes tried to program is the feeling of numbness. This transitional feeling has always felt uncomfortable to me, and I would try to shift it into some other feeling—even a painful one, just to get the ball rolling. This was resistance to what existed, so the numbness persisted.

Numbness (not feeling) *is* a feeling. When you stay with it, you will eventually notice a fragment of something different than numbness, and that new feeling will build. This piece is what moves you into your next step.

When my brother called me to tell me that my father had died, I chatted with him, hung up the telephone, and felt nothing. William came into the room and asked what was going on. I said, "Dad died, and I don't feel anything yet." I knew the waves would come, and of course they did, wave after wave of the cycles of grief. This time I didn't try to intervene in the process of the transitional numbness. Numbness is a feeling to be respected and experienced just as any other feeling.

OBSERVE THE SENSATIONS IN YOUR BODY

If it is difficult for you to feel sensations in your body, place your hand in the center of your chest at the level of your heart. Feel the sensation that occurs anywhere in your body when you focus on something that evokes a feeling or memory of joy. Then do the same exercise and focus on something that you associate with feelings of sadness, grief, anger, or fear.

You can also briskly rub your hands together and feel the energy that you have just created. Then hold that energy over your heart, belly, throat, etc., and notice how you feel.

Make a commitment to tune into the sensations in your body frequently during each day. Observe the energetic feelings in your heart, stomach, throat, head, etc. Notice when you feel yourself constrict the energy in parts of your body. The constriction provides a clue that you are resisting feeling.

TO MOVE BEYOND STRUGGLE, ALLOW YOURSELF TO BE IN MORE THAN ONE PLACE AT A TIME

Be open to the possibility of experiencing more than one type of emotion at once. For example, when you sincerely feel an area where you feel powerless, you will notice that you simultaneously begin to feel a new wave of empowerment coming online. After you have truly begun to experience your grief, you will notice that sweetness is simultaneously present. This may be in the form of sweet memories or a knowingness of what is to come. The list below portrays emotions which frequently exist in pairs.

EXAMPLES OF EMOTIONS THAT FREQUENTLY OCCUR IN PAIRS

Grief .... Sweetness	Powerless ..... Empowered
Sadness .... Joy, relief	Fear .... Fearless
Hatred .... Love	Fear .... Love
Self-hatred .... Self-love	Numb/dead ... Vibrant
Fear .... Excitement	Depression .... Hope
Sadness .... Happiness	Death .... Rebirth
Lonely .... Self-sufficient	

When we don't judge our emotions, we function from the center of a triangle, viewing both ends of a polarity from an objective position. If we don't judge agony, we can feel ecstasy at the same time. If we aren't willing to feel agony, we will never have access to ecstasy, and we will continue to re-create opportunities to feel agony. We can ask ourselves a simple question: "Why not now?"

Allowing yourself to be aware of and to feel both extremities means that you are positioned at point zero, a neutral area illustrated in Figure 8 on the next page. It is as if you are feeling your emotions as an impartial observer because you do not judge them. It is an illuminating experience, and it will greatly enhance and speed your personal transformations. You feel both ends of the continuum, yet you are emotionally detached from both of them.

Practice not judging your emotional experiences as positive or negative. Feel your emotions and watch the positive and negative polarities collapse. Notice that as soon as you acknowledge the swing in the polarity, it stops swinging!

Once you are aware that emotions travel in pairs, you will also notice that grief is always paired with rage. The rage is because we feel betrayed. Our Guardians feel that we were abandoned when we lost something or someone and needed to grieve. When we hate, we also naturally feel rage. If you want to drive in the fast lane, just feel these emotions as twins without trying to separate or make sense of them. Feelings are feelings; they are not intellectual or linear.

If your mind demands that you be rational, remind yourself that Madison Avenue attempts to sell us over 80 percent of what we buy strictly based on emotional appeals. Don't try to make your emotions linear or rational—be grateful that they aren't! Do we want our wholeness, or do we want to become a human computer making sense of all of our feelings? It can't be done, but we still have the choice to travel in the slow lane anytime we want to.

Point Zero

Fear	Excitement, confidence
Sadness, grief	Sweet memories, joy
Anger	Love, compassion, joy
Hate	Love
Agony	Ecstasy

Point Zero
Figure 8

Point zero is a neutral area in our consciousness in which we do not judge our emotions. We function at a point equidistant from both ends of a polarity knowing that each is essential for our personal growth (In fact, each is necessary for the other to exist.) We move rapidly through our transformations because we simply see the mechanics of how life operates instead of judging one end of a polarity as good and the other as bad. We also feel both ends of the emotional continuum simultaneously.

If you want to graduate from struggle, understand that the concept of emotional pairing proves that there is no such thing as a negative feeling. There are only polarities. The "positive" and the "negative" feeling are always both equally present. It is only our judgment of our emotions that prevents us from feeling both ends of a polarity at once. Thus, in reality, there is no pain in life! There are only new levels of upper-end polarities to be experienced, and the way to experience these is to also feel the lower ends.

MIRROR, MIRROR ON THE WALL—WHERE ART THOU?

When I don't know what I'm feeling, I look for mirrors. They are always available, whether they exist in the form of close friend, stranger on the street, spouse, pet, nature, movie character, work of art, etc. The choices are endless.

This is because we can only perceive in our mirrors what is on the surface for ourselves. It's another example of the illusions of life.

At one point when I was in denial of my fear concerning my future, William and I were camped at a secluded spot with a beautiful rushing creek. I could tell by my swollen belly and my feeling of deadness that I was in resistance to feeling something, but I didn't know what. I was open for the mirror to present itself and walked toward the stream. My instincts said to stop and be silent, so I knelt down and observed the surroundings.

A small, frightened rabbit darted in and out of brush by the creek. It appeared to be quite thirsty, but every time it neared the flow of water and pushed its head down close enough to drink, it scampered away in fear. This continued for about 15 minutes, and it never took a drop of water. I listened and watched for signs of predators or even competitors for the ample water supply and found none. The mirror became quite clear to me. I was too afraid at the time to reach for what I needed and wanted next in my life even though it was right in front of me and readily available. I was profusely grateful to the bunny for such a clear reflection. Once I saw the mirror, I was able to feel my fear. It had been close to the surface just waiting to be acknowledged, but I had been confused. My belly resumed its normal size, my energy level escalated, and my next level of empowerment emerged.

> Your life will be your best teacher, for you will discover that you are always putting yourself into learning situations that are ideal for your growth.
> Ken Keyes, 1972, *Handbook to Higher Consciousness*

WATCH FOR JOY ALARMS

When our joy and peace of mind threaten our Guardians, they react by leaping on our shoulders, gingerly draping their hands around our throats, and squeezing our jugulars—just to get our attention. Then they croon to us in four-part harmony, "It's not OK to have this much joy. Things can't really be this easy. WATCH OUT!"

We are being given a choice. We can respond by firmly removing our Guardians' hands from our throats and clearly telling them that we have already experienced that level of insecurity. We can add that we are ready for a new experience, rather than hanging out singing the latest rendition of *Living in Fear*.

We have all been programmed to think that joy is available only in limited quantities, and the unfamiliar still frightens us. The unknown here is *too much joy*. Are we willing to experience new realities? Remember, we can always change our minds and call in more pain.

Laughter is contagious except to the Guardians. The longer we stay in bliss, the more impermeable we are to our Guardians' antics. They become so uncomfortable that they take a long-needed vacation. So, welcome your bliss. You deserve it. The following poem indicates that we have been encouraged to accept this "new" unknown—feeling joy—since the 16th century.

ACCEPTING JOY

The gloom of the world
Is but a shadow.
Behind it,
yet within reach,
is joy.
Take joy.

Fra Giovanni, 1513

Joy is a major creative force, and it also sustains what we build. Bliss can be an endless cycle because everything that we create will naturally advance toward and return to it. Allow yourself to feel your joy and to choose bliss. At such times, you won't encounter your Guardian! It is repulsed by periods of joy only because bliss is not its customary reality.

TO DRAMA OR NOT TO DRAMA . . . THAT IS THE QUESTION

When some people first become willing to feel their emotions, they generate a roller coaster of drama. Drama means resistance to feeling the depth of emotions. When we "do drama," we continue to re-create experiences that provide us additional opportunities to deal with the same emotional content.

Drama or recycling differs from the onion-peeling process. When we peel the onion, we feel more submerged layers of material that may be similar on the surface but are different because we are actually experiencing deeper overlays of polarities.

For many people, the roller coaster of drama makes them feel alive because they have been numb for so long. Now, they can finally recognize and experience the surface of some of their emotions. They feel alive, and they want their new excitement to continue.

Drama becomes their new comfort zone. Dealing with the same issues over and over may feel safe because they think they know what to expect. They feel in control because they think they know what emotions will surface and how they will experience them. In reality, this doesn't happen. Our emotional material eventually expands, and it does so in small enough degrees that it doesn't alarm us.

This is sometimes related to a joy alarm. We may create problems to deal with because we feel we don't deserve to be happy. Extended bliss may be too big a stretch for our comfort zones. At other times we really aren't finished dealing with a piece of major emotional content. Sometimes, our Guardians are trying to pull us back into our past. This is common when processing child abuse or domestic violence issues. When that is the case, we simply need to remember that our Guardians are illusions. They are old distortions that belie the awesomeness of who we really are.

Sometimes we feel the same thing over and over out of habit, or we don't know how to move beyond Victim 101. It takes courage to feel past pain that hurt so much or was so frightening that we repressed it. It also takes courage and a genuine commitment to ourselves to take full responsibility for our own lives and move forward. There is a perfect time for both experiences.

I remember going to a self-help group many years ago and wondering why everyone was still living in the past, labeling themselves as dysfunctional, and blaming their parents for their present circumstances. The thoughts kept running through my mind, "It's cleansing to experience unexpressed emotions, but how long do you want to stay imprisoned by limiting yourself to your past? Can't you see how the past served you? Notice how strong and compassionate you are and how much you've learned from your experiences. What about owning your responsibility for your own life now?"

I saw the mirrors around the room and knew I must be doing the same thing. In that moment, I graduated myself and never attended the group again although it had served me up to that point. It was time to strike out on my own and to be my own support system as I found a new way to live. It was time to own my power and find the courage to be who I really was instead of continuing to limit myself by saying, "I can't _____ because in the past _____."

Our mirrors are precise. Up to that point, all I had seen was the pain that the members of the group had experienced. Because it was time for me to move into a different phase of my life, the mirrors I saw changed, and they would never have been the same again, even if I had attended the group a hundred more times.

Recycling the same issues over and over is similar to being afraid to try something new because we aren't sure we will like the new activity as much as we enjoyed the old one. How many times do we go out to dinner and order the same food because we are familiar with it or know we will like it? Sometimes we hesitate to finish reading a novel because we don't know if we will be able to find another one that we will enjoy reading as much. We savor each page in the last chapter, slowly digesting each paragraph and reflecting on selected phrases.

It is not necessary to judge the experiences that you have continued to repeat. Just have the intention to participate in something different. To prevent additional internal resistance, you can talk to your Guardian and say that you've fully experienced and integrated the previous chapters of your life. You can even think of them as books you have read and place them on a bookshelf in your mind. They will be available to you again should the need arise to resurrect or re-experience them.

In truth, your recycled experiences are just tired old thought forms that don't serve you anymore. They just need to be recognized, not fought. Your Guardian is incredibly strong. You can negotiate with it to take on a new job description—to be your servant instead of your master.

Energy is inherently neutral. Only our focus makes it take a certain form. We gave birth to our Guardians because we felt powerless. They were simply thought forms, and we provided their life force. Focus, will, and passion for ourselves are our tools to become all that we truly are, to own our full capabilities by being self-responsible. The reality of everything in our lives is based on our focus and the accuracy of our perceptions. We define it all.

There is a big difference between feeling pure emotions such as current grief, loss, or anger and recycling the *distortion* of who you really are. Just feel what you feel and be open to the transitions that will naturally occur in your emotional content. If you feel sensation in your body, your emotions need to be felt. If the stimulus is only in your mind and doesn't shift when you know that you have already processed a particular experience, it is your Guardian attempting to hold you back.

All that is necessary is to comprehend that the Guardian is endeavoring to keep you from changing. Your recognition of this fact will require it to change its configuration into something that serves you. It is no longer needed in its old form. It just doesn't yet know another way to live.

Once you perceive its presence, it has no choice but to change. It feeds back into you as liberated energy that you can employ to propel you down the fast lane (or to savor the slow lane, if that is your choice). Once again, there was nothing to get rid of. Everything serves us.

Although completing an emotional phase doesn't require drama, it is best not to judge its occurrence. Judgment delays your process, erects an energetic roadblock, and fatigues your body.

Just feel what you feel, and know that drama can be just another tool. It is a bridge in itself because we are finally feeling something that we weren't able to allow ourselves to experience in the past. We simply want more sensation, and this is the only way that we know how to achieve it at this time.

At first, drama and recycling serve us. Eventually we notice that we are repeating the same patterns instead of moving forward. We perceive this phase and step past it, saying to ourselves, "I've done this so many times before. Sure, it's scary to move into an unexplored area, but I'm ready for something new." Boredom is a powerful motivator.

Our feelings become current versus recycling our yesterdays. We move beyond our drama. We grow tired of playing in the past, starring in only one movie, when there are hundreds of roles to play in thousands of movies. Emotional expression becomes a fulfilling and automatic process. To our delight, we discover that there really is more to life than pain and fear. There are so many variations of feelings available, so many chapters in our lives.

Drama melts when we completely experience what we need to. Once again, we use everything as tools to become more of who we really are. Our dramas become building blocks for our bridges from our past to our future.

HANG IN THERE! EMOTIONS ARE ENERGY IN MOTION, SO KEEP MOVING

Just keep feeling whatever layers of emotions that emerge. Treasure each layer even when it feels painful. There are brilliant nuggets of gold and wisdom contained in each of them. Know that there will be an endpoint at the bottom of each polarity, but the high ends have no ceilings. They touch the sky, pierce the clouds, and then spiral infinitely higher.

Be patient with yourself. That's loving yourself. Our thoughts and belief systems took years to establish. When you try to rush, you cheat yourself out of receiving the very gifts that it is time for you to acquire.

DON'T MISS THE GRAND FINALE

Eventually, we finish our work regarding a particular issue. We just know that we have completed a milestone in our lives, a major piece of emotional work. We can clearly see the same issue in someone else, but it no longer sparks an emotional response within us unless it is compassion for their experience. We see the mechanism, but it has no entry point into our consciousness.

For example, when I grieved my father's death, there were major cycles of denial, anger, guilt, depression, and calmness until I was complete with the experience. The big original waves of feeling were followed by smaller aftershocks until all of the phases had been felt.

Because I practiced the techniques discussed in this book, the entire process of fully grieving his death was quite short. After that, there was no emotional trigger for me anymore. Movie scenes about death or conversations with others about their parents' deaths no longer contained an emotional stimulus for me.

ENJOY YOUR NEW LEVELS OF AWARENESS

Notice your added awareness when you feel your emotions. The energy that you have used to repress your pain is now available to absorb clues from every aspect of your environment. We are so much more present when we are feeling. We now easily sense the myriad of clues that our bodies and our outside world *have always been giving us*. We perceive both external mirrors and internal sensations quickly and efficiently, using them as tools.

We know what other people are going to say before their mouths begin to move. We can read the energy in their bodies, noting their moods and how fully present they are willing to be in each moment. All of this is done without judgment. We know so clearly that all of us on this planet are interconnected.

Our senses are a cornucopia of delights. Never before have we seen so much beauty, smelled the depth of aromas, and heard the soft variations in sounds. We thrive on the diversity of what we touch. How could we never before have noticed the dramatic difference between touching one thing that is soft and delicate and another that is hard and rough? How could we have thought that the leaves of the trees are blown by the spring winds? No, they dance with fairy-like ecstasy, chattering and celebrating their very existence.

We know instinctively our next moves, and we easily follow them to completion. The gold mines that we have given ourselves by getting out of our heads and our resistance and allowing ourselves to feel are so profound that they are almost overwhelming. This increased awareness brings a sense of humility that I won't even attempt to describe.

How could I have lived all of these years and cheated myself out of these feelings, sensations, and insights? How could I have thought I was alive when I was so dead?

Only my perceptions have changed. The things that I didn't notice or experience have always been there, patiently waiting for me to perceive them. I can only be filled with awe and wonder regarding what I still do not sense and comprehend about life.

How long can we continue to deny how awesome all of us really are?

EXERCISES

1. Describe your current areas of resistance to feeling and expressing your emotions. Are there situations in which you would rather analyze or try to figure out why you feel a certain way instead of feeling?

2. How is your resistance serving you?

3. What is the best way to deal with your resistance?

4. Can you recall an experience in which you allowed yourself to function at point zero?

5. Describe some joy alarms you have experienced.

6. Describe your most recent mirrors at work and in your personal life.

TWENTY

EXAMPLES OF EXPRESSIVE TECHNIQUES

I want to unfold.
I don't want to stay folded anywhere.
There, I am a lie.

Ranier Maria Rilke

There are as many ways to express your feelings as there are people on this planet. This chapter contains examples to stimulate your thinking regarding tools that will assist you in giving yourself permission to fully feel.

The techniques that work best for you may differ from the methods favored by your friends and colleagues. There are no right or wrong ways to express yourself as long as you are not hurting yourself, another person, or valuable property. You cannot possibly make a mistake. Just try a variety of techniques and see which ones assist you at this time. As you change, your favorite methods will also evolve, so stay open.

If you are in resistance to expressing yourself, simply notice your resistance and trust that it will transform when it is time. Just renew your commitment to yourself to experience your emotions so that you can receive the many gifts they offer you.

Your body and your intention to live consciously (be aware) are the only tools that you will truly need, so always be sensitive to what is occurring in your body. Chapter 15 provided examples of physical sensations related to various emotions. These can assist you in determining your personal reference points related to your feelings.

Because you have made a commitment to feel, you will find all kinds of external tools ranging from mirrors (people, nature, etc.) to art supplies available to you. The list below is not intended to be exhaustive but provides examples of tools to assist you in expressing yourself. Have fun adding your own favorite techniques to those listed.

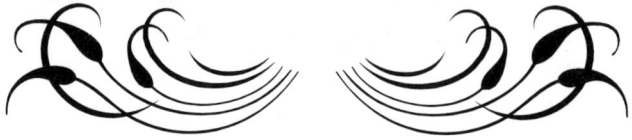

BASICS

Feel and express your emotions and sensations. Laugh, scream, cry, roar, rage, smile, sigh, languish, talk, and jump for joy. Ride your emotions like fish ride the swells of the ocean, giving the waves total permission to transport food right to their mouths. Allow your feelings to carry you to the home inside of yourself.

PHYSICAL MOVEMENTS AND SOUNDS

Spontaneity is the only rule here. Your body's innate intelligence knows exactly what to do, so move it however it wants to express itself. When possible, involve your whole body, including your limbs and torso as well as sounds (singing, screams, primordial sounds, tones, etc.). Notice your breath without trying to change it.

Work by yourself or with one or more trusted partners who have also made a commitment to experience more of who they really are. Activities involving physical movements and sounds are wonderful to do with children. They are usually uninhibited, and their playful, honest, and creative energy can be contagious. (They also don't take life "too seriously.")

If you judge yourself or your activities, just notice your resistance. If you begin to analyze why you want to move a certain way or what a specific movement means, just know that this is indicative of traveling in the slow lane.

Examples of physical movements and sounds to express yourself are described below.

♦ Freestyle movement or dance to music; vary the tempo and type of music you use.

♦ Beat a drum.

♦ Lie on the floor and kick your feet in the air.

♦ Pound a pillow.

♦ Jump on a beanbag chair or lie on the floor and kick it. Allow sounds to emerge from within you.

♦ Induce laughter. (One person begins to laugh, and suddenly the whole room is filled with chuckles and howls.)

♦ Act out animal movements and sounds.

♦ Design safe ways to physically strike objects. Examples: kick or stomp empty plastic jugs, hit empty cardboard boxes with plastic baseball bats, beat a chair with a dishtowel, etc.

ENTERTAINMENT MEDIA

The following are external stimuli that will assist you as you allow your emotions to surface. Use your intuition. Don't analyze why you choose what you do. Enjoy the surprise of simply selecting whatever appeals to you and then learning what it brings to you. You will see other individuals or story characters as mirrors, and various emotions will be triggered.

♦ Movie

♦ Video

♦ Library book—children's books are wonderful for this purpose. They are short and quick to read.

♦ Music

♦ Art exhibit

CREATIVE PROJECTS

Allow your creativity to flow through use of a variety of artistic supplies. Spontaneously design anything, and you will begin to feel and express your emotions. When possible, give yourself a variety of color selections.

Just look at your creations without analyzing them. Place them in an area where you will see them frequently, and allow the insights from what you have produced to be revealed to you when the time is right.

♦ Crayons, colored pens and pencils, paints, fingerpaint, chalk, etc.

♦ Construction paper, glitter, paints, glue, tape, crepe paper, feathers, shells, etc.

♦ Clay is very empowering. You can mold and shape it as well as express yourself in other ways.

♦ Cut pictures that appeal to you from a variety of magazines or catalogs and glue them on posterboard.

♦ Sand tray. Put several inches of sand in a plastic container or a cardboard box. Play with the sand with your fingers, lift it up, and move it around. An option is to have available a variety of objects such as small rocks, pictures, shells, leaves, and miniature representations of people, houses, cars, animals, and furniture. Place them in the sand tray as your instincts lead you to do. Allow your design to talk to you versus analyzing it.

♦ Remember how children fully express their anger one moment and have a peanut butter and jelly sandwich with their "opponent" the next. Act out that scenario (with or without a partner).

JOURNALING AND WRITING

♦ Factual and creative writing have been used for centuries as expressive techniques. You can have an agenda or do free-flowing writing.

♦ Write to an aspect of yourself that you have judgments about.

♦ Write to yourself as a child.

♦ Have no agenda, and write with your non-dominant hand. (This stimulates your brain and is also very transformative regarding your emotional issues.) Promise yourself that you will write for 15 minutes without stopping. If you have nothing to write, scribble until thoughts come to you. If nonsense words appear, record them. Just keep writing. Read the results without analyzing them, and insights and emotions will be revealed to you.

♦ Write a story beginning with "Once upon a time . . . "

♦ Answer a series of questions such as those listed below. Use your dominant or non-dominant hand. Be with your feelings when they surface. The sentence stems below are examples. Also develop your own.

- My biggest fear is . . .
- If I could feel what I am most afraid to feel . . .
- I don't want to change because . . .
- I love myself when . . .
- I don't love myself when . . .
- I am angry about . . .
- I have judged my feelings about . . .
- I feel anxious when . . .
- I feel happy when . . .
- I feel worthy when . . .
- If I could say what I really want to say . . .
- I feel good about . . .
- I accept that I have been feeling bad about . . .

When you have completed your answers and have felt any emotions that surfaced, you may want to confirm your intention not to judge yourself by saying, "And that's the way it is right now."

DREAMWORK

Before going to sleep, ask your dreams to assist you in expressing yourself. Keep a pad and pencil by your bedside in case you want to record any middle-of-the-night insights that flow through your consciousness, but don't try to wake up to receive or record them. Anything you need to know will be available to you. Our intentions are so powerful that this technique will work without struggle or effort.

BREATHWORK

Our breath is our life force and is a powerful tool for expressing ourselves. There are a number of excellent breathwork techniques which can be investigated at your local bookstore or public library. Peruse books on yoga, stress reduction, and more specialized approaches to breathwork. There are a variety of theories concerning the effects of increased or decreased oxygen to the centers of the brain that deal with our emotions. Experiment with the following ideas and then design your own by paying attention to the signals in your body.

♦ Long, slow, deep rhythmic breathing to relaxing music.

♦ Fast breathing with the intention of inhaling and holding as much air as possible in your chest before exhaling.

♦ Breathe in as much air as you can retain in your chest cavity. Hold your breath, and then breathe in more before releasing it. Repeat and continue to extend the length of time that you retain your breath and the amount of air that you can hold. Relax and repeat. This is an expansive and revealing exercise that can also be used for relaxing or energizing the entire body.

♦ Exhale all of your breath. Then bear down on all of the muscles in your body (push your muscles against themselves), forcing any remaining air out. Hold your breath as long as possible before you inhale again. Repeat this 10 times, relax, and repeat. This is a very expansive technique that will cause your emotions to surface, particularly those relating to how much passion you have for your Self.

EXPRESSION ON THE RUN

Perhaps at some point, we will all give ourselves permission to be who we are in every circumstance. Until that time, if you are trying to figure out how to express yourself in crowded places or situations where you do not wish to be observed, experiment with strategies such as the following.

♦ Scream in your car with the windows rolled up.

♦ Scream into a pillow.

♦ Yell or cry at a sporting event or on a crowded dance floor and discover that no one notices!

♦ Express yourself however you want to, wherever you want to, and notice that everyone is so busy judging themselves that they never bothered to notice or judge you.

♦ Fully express yourself in a public setting, and discover that your openness gave others permission to express themselves.

EXCELLENT CARE OF YOURSELF

The more fully you express yourself, the more your self-love will spontaneously expand. Know that you deserve an excellent support system and that it begins with yourself.

Our bodies are the homes we live in. They also house all of our memories and the clues and sensations that lead us toward our next steps. Be gentle and loving with yourself when you are experiencing major transitions. The cells in your body are reconfiguring as your molecular structure changes.

Your body will tell you what it needs and wants. It may want to breathe fresh air in a park, on a mountainside, or by water. It may want extra sleep so that you can become refreshed and express yourself through your dreams. Maybe mild or rigorous exercise is today's desire. Spontaneously treat your body to the loving respect it deserves such as massage or other bodywork, special baths, and a variety of yummy, nutritious foods. Your body will tell you exactly what it wants and when. You will discover that your body even wants to express itself through the foods that you eat.

IMAGINE THAT!

Use your imagination to construct situations like the examples below. Have fun! Play! Our lives are constantly reshaping themselves. Most of the challenges we perceive to be problems are just tired old thought forms (our Guardians).

♦ Imagine that someone has handed you an object with which to express yourself. Accept the object and act out your use of it.

♦ Imagine that a wizard is standing in front of you, wearing a gorgeous purple robe and holding a glittering magic wand. The wizard looks at you with that expression that you know gives you permission to blossom into your full empowerment, saying, "Now is the time!"

♦ The next step is yours. Fully express yourself. Tell your Guardian anything you need to. Feel your emotions and watch them transform your life.

♦ Your Guardian is standing in front of you, wearing a mischievous expression and a snaggle-toothed smile. Express yourself physically, but without words, to your Guardian.

PAUSE TO ANCHOR YOUR NEW SELF

It is the pause between notes that creates beautiful music. After major emotional breakthroughs, you can allow yourself time to anchor your new self by feeling your cellular structure radiate its newness. Exactly how you do this will be your individual preference. Sometimes you may want to close your eyes and feel your body tingle with vibrant new sensations. You may choose to draw a picture symbolizing your experience or write about new insights or perceptions. At other times, you may wish to stretch your muscles, cherishing the new freedom in each limb and organ. You may go to sleep and dream or jump up and shout with joy. All that matters is that you anchor your internal transformations. Experience your rewards consciously and know that your awareness and your pause have provided you a reference point—you can return to this safe and special place inside of yourself at any time.

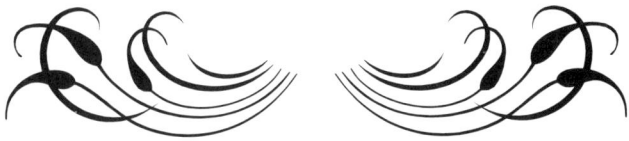

The emotional component of each of us is bursting to break free from our denial of our real selves. Allow this creative critter its freedom, and you will effortlessly receive your personal empowerment. It will latch onto you with the swiftness and grace of an eagle swooping down to snatch its prey. You will simply no longer be able to deny the awesomeness of who you truly are.

Your emotions will bring you a myriad of gifts, including release of physical constrictions, greater energy, catharsis, clarity, a sense of relief and rebirth, insights, and fresh perspectives. You will suddenly discover that you have given birth to your real self.

These things most of us have been so afraid of, our feelings, are just energy. Their sensations are our personal languages, and there are different intensities in our individual dialects. Some emotions vibrate faster and some slower. They vary in power, weight, intensity, temperature, yield, and malleability. Feelings penetrate our entire bodies, although at specific times we feel them more in one area than another. Diverse amounts of energy run through us at different times and in unique ways. It is like a computer is working with distinct bits of energy that flood our subconscious minds before the sensations become conscious.

The language of emotions is fascinating, and we can analyze our feelings endlessly. When we want to travel in the fast lane, we will simply experience them. We will understand that by allowing these basic electrical components of ourselves to flow in safe and constructive ways, we are allowing ourselves to vibrate with our full frequency. We are calling for our self-actualization by allowing ourselves to be the holistic beings that we are.

EXERCISES

1. What are the easiest ways for you to express your feelings at this time?

2. Describe your greatest areas of resistance and how these are related to your self-judgments.

3. What are some different ways that you are willing to consider expressing your emotions?

4. Outline specific ways you can express yourself at work or in another public setting.

Examples:

a) Hold a red or black pen in your non-dominant hand during a tense meeting. Allow your hand to doodle without analyzing what it draws or writes. Stay in touch with your feelings. Notice that you can be fully attentive to the meeting, feel your emotions, and express yourself at the same time. What freedom!

b) Sometime when you are frustrated, take a break and go into a bathroom stall or other private area and vent your frustrations. For example, swiftly blow out your breath several times, as if you are blowing out candles. You might pummel your fist into an object in a way that doesn't damage you, another individual, or property of value. Remember the ball of clay from exercise #8 in chapter 5? You may want to swing your arms or stomp your foot. You can also shove one fist into the palm of your other hand or play the "silent scream" game. Have you ever tried furiously scribbling with a red pen? Feel your energy level rise as your frustration is expressed and the opposite emotion (joy) becomes available to you. Because pain and pleasure are side by side in the brain, most people begin laughing very quickly and go back to work feeling more energetic.

TWENTY–ONE

TRANSFORMING PAIN INTO POWER—
THE STORY OF A WATER DROPLET

The following story illustrates some of the concepts described in this book.

When I was formed by the moisture in the sky and became a water droplet, I relished having a molecular structure of my own, getting to be whole and complete within myself. To my surprise, I gained weight, descended from the sky, and became part of a puddle fed by a cloudburst.

I danced around and around, exploring my new form. Freedom surged through every molecule in my body as I wriggled around with glee. "I have a body!" I exclaimed. "What fun! Now I can laugh and play and sing in my little pool of water." As the fine mists of the storm continued, the ripples from other falling water droplets gently caressed my form. I giggled as their tiny waves tickled my soul as well as my body.

My ecstasy was short-lived. "OUCH!" All of a sudden, every sub-atomic particle in my anatomy ached. A heavy rainstorm was furiously pounding me. Instinctively, I sank to the bottom of my puddle to hide and wait out the storm.

Then the sun came out, so I lazily glided to the top of the runoff and devoured the warm rays. How relaxing!

"Whoa!" I recoiled. "I guess I was in a sunbathing trance too long. It's dangerous here. I barely survived that one. Where did that huge paw come from? And that big tongue? It tried to suck me into its vacuum!" I raced as fast as I could to the bottom of my puddle and tried to avoid the hairy paws that seemed to be everywhere I wanted to be.

I could have been carried off by that dog—I would have disap-peared into the air! I decided to be much more cautious.

That night and the next few days offered a period of peaceful transition. What a relief to rest, spin around in my pool, and think through my survival strategies. No more rainstorms and dog paws for me!

I thought I had it all figured out when a drought settled in. I al-most lost all of my substance when powerful winds and scorch-ing heat sucked on my cells. I learned to be careful not to be on the top of my decreasing puddle any longer than necessary, or I would just be part of the air again. I learned how to stay clean even though most of the dingy pool was becoming so small that I felt dirty.

As the summer passed and autumn rains began, I thought that I had finally mastered this demon called change. The rainy sea-son ensured my survival. I was comfortable and happy as long as I darted lower into the puddle at the first signs of heavy thun-derstorms that otherwise produced great pain.

Then my pristine solitude and smug self-confidence were totally shattered—in a flash—a flashflood! Wow! All of a sudden, my puddle joined with all of its neighbors in a torrent of the most frightening and dangerous mudslide. Debris of all kinds pummeled me from every direction—tree limbs, sticky piles of leaves, pebbles, and even large, heavy rocks. As if that weren't traumatic enough, lightning cracked overhead with a vengeance and struck several trees that I was whirled around.

My heart ached with a desperate longing for the small puddle that I had so carefully mastered. All of my study and training were for naught. I had no future.

Even though in my heart I was kicking and screaming, my body felt lifeless because I had no choice but to be swiftly and mercilessly carried along by the violence of the flood. I was a dead water drop, and I knew it.

Hour after hour, I "checked out" because my emotions and physical trauma were too painful to endure, but my mind agonized over my future. I knew in my heart that I would never be the same again.

Would I even exist? Surely not in my former molecular structure because I had been so violently mixed with other water droplets, mud, slash, and other stench.

If I survived, would I be glad that I did? My very soul had been ravaged.

As three days of flooding dragged on with excruciating agony, I checked out of my body more frequently. I just didn't want to be present for any additional trials.

Finally, the flood subsided, and my molecular structure reformulated. With great caution, I became aware once again. I peeked out to ascertain the composition of my environment. I was now in the central part of a beautiful green river bordered by huge ancient trees and clean, shapely boulders. My new home was deep enough that I would never again need to worry about being in a puddle that could dry up at any time. Great blue herons and bald eagles soared overhead, welcoming my arrival and providing evidence that the river was teeming with life.

As further evidence of my good fortune, jolly speckled trout and salmon were cavorting and displaying their leapfrogging skills while they enjoyed the bounteous cuisine that we, the river molecules, brought to them. The perfect temperature of the river invigorated my reformulated body while the rhythmic current gently massaged and rejuvenated it. I felt I was the safest that I had ever been.

How could I have doubted myself and my process of transformation? Just as it had been so perfect when I descended to the earth and landed in the puddle so that I could begin to teach myself more lessons, now I had once again proven to myself that change only brings a higher sense of evolution.

I began to talk to the many other water droplets in this river and they agreed with my conclusion. We had all had enough conscious experiences by this time in our journeys of life that even when we wanted to or did "numb out," we knew that transformation was an inevitable part of our existences.

In the ensuing days, I so greatly enjoyed my new home and friends that I forgot that transformation is the nature of reality. I awoke each morning with such zest for life; so grateful that my physical structure was now sparkling, clean, and healthy. All of my pain had been cleansed by this river and carried downstream. I swam and floated, I danced, and my heart opened to and celebrated the adventure of life. It was an exquisite and memorable time.

And then, of course, you know what occurred. Everything changed once again, and the next transition provided the greatest lesson of my life. One day, I was casually drifting downstream when the momentum of my travel was greatly escalated. Faster and faster, I was carried by the river. With terror in my heart, I panicked. I anxiously searched for sounds or other signs of another flashflood, but there were none.

"Whatever is going on?" I frantically asked myself and the river. "What should I do? I sense yet another change, and I feel so out of control."

Mother River promptly responded, "Float! Give up trying to control anything this time. You already know that change is the nature of existence. If you want to experience the ride of your life, surrender and trust yourself and your process of transformation."

"That's easy for you to say," I retorted, as I watched my friends scramble and try to position themselves as they invariably lost their sure footing. Without exception, they were carried faster and faster downstream, against their will.

As I resisted yet another change in my life, I cried out for them. The distance between us was expanding rapidly. Soon we would have only our memories of each other.

"Why? Why can't I have what I want? Why can't I create my reality to fit my pictures of how I think life should be?," I cried as I realized the depth of my opposition to change. I was kicking and screaming just as much as I had during my previous life transitions, whining, "*How* do you give up control? I don't even know what that means."

Again, Mother River quickly came to my rescue, responding, "You're doing it! Just feel your emotions and don't check out this time. You will soon find that by having the ride of your life, you are giving yourself the *gift* of life. You will be more aware, happier, and more powerful than you ever could have imagined."

"That's easy for you to say—you're the whole river—not just one little water droplet!" I moaned. "You would never know what it's like to be a tiny droplet and have your whole body—your whole world—torn apart, and there is nothing you can do about it!" Right now, I hated the power of this river. Every molecule in my body was rebelling against her.

"How do you think I got to be the whole river, little droplet?" asked Mother River, as she churned and roared with her outrageous, mighty force. "Don't you think I experienced the same rights of passage? Don't you think I felt like you do before I learned to surrender to my evolutionary process as I prepared to dump into the ocean?"

Her comments goaded me into new understanding. Even now as I was being whirled around and around, cascading toward an unknown destination at an ever-increasing rate of speed, I knew she was right. I had learned basic survival skills, I had felt victimized, and I had learned some things about my power. Now, it was time for me to learn to surrender to my process. This was my opportunity to be fully conscious during this thing called change—my transformation process—instead of being in resistance. This time, I could learn to perceive where I was in denial, numbing out, or unconsciously following my old patterns of fighting transition.

"It takes far more courage to be conscious of change and surrender to it than it does to play the role of victim," instructed Mother River.

I screamed because I knew I was being yanked out of my complacency into yet another stage of growth.

"The reason you feel like you are being jerked around is because of your resistance to a different way of life," bellowed Mother River. "Stop trying to maintain your current footing. Allow yourself to be carried along with the natural flow of the river. Your battle with the inescapable is wearing you out. Just feel the sensations in your body and watch for their natural clues regarding your proper position. You really don't have to do anything but watch yourself change."

It was her last phrase that finally got through to me. "There is nothing to do in life but watch myself change," I reminded myself.

I watched myself try to cling to sharp rocks in the river, to other droplets—to anything that was familiar. I stayed aware during the process. It must have been at least a half hour that I observed it, wondering all the while *how* to let go of control. I coached myself, "The only thing that exists is change. There is nothing to do but watch myself change."

Slowly, I relaxed the molecules in my structure and found that I could still feel the layers of my fear when they wafted through my consciousness. All of a sudden, I realized that I was simultaneously feeling fear *and* excitement. I was enjoying a new experience—a neutral stage where I simply appreciated the range of feelings in my body.

Wow! What a trip! One moment I was rapidly and flawlessly gliding over a well-worn rock, and the next I was laughing with thousands of other droplets as we swirled around in circles. Sometimes we were scattered high into the air by the sheer force of our speed as we collided with huge rocks. It was glorious!

Mother River had been right. I could never have imagined the new life force I felt and the ecstasy of being carried ever higher into the air as I surged further on each leg of the journey. Letting go of my resistance ensured that my molecular structure became more energized. Its vibration became higher and more intense as the negative ions from the water added greater electrical frequency to my body. Sometimes the rate of change made me dizzy. Yet, I was feeling a level of ecstasy I had never dreamed existed.

"I love living in the fast lane!" I announced to Mother River. "I want an even higher rate of vibration."

Then Mother River gave me a choice. "Well, now you are beginning to understand the evolutionary process. Look ahead of you. In about 300 yards, we become a waterfall. It will appear to you that the river drops off the face of the earth."

I gazed ahead and gulped. A huge wave of panic washed through me. I knew I couldn't live through what lay before me. The river became torrential and did indeed plummet from the surface of the earth and disappear into a giant vacuum. I had been so busy playing that I hadn't even noticed the crashing sound of the waterfall ahead. Surely all of the drops that were carried down it died. "I can't do it, Mother River. I've never done it before, and I'm certain I will die."

"I understand," she responded with the utmost compassion. "Life is all about choice. You can choose to dissipate into the air at any time on this journey. Because there is really no such thing as death, if you do so, you will re-emerge at some time. That's what happened when you solidified, fell from the sky, and entered the water puddle."

"Whew!" I sighed with relief. "Yes! I know how to exist in a tiny pool of water. I can do that again."

Then my memory kicked in. I remembered my terror of the rainstorm beating my body, the dog's slurping tongue and hairy paws, and the flashflood. I had developed tools by living through all of those experiences. Yet, now I knew so much more. I finally knew how to surrender to my process—or did I?

Mother River was right. There was no wrong path. Which path did my heart choose?

Would I want my familiar realm of avoiding the rainstorm and the dog, of being torn apart by the flashflood or something similar? I knew enough now that perhaps I wouldn't even wrestle with the events in my life. Surely a journey in a flashflood would be easier next time and I wouldn't numb out anymore. I would trust myself and my process even when I was afraid. I knew I could repeat my past and still learn more about life.

My thoughts raced as fast as the speed at which I was being transported downstream. My heart pounded, but this time it wasn't with fear but with the exhilaration that emerged with my new clarity. My heart was speaking to me.

"Life is all about choice. At any moment, I can choose to dissipate my structure, be part of the air, and no longer exist as a distinguishable water droplet. *And*, if I do that, I will never know what's on the other side of the waterfall or what's around the riverbend." I concluded. "I will cheat myself out of the adventure of being even more alive."

I was more passionate and spirited than I had ever been. I had reached new heights of frequency and had a greatly expanded life force.

"I want even more!" I screamed to Mother River above the formidable sound of the turbulent waters. "Now that I have tasted being even more alive, I can't settle for anything less. I can't go back to being just part of a puddle or being carried along in a flashflood."

My decision had been made just at the brink of the cliff. I breathed deeply and plunged into my new flow of life. Faster and faster, I was swept downstream by the river. Even though the pace was the fastest I had ever experienced, it didn't make me dizzy this time.

I laughed and sang as I played in the rapids. When I saw that I was literally about to drop off the edge of another steep ledge, I leaped high into the air with a divine combination of fear and excitement. I knew I was protected because I had made a firm decision to experience life.

In my wild excitement, I was carried from one descending rock shelf to the next as I cascaded down the waterfall. During the entire journey, I heard the voices of other water droplets. Some were screaming in panic, and others were shouting with sheer delight. Many had chosen to numb out and weren't feeling anything at all. They were simply existing, waiting to re-emerge at the bottom of the cliff so that they could assess what life had brought to them.

Every particle in my body felt the sheer force of my new power as I turned cartwheels and somersaults all of the way down the next cliff. I was now part of a fine mist of negative ions spewing rapturously above the gushing waterfall. Sometimes I dipped deeply into the splash of the fall and then vaulted high into the air with the greatest of mastery. The sun protruded through the mist and produced beautiful rainbows that winked at me and reinforced my courage.

With wild abandon, I proclaimed my new self, screaming, "Freedom! I'm *alive!*" Every part of me commemorated this new force

I had become. I was no longer being carried downstream by a river or a waterfall. I would never again experience a perilous journey down a sharp cliff.

I was now an active participant in my own life. My new power came from the fact that I had *become* the waterfall, just as I would later *be* the lower part of the river.

"And just think," I laughed, "there was a time when my wildest dream was to *exist* in a small dirty puddle, dodging rainstorms and hairy dog paws!"

TWENTY–TWO

A PARTING MESSAGE FROM THE AUTHOR

This book tackled the stormy areas of our lives—our painful experiences and emotions—and described simple principles for fully using both to enhance our personal growth. Transforming our pain into power becomes effortless with experience. We mine the gold nuggets of wisdom and joy that are available in our most dismal experiences, and we liberate ourselves from the prisons that we create when we judge our circumstances and feelings.

We just feel, without judgment, and the ever-changing flow of our feelings is as automatic as it is for babies. Our emotions become one of our most joyful tools. We become aware of the sweetness of sorrow, the power and fun of constructively expressed anger, and the way our personal empowerment travels hand in hand with our fears.

As we feel our fears of unexplored realms of life, we simultaneously experience our excitement concerning our next steps. Our energy is fully available to us, and with the curiosity and excitement of a small child, we ask ourselves, "I wonder what's next?"

When we no longer dread life's uncertainties, we graduate ourselves into our next steps in life, and then the next, and the next, into eternity. This, my friends, is real freedom.

Because we have the intention to live in a conscious manner, rich insights and exceptional clarity become available to us. We discover that truth has never been hidden from the masses. We have merely been afraid to acknowledge its presence. All we have to do is perceive the distortions in our lives and they become neutral energy awaiting our next use of them.

Our focus and our passion for ourselves transform this free energy, and we use it to expedite our growth and to function at much higher levels. Once again, there is nothing to get rid of. Everything in our lives serves us.

My experiences and the perceptions I have gained during the past 20 years while living and collecting data for this book have struck me with such an explosive force. I am filled with awe and wonder regarding what I still do not sense and comprehend about life.

Life will surely be even more profound and powerful than what has already become apparent. Knowing that, I choose to remain totally open and conscious and to *fly* into my next steps with full focus. I am filled with an exquisite passion for *life*.

The day before William and I mailed the final manuscript, brisk Chinook winds wafted through our beautiful valley heralding the arrival of spring and hastening the melting of our beloved snow. We went to sleep in ecstasy that night, exhilarated by the vibrations and sounds of cracking ice flows tumbling down rejuvenated creeks and the smells of new life all around us. The sensations were almost overwhelming. I awoke in the wee hours of the morning compelled to record the following message that had filtered through in a dream. Afterward, I realized that it was March 21, the first day of spring.

> The winds of change blow,
> and we are transformed.
> We are *feeling*,
> and our lives will never be the same.

> We notice the brisk breezes on our cheeks
> and smell the arrival of Spring—
> deep transformation, change, and rebirth.

It is too late for the past.
It has come and gone
and will never return.

The moment of choice has arrived—
to be strangled by the past or
blaze a trail into the future.

The past is death,
and the future is ours.
It is life itself.

The moment of choice
presented itself,
and this time
there was no choice.

We have all of the tools that we will ever need to face our challenges. It is our decision whether to continue to avoid the majestic wild horse of life or to become one with it and to dance into *our* freedom.

From the depths of my heart, I thank you for the opportunity to have shared with you this most treasured part of myself.

May you live and love with the highest level of passion for your Self.

Give a Gift of Love to a Friend

ORDER FORM

Transforming Pain Into Power, ISBN: 1–8855–98–88–2
You may order 24 hours a day, so *act now!*
Telephone orders: 1-800-218-6110

E-mail: http://www.amazon.com
                                or
                                shimodapub@mindspring.com
                                URL: http://www.mindspring.com/~shimodapub/
Mailing address: Shimoda Publishing
                                c/o 1225 E. Sunset, #317
                                Bellingham, WA 98226-3529

Please send me _____ **copies of *Transforming Pain Into Power*** @ $16.95 per copy. I understand that I may return any books in good condition for a full refund—for any reason, no questions asked.

Shipping and handling costs: $3.00 for the first book and $2.00 for each additional book.

I am enclosing a check or money order for $_____

Name:_____

Address:_____

City:_____ State: _____ Zip: _____

Telephone:(   )_____-_____Fax: (   )_____-_____

E-mail:_____

Purchase order number (if applicable) _____

Call toll free and order now!

Bookstores and libraries may also order from New Leaf, Bookpeople, Ingram, DeVorss, Quality, or Unique.

GLOSSARY

The way most of the words and phrases itemized below are used in this book expands upon classic dictionary definitions. If a meaning has been extracted from *Webster's New World Dictionary (10th Ed.),* the dictionary reference is noted. The other definitions below are specific to the context of this publication and are explained in greater depth within the book.

Approach-avoidance: This phrase means simultaneously moving toward and away from something. We may be in approach-avoidance regarding a goal or experiencing something different than our current reality. We are saying, "I want it" and "I don't want it" at the same time. This usually means "I'm afraid to have what I say I want" or "I'm afraid I don't deserve to have what I want." Another term for approach-avoidance is "push-pull."

Aware: knowing, conscious, realizing *(Webster's New World Dictionary, 10th Ed.)*

To move beyond struggle in life, we need to do two things: 1.) have the intention to live in a 100 percent conscious (aware) manner, and 2.) not judge ourselves or our experiences.

Bridge: a structure built to provide a way across, a thing that provides connection or contact *(Webster's New World Dictionary, 10th Ed.)*

Our emotions are the building blocks that are used to construct the bridges from where we are now to where we are going.

Comfort zone: Comfort zones are not necessarily comfortable! They are merely what we are used to. They are our known realities. We are constantly exiting our comfort zones and moving into our unknown realities—our next steps in life. Because of our fears of change, even when we are in difficult or painful situations and change is clearly to our benefit, we tend to cling to our comfort zones. This is because we have learned how to act and feel when we are in these realms. There is a part of each of us that does not yet want to learn new behaviors or have different experiences. Thus, we experience approach-avoidance.

Compensating Strategy: This is a defense mechanism to compensate for our feelings of inadequacy or insecurity. We project an external image such as workaholic or perfectionist to compensate for feeling inadequate or insecure. One example is a superachiever who does not have a balanced life or a true connection with him or herself. Another example is a person who plays the role of a victim or a martyr who feels powerless.

Conscious: having an awareness, able to feel and think, awake, aware of oneself as a thinking being, intentional behavior *(Webster's New World Dictionary, 10th Ed.)*

When we experience our lives with the intention to be 100 percent conscious, we discover more about ourselves, and our personal growth rates escalate significantly.

Conscious choices: When we assume responsibility for our own lives, we consciously make our choices and decisions and enjoy the personal freedom that ensues from doing so.

Consciousness: the state of being conscious, awareness, the totality of one's thoughts and feelings *(Webster's New World Dictionary, 10th Ed.)*

Construct: Constructs are distortions that we have fed with our belief systems. They are not real; they are thought forms that we have given life by believing in them. They were created throughout time by social beliefs and dogma, generation after generation.

We have unconsciously accepted them as our own, and we can choose to continue to function with them or not. They are based on ignorance, insecurity, and associated emotions such as fear. They are extremely hardy, yet they need our cooperation to feed on us.

They become more discreet—harder to perceive—the more conscious we become so that we can pass more difficult tests of detecting them. It is necessary to recognize social constructs and not to allow them to feed on us. Constructs cannot abide in the presence of joy, ecstasy, and laughter.

Constructs want you to secede from the union of you with yourself. Once they are detected (acknowledged), they change form and become usable, neutral (free) energy. Simply recognizing them for the distortions that they are means that you are not resisting them or setting in motion a battle inside of yourself.

Core identity: A core identity is a central identity. Who we really are (unlimited beings) is usually masked by the compensating strategies and identities that we have adopted to survive in a particular social or family structure. To discover the beauty of who we really are, all we have to do is experience our unfelt emotions, layer after layer, until we reach our core selves.

Denial: refusal to believe or accept, same as self-denial *(Webster's New World Dictionary, 10th Ed.)*

When we deny what exists, we negate our Selves and repress our emotions. We store these unfelt emotions in our bodies, and that allows us to live in our denial.

When we refuse to accept what exists, we are unable to see who we really are. It takes energy to hold our denial in place, so we create situations to support our insecurities and to refute the fact that we are afraid. We resist feeling our emotions, and this creates internal struggle.

The mechanism of denial splits our creative potential. We feel split inside of ourselves, and we don't know it. We feel insecure. This is demonstrated by anxiety or depression. We try to compensate for our insecurities by projecting images such as superachiever, victim, martyr, or perfectionist.

Distortion: illusion, false idea or conception, unreal or misleading appearance or image *(Webster's New World Dictionary, 10th Ed.)*

Our lives are filled with distortions based on our belief systems and our inabilities to perceive things as they are. Once we recognize distortions, they are compelled to change their forms. For example, our Guardians are distortions. Once we see them for what they are, they must change and become neutral energy. That neutral energy is transformed by our focus and passion. It is free energy that we can use to expedite our growth.

Most of us can only perceive in other individuals what exists within ourselves because we comprehend our own characteristics as they are mirrored to us by others. Generally, we also interpret new information based on what we already know—our known realities. Because our unknown realities are greater than our known realities, it is understandable why we have so many distortions and misperceptions in our lives.

Drama: Drama is resistance to feeling and expressing the depth of our emotions. When we "do drama," we re-create experiences that provide us additional opportunities to feel emotions or process emotional material that we have already dealt with.

Drama differs from *Peeling the onion* (see below), which means experiencing deeper layers of a polarity.

Drama can be a bridge toward learning to express emotions in the moment without recycling them. In other words, it is important not to cheat yourself out of feeling. When you are recycling emotional content, be aware that you may have an unconscious desire to control how you experience emotions or to stay in your comfort zone.

Emotions: feelings such as love, hate, fear, anger *(Webster's New World Dictionary, 10th Ed.)*

Other examples of emotions are happiness, depression, insecurity, ecstasy, sweetness, freedom, aliveness, hope, wholeness, sadness, lust, loneliness, self-confidence, ecstasy, guilt, and excitement.

Emotions are the language of you talking to yourself. They are energy in motion, the essence of fully experiencing life, and the glue that connects us to ourselves and others.

Our emotions are our spontaneity, and they empower us when we own, feel, and express them. They need to be felt and expressed, but it is not necessary to endlessly process or recycle them.

We feel our emotions by being aware of sensations in our bodies and then expressing them in a variety of ways, including physical movements, talking, laughing, crying, screaming, etc. Allowing ourselves to feel however we feel makes everything easier because we are not fighting with ourselves. (We have not set up internal resistance.)

Feeling our emotions frees energy in our bodies, so it energizes and empowers us. Releasing energy blocks in our bodies where we have repressed feelings reduces stress and improves our health. This is because we are holistic beings with connections between our minds, bodies, and spirits.

Feeling our emotions improves our relationships because we stop carrying around stuffed feelings when we relate to other people. Our emotions connect us to others by removing our feelings of separateness.

Emotional Expression: This is an individual's style of expressing his or her emotions. Our emotions can be felt as sensations in our bodies and expressed by physical movements, crying, talking, screaming, laughing, etc.

Empowerment: When we are empowered, we are willing to acknowledge our full capabilities. We have the intention to live in a 100 percent conscious manner and to be totally self-responsible instead of blaming others for our lives or our choices. This entails owning our power versus "playing victim" or feeling powerless.

Energy: capacity for action, inherent power, force of expression, the capacity for doing work *(Webster's New World Dictionary, 10th Ed.)*

Energy is raw power harnessed by our focus, will, and passion for being all that we truly are. Everything in life is composed of energy, and it is inherently neutral and waiting for our use. As soon as we perceive distortions, they must transform so that we can use them in other ways for our growth.

Feeling: experiencing emotions *(Webster's New World Dictionary, 10th Ed.)*

Frequency: Frequency is the level of the energetic vibration of matter. We are most comfortable around others who vibrate at a level similar to our energetic vibration. We resonate with them.

Funnel: A funnel is a key growth experience in life in which a person moves from one known reality to their next step—their next unknown. When we are close to achieving a major goal in our lives, we enter a funnel in which we acquire essential knowledge and experience. The funnel involves an intense process in which our comfort zones are stretched. Our self-doubts, fears, and self-judgments surface so that we can transform them and move into new stages of our lives. Our experiences in funnels are our passports to our next phases of life.

Going around the wheel: This term means repeating past behaviors or experiences similar to the way a hamster plays in a plastic wheel. We recycle instead of gaining the wisdom inherent in events and advancing to our next steps in life.

One of the most common ways that we tend to go around and around the wheel is that we judge ourselves as inadequate. This creates an internal resistance that inhibits our development. It guarantees that we will continue the cycle of trying to change or "fix" ourselves. We also tend to judge others because we are judging ourselves.

Guardian: Our Guardians are distorted thought forms that we created because we didn't know how powerful we really are. Unlike the *Construct* (see above), our Guardians were defense mechanisms that originally served us. They were designed to protect us from knowing or owning our power. In fact, their original jobs were to keep us from feeling, from experiencing life. The Guardians took on lives (energy) of their own and became our masters instead of our servants. All we have to do is perceive them as distortions and give them new job descriptions.

Our Guardians are primarily connected with our feelings of shame, blame, self-doubt, and self-judgment. They fight our changing—no mater how beneficial change will be for us because they like to be in control of our lives and don't like change of any kind. The Guardians must alter once we perceive them as distortions. They transform into neutral energy that we can use to speed our growth.

Identity: Our identities are the ways we perceive ourselves or the ways we want others to view us. Examples include super-achiever, non-achiever, workaholic, caretaker, perfectionist, victim, martyr, and loser.

We outgrow elements of our personalities (identities) as we advance in our lives. Some of our identities originated because of our needs to be viewed certain ways so that we would feel "good enough." In other words, we created identities designed to compensate for our feelings of insecurity. Other components of our personalities were established to validate our erroneous self-perceptions that we were "not good enough." During major life-changing processes, most of our identities are gradually broken down and transmuted. Even though this can be frightening, it produces tremendous freedom because we lose our limiting self-definitions.

Our identities would be harmless if we did not think they were real. In a similar vein, we sometimes resist feeling our emotions because we believe that we will become them. We are not our fears, insecurities, etc. We merely experience them so that we can then feel their opposites—empowerment, self-confidence, etc. Living with polarities is an essential tool for our personal growth.

Illusion: distortion, false idea or conception, an unreal or misleading appearance or image *(Webster's New World Dictionary, 10th Ed.)*

See *Distortion* above.

Joy alarm: The belief that we cannot have ongoing bliss and that joy can only exist in our lives in limited quantities can initiate a joy alarm. When we feel uncomfortable with joy or think we don't deserve it, we re-create pain in our lives. This ensures that we are in our comfort zones of *not too much joy*.

Judgment: an evaluation or critique (often a criticism) of ourselves, others, or the experiences in our lives.

Our self-judgments are one of the primary ways that we hold ourselves back from being all that we are. We rate ourselves or others as insufficient. When we feel inadequate, we frequently project our feelings of inferiority onto someone else rather than feeling our own insecurities. Our judgments of others and of ourselves hold us back because our focus is on blame instead of gleaning the wisdom available and moving forward. The judgments also create an internal resistance to what exists, so we spend significant energy battling rather than accepting it. When we accept things as they are, everything that we have been wanting to change automatically begins to transmute.

Judging our experiences as negative is one of the primary ways that we cheat ourselves out of the wisdom they offer to us. We either focus on blaming someone else or trying to change or repair something. In truth, all of our experiences in life serve us, so there is never anything to fix.

Our judgments of our emotions and experiences are our self-created prisons, and our judgments pave the roads to our pain.

Judgment 101: A course most of us enroll in. We judge ourselves, our emotions, and our experiences until we learn that judgment ensures that we will struggle with life instead of understanding how very simple it really is. When we understand that everything in life is purposeful and that there is gold to be mined in all that appears dark on the surface, we graduate ourselves from the course. At that point, our learning becomes more spontaneous and joyful. In fact, it is almost effortless.

Known reality: This is what we know at this time or what we have experienced to date.

Leapfrog: We are all interconnected. Each time we change, we cut a groove in consciousness which makes it easier for the next person to more easily or quickly (if they choose) gain the wisdom from a similar event. Sometimes, they can even omit that occurrence by experiencing us as a tuning fork. (See *Tuning fork*.) When we are around others, we sense their frequency (their electrical vibration). A third frequency is spontaneously born from our two energies.

Sometimes we resist another person's higher vibration. We reject them, attempt to project our own emotional issues onto them, or try to prove them wrong simply because we are resisting our own growth. This is usually an unconscious mechanism so we can't see that we are cheating ourselves out of a valuable interaction with the other individual.

Letting go of: Rather than letting go of or getting rid of anything, this book stresses using everything as a tool. All things are part of us, and everything in our lives can assist with our personal growth. The philosophy of letting go of or getting rid of events or feelings that are unpleasant assumes that there is something wrong with what we are experiencing, and this is not true. Everything in our lives is purposeful. Once we see distortions for what they are, they automatically change into neutral (free) energy that we can use to accelerate our growth.

Mechanics: the science of motion and the action of forces on bodies *(Webster's New World Dictionary, 10th Ed.)*

The principles of mechanics are concerned with how things work in everyday life. In this book, the term mechanics refers to understanding emotional energy and how it is transformed so that we can better function on a daily basis. As an example, when we don't resist what exists in our lives or battle the necessity to feel our emotions, they transform automatically into other forms— neutral energy that we can use. Then we consciously or unconsciously shape that energy by our focus and our passion.

Mechanism: any physical or mental process by which a result is produced *(Webster's New World Dictionary, 10th Ed.)*

The Guardian is an example of a mechanism. Originally, the Guardian was merely a thought form that we were powerless. We fed our Guardians with our beliefs, and they took on life (energy) of their own. All that is necessary to transform the energy of our Guardians is to see them for the distortions that they are. They will automatically change into neutral energy that we can use to further our growth.

Mining the gold in the darkness: This is a concept based on the understanding that all of life's experiences, no matter how dark they may feel or appear in the moment, serve a purpose. For example, our sadness, disappointments, depression, anger, guilt, and hurt are all tools for learning and growth.

Mirror: a smooth, reflecting surface; anything giving a true representation; to reflect, as in a mirror *(Webster's New World Dictionary, 10th Ed.)*

We are all mirrors for each other. What I see in you exists in me or I could not perceive it in you. Thus, we are tremendous personal growth tools for each other.

New Paradigm: See *Paradigm shift.*

Next step: When we move from where we are now, our known realities, into where we are going next, our unknown realities, we move into our next steps in life.

Numbness: This is a transition feeling in which we don't think we feel anything. This is different than the concept of the *Walking dead* (see below), because numbness is a feeling. It is the emotion of not feeling. We may feel dead, but we are very much alive and are preparing to move into our next steps.

Old Paradigm: See *Paradigm shift*.

Owning our power: This term means being who we really are— magnificent and capable individuals. Owning our power entails accepting personal responsibility for our lives and our well-being. Most of us don't fully own our power because it is easier to blame others for our circumstances than to be self-responsible.

Pain: physical or mental suffering caused by injury, disease, anxiety, grief, etc. *(Webster's New World Dictionary, 10th Ed.)*

What is painful for one person is not necessarily perceived as painful to another individual. We each define pain differently because of our unique perceptions, knowledge, and experiences and the degree to which we are aware of the sensations in our bodies.

When we experience our emotions, we can choose to feel both ends of a polarity, such as fear/empowerment or self-confidence/insecurity, simultaneously. When we do so, it becomes very clear that there is no real pain in life. There are only polarities to experience.

Paradigm shift: A paradigm is a model or framework, and a paradigm shift related to the content of this book is now occurring in our society.

In the Old Paradigm, we blame others for our circumstances, judge our feelings or experiences as positive or negative, repress or deny our feelings, and avoid self-responsibility. We think we need to fix or change ourselves.

In the New Paradigm, we choose to take responsibility for our own lives. We allow ourselves to feel and express all of our feelings, and we know how to do this in safe and constructive ways. This energizes us and allows us the freedom to be the masterful beings that we are. We know we each have the choice to be as whole, real, and alive as we are willing to be. We welcome life. We feel connected to ourselves and each other. The self-responsibility we practice in the New Paradigm brings us tremendous personal freedom and empowerment.

Patterns: a regular way of acting or doing; a predictable route, movement, etc. *(Webster's New World Dictionary, 10th Ed.)*

We all have predictable patterns of behavior and of interpreting events in our lives. They developed as we grew up, and many were based on inaccurate perceptions of who we are. Many patterns were defense mechanisms to compensate for our insecurities. As we peel off layers of insecurity and fear, we become more open to new ways of thinking and of doing things. We spontaneously free ourselves from obsolete patterns and more freely walk into our unknowns.

Peeling the onion: This is an expression referring to the fact that we experience layers of our emotions before we comprehend who we really are. This process is similar to peeling off the layers of an onion. As we encounter the tiers of our emotions, our feelings may appear to be resurfacing. In reality, we are simply feeling more submerged layers of emotional material. They may be similar on the surface, but we are actually experiencing deeper overlays of polarities. We shed our identities—formulated because of our insecurities—and reach our core, discovering how profoundly beautiful and capable we are.

Playing victim: When we play victim, we avoid owning our personal responsibility for our lives and our circumstances. We blame others; we give away our power. This is because we have unconsciously looked outside of ourselves for permission to live our lives a certain way. When we play victim, we are in essence saying that we are incapable of making our own decisions and choices. Often we blame others because they don't fit our image of how they should perform in relationship to us.

Point zero: This is a neutral place where we don't judge our emotions. We function at a point equidistant from both ends of a polarity, knowing that both ends are vital to our personal growth. We move rapidly through our personal transformations because we simply see the mechanics of how life operates versus judging one end of a polarity as good and the other as bad. We feel both ends of an emotional continuum simultaneously.

Polarity: the property of opposites; the tendency to grow, think, feel, and turn in contrary directions as if because of magnetic repulsion *(Webster's New World Dictionary, 10th Ed.)*

Polarities are naturally occurring opposites in life such as happy/sad, fear/empowerment, and love/hate. Polarities are contradictory life circumstances and emotions, and they allow us to fully experience life. Once we have fully experienced one side of a polarity (unpleasant feelings such as fear or self-doubt), we can fully experience the other side (enjoyable emotions such as self-confidence or empowerment). Polarities are principal tools for our empowerment. If I do not allow myself the experience of feeling fearful and powerless, how can I feel and experience the full breadth of my power?

The way to experience the upper levels of a polarity is to feel the lower levels of it, and we do this is degrees. Once we have completed our encounter with the "bottom of the bottom," we discover all that is left is to feel new levels of the upper end of the polarity. There are no ceilings on the high ends of polarities, although there are endpoints on the lower extremities.

Polarities provide a frame of reference for measuring our experiences not as good or bad but by the distinct difference between the two. As an example, if I had never experienced hot, I would have no frame of reference to fully understand cold.

Power: ability to do or act, vigor, force, strength, influence, authority *(Webster's New World Dictionary, 10th Ed.)*

Note that all of these qualities are internal attributes. Our society has promulgated the illusion that being a powerful person means having dominion over others. This refers to external power such as a person in a certain position who manipulates people so that they will do something that they wouldn't otherwise do. It is not true that one person must be disempowered for another to be empowered.

Genuine power is an innate quality. It embodies soft and vulnerable qualities as well as the ability to be firm and tenacious. It includes the ability to be who we really are, no matter who is in our presence. Compare this to "power over" which involves a facade of power that comes from feeling insecure or powerless. When we attempt to exert power over others, we demean them or demand that they succumb to our point of view.

People who are self-secure are real, vulnerable, and honest with themselves and with others. They are true to themselves. They do not need to prove themselves or their abilities to others, nor do they need their approval.

Power over: This is a misperception of empowerment and a false definition of power that is frequently used in our society. It is based on the belief that an individual is powerful if he/she can manipulate the behavior of others or have them fear him/her. It is a facade. The person who needs to have power over others actually feels insecure or powerless.

Push-pull: See *Approach-avoidance.*

Push your buttons: We all have sensitive areas in our psyches—aspects of ourselves that feel insecure, inadequate, fearful, or guilty. When we are in resistance to acknowledging or feeling these components of ourselves, other people push our buttons. They remind us that we have emotional issues to deal with, even though we would rather deny this or postpone allowing ourselves to experience them. For example, other people might trigger an emotional response in us by making conversations related to an area of our denial. They might serve as a mirror so that we can perceive a component of ourselves that we would prefer to deny.

Recycling: to pass through a cycle again, to use again and again *(Webster's New World Dictionary, 10th Ed.)*

When we recycle, we re-create opportunities to process emotional material that we have already dealt with. (See *Drama* above.)

Resistance: fight against; opposition of some force or thing to another, as to the flow of an electric current *(Webster's New World Dictionary, 10th Ed.)*

Our Guardians oppose our transformations even though they will be advantageous for us because they distrust change, and they want to continue to control our lives and the ways that we perceive ourselves. If we fight our resistance to change, we create an internal war because we are defying what exists inside of ourselves. When we simply notice our resistance, it has to change because it is a distortion. It melts and becomes neutral energy that we can then use for our growth.

Resonance: We are in resonance with people who are vibrating at a similar electrical frequency. We usually have common belief systems and/or circumstances in life. Like the frequencies on a short-wave radio, we connect with those who are also tuned to a certain channel. We are comfortable associating with the people we resonate with. We are less likely to project our own issues onto them than onto people who are vibrating at a different frequency. When we resonate with someone, we are particularly valuable mirrors for each other.

Self-acceptance: Self-acceptance involves accepting ourselves just as we are right now, without needing to change anything about ourselves or our lives. Self-acceptance is the opposite of judging ourselves to be inadequate.

Self-actualization: Self-actualization is being all that we are, fully using our abilities, owning our personal power, and being self-responsible. It involves developing ourselves to our fullest—physically, mentally, emotionally, and spiritually.

Self-responsibility: When I know that I am in charge of my life, including my decisions and choices, there is no one to blame for the things in my life that I dislike. Total self-responsibility results in personal freedom and is accompanied by feelings of bliss.

Sensation: the receiving of sensory impressions through hearing, seeing, feeling, etc.; a conscious sense impression; a generalized feeling such as a sensation of joy *(Webster's New World Dictionary, 10th Ed.)*

We receive information about our emotions through sensations in our bodies such as feeling "lumps" or constrictions in our throats when we want to cry. Another example is feeling fullness in our bellies or dramatic sensations or palpitations in our hearts when we are frightened.

Struggle: to make great efforts, strive, labor, conflict, strife, to fight violently with an opponent *(Webster's New World Dictionary, 10th Ed.)*

Life was never meant to be a struggle even though our culture has developed strife into an art form. The greatest reason we struggle in our lives is that we judge and label our experiences as painful or difficult. We forget or don't yet know that life is exactly as it should be and that there is something to be learned in every experience. Neither we nor our experiences are ever off course.

When we understand how truly simple life is, all of our struggle dissipates. There are only two things to do in life: 1.) live consciously, and 2.) not judge ourselves or our experiences. If we are living consciously, we automatically experience our emotions. We allow their spontaneous flow, and this provides the fuel to propel us down our path of growth.

Tapes: Most of us have old tapes that play in our heads saying that we aren't good enough or capable enough to have what we want in our lives. The tapes are potentially harmful because it is an old habit to believe their content. Most of the time, we are unaware that they are playing. All we have to do is be conscious of them. Then they have been acknowledged, and our opinions of ourselves begin to shift without our having to try to alter our self-perceptions. Attempts to change them create resistance, and this inhibits our growth.

Thought form: Our thoughts are energy, and we create our lives and reshape energy via our thoughts as well as our actions. When we unconsciously empower thought forms that are distortions (such as our Guardians or social constructs), we feed them, breathing new life into them. This occurs because we have unconsciously accepted the distortions as real and placed focus on them; we have incorporated distortions into our lives.

When we live consciously, we notice distortions versus empowering them. Once they have been perceived, they are required to change form. We then have neutral (free) energy that our focus, will, and passion transmute. The new configurations become building blocks for the bridges from our known realities to our next steps.

Transform: change the form or appearance of; change the condition, character, or function of *(Webster's New World Dictionary, 10th Ed.)*

Our personal transformations happen spontaneously when we live in a conscious manner, don't judge ourselves or our experiences, and feel our emotions. On the other hand, when we "try" to transmute a pattern or identity, we create resistance that inhibits our changing.

Regarding transformation of distortions, once we perceive them, they must change form. They become neutral (free) energy that is then shaped by our focus, will, and passion.

Tuning fork: We all serve as tuning forks for each other. Each time we are in another person's presence, we consciously or unconsciously sense each other's energy. A third frequency is formed as our two energies merge because we are all interconnected.

Sometimes we resist opportunities to increase our frequencies via our interactions with other individuals. Often, this is because we don't wish to perceive the mirrors they reflect to us. At such times, we may reject them, try to make them wrong, or project our own emotional issues onto them.

Also see *Leapfrog.*

Unconscious: 1.) deprived of consciousness, not aware, not realized or intended—an unconscious habit; 2.) in psychoanalysis, the sum of all thoughts, impulses, etc., of which the individual is not conscious but which influence his or her behavior *(Webster's New World Dictionary, 10th Ed.)*

Both of the above definitions are used in this book. 1.) The concepts presented herein stress the importance of living consciously versus unconsciously because that terminates the aspects of struggle in our lives that are created when we live with distortions. 2.) Our bodies house our unconscious emotional material so that we can resurrect it at the precise time that we need to experience it.

Unknown reality: Our unknown realities are what we have not yet experienced. Our known realities are "where we are now," and we are always moving from our comfort zones into new unknown realities—our next steps.

Upside down and backward: This is a term indicating that much of what we have learned about life is a distortion of the truth. One of the saddest distortions of all is that we have been taught that our abilities are limited.

Victim mentality: See *Playing victim.*

Victim 101: A course most of us enroll in. We continue to blame others for our life circumstances or personal characteristics until we learn to take personal responsibility for our own lives. When we decide to acknowledge our power instead of blaming others, we graduate ourselves from the course and experience our freedom.

Wake-up call: A signal to look at one's self and one's life. An opportunity to garner insights and enlightenment from an experience even if it feels painful on the surface. Examples include the loss of a relationship or a job.

Walking dead: We experience being the walking dead when we are alive and breathing but in resistance to feeling and expressing our emotions. We are cheating ourselves out of the wisdom, power, and energy that emotional expression brings to us. We don't risk feeling because we fear pain. The paradox is that we therefore retain our emotional pain, and our physical energy is blocked because we have resistance in our bodies. Thus, we deplete our energy levels and we may even develop physical illnesses. Because of our unwillingness to experience our lives (unpleasant feelings and the lower ends of polarities), we cheat ourselves out of feeling pleasurable emotions and the upper ends of polarities.

Yet-to-be-known reality: Some part of each of us is aware of our future because time and space do not really exist. Even though I discuss our unknown realities in this book, I am quite aware that they are actually our yet-to-be-known-realities. We know everything, even though we are not yet conscious of all of our knowledge.

Index

BIBLIOGRAPHY

Bandler, R. *Using Your Brain for a Change.* Moab, UT.: Real People Press, 1985.

Bean, R. *The Four Conditions of Self Esteem.* 2nd edition. Santa Cruz: ETR Associates, 1992.

Berman, J. *Uninvited.* New York: Warner Books, 1995.

Branden, N. *Honoring the Self.* Los Angeles: Larcher, Inc., 1983.

———. *How to Raise Your Self Esteem.* New York: Bantam Books, 1987.

California Task Force to Promote Self Esteem and Personal and Social Responsibility. *Toward a State of Esteem.* Sacramento: California Department of Education, 1990.

Castenada, C. *Fire From Within.* New York: Simon & Schuster, 1984.

Chopra, D. *The Return of Merlin.* New York: Harmony Books, 1995.

Cole, D. *After Great Pain: A New Life Emerges.* New York: Summit Books, 1992.

Cousins, N. *Anatomy of an Illness.* New York: W.W. Norton, 1979.

Damasio, A. *Descartes' Error. Emotion, Reason, and the Human Brain.* New York: Grosset/Putnam, 1994.

Dubos, R. *Celebration of Life.* New York: McGraw-Hill Book Company, 1981.

Gerber, R. *Vibrational Medicine.* Santa Fe: M.D. Bear & Co., 1988.

Guralnik, D., ed. *Webster's New World Dictionary of the American Language.* 10th Edition. New York: Warner, 1993.

Hermann, N. *The Creative Brain*, Lake Lure, N.C.: Brain Books, 1991.

Hillman, J. & Ventura, M. *We've Had a Hundred Years of Psychotherapy and the World's Getting Worse.* New York: Harper Collins Publishing, 1992.

Hutchison, M. *MegaBrain.* New York: Beach Tree Books, 1986.

————. *Megabrain Power.* 1st Edition. New York: Hyperion, 1994.

Kenyon, T. *Brain States.* Naples, FL: U.S. Publishing, 1994.

Keyes, K. *Handbook to Higher Consciousness.* 7th Edition. Coos Bay, OR.: Ken Keyes College, 1975.

————. *The Hundredth Monkey.* 2nd Edition. Coos Bay, OR: Vision Books, 1987.

Kübler-Ross, E. *Death and Dying.* New York: Macmillan, 1969.

Legrand, M., Bergman, A., and Bergman, M.*A Piece of Sky.* Streisand, Barbra, Columbia C2T66109, CT66457.

Levoy, G. *This Business of Writing.* Cincinnati: Writer's Digest Books, 1992.

Lowen, A. *Depression and the Body.* Harmondsworth: Penguin Books, 1973.

————. *Fear of Life.* New York: Macmillan, 1980.

————. *The Betrayal of the Body.* New York: Macmillan, 1967.

————. *The Spirituality of the Body.* New York: Macmillan, 1990.

Lowry, R. *Abraham Maslow: An Intellectual Portrait.* Monterey, CA: Brooks/Cole Publishing Co., 1973.

Marston, S. *Building Children's Self Esteem.* Santa Monica: Hay House, 1991.

Maslow, A. *Toward a Psychology of Being.* New Jersey: D. Van Nostrand, Inc., 1962.

Morgan, M. *Mutant Message DownUnder.* Lees Summit, MO: MMC, 1993.

Moyers, B. *Healing and the Mind.* New York: Doubleday, 1993.

Muller, W. *Legacy of the Heart.* New York: Simon & Schuster, 1992.

Ornstein, R. and Thompson,R., *The Amazing Brain.* Boston: Houghton-Mifflin Company, 1984.

———— and Sobel, D. *The Healing Brain,* New York: Simon and Schuster, 1987.

Pearson, P. *You Deserve the Best. How to Stop Self-Sabotage and Deserve More.* Dallas, TX: Conmemara Press, 1993.

Richards, William. *Pearls of Wisdom.* Ontario, OR: Shimoda Publishing, 1998.

Rilke, R. *Selected Poems of Ranier Maria Rilke* translated by Robert Bly. New York: Harper & Row, 1981.

Rossi, E. *The Psychobiology of Mind-Body Healing.* New York: W. W. Norton, 1986.

Satir, V. *The New Peoplemaking.* Palo Alto: Science & Behavior Books, 1988.

Siegel, B. *Love, Medicine, and Miracles.* New York: Harper & Row, 1987.

Sinetar, M. *Elegant Choices, Healing Choices.* Mahwah, N.J.: Paulist Press, 1988.

Tzu, L & Ni, H. *The Complete Works of Lao Tzu.* Santa Monica: Seven Star Communications, 1995.

Wilde, S. *Life was Never Meant to be a Struggle.* Taos, N.M.: White Dove International, Inc., 1987.

Williamson, M. *A Return to Love.* New York, NY: Ballantine Books, 1994.

Winter, D. *Alphabet of the Heart.* San Anselmo, CA: The Meru Foundation and Crystal Hill, 1993.

Wotitz, J. *Healing Your Sexual Self.* Deerfield Beach, FL: HCI Audio Books, Health Communications, Inc., 1989.

Zevin, D. *Into Adolescence: Enhancing Self Esteem. Network Publications' Contemporary Health Series.* Santa Cruz: Network Publications/ETR Associates, 1989.

Give a Gift of Love to a Friend

ORDER FORM

Transforming Pain Into Power, ISBN: 1–8855–98–88–2

You may order 24 hours a day, so *act now!*

Telephone orders: 1-800-218-6110

E-mail: http://www.amazon.com
                                or
                                shimodapub@mindspring.com
                                URL: http://www.mindspring.com/~shimodapub/
Mailing address: Shimoda Publishing
                                c/o 1225 E. Sunset, #317
                                Bellingham, WA 98226-3529

Please send me _____ copies of *Transforming Pain Into Power* @ $16.95 per copy. I understand that I may return any books in good condition for a full refund—for any reason, no questions asked.

Shipping and handling costs: $3.00 for the first book and $2.00 for each additional book.

I am enclosing a check or money order for $_____

Name:_____

Address:_____

City:_____ State: _____ Zip: _____

Telephone:(   )_____-_____Fax: (   )_____-_____

E-mail:_____

Purchase order number (if applicable) _____

Call toll free and order now!

Bookstores and libraries may also order from New Leaf, Bookpeople, Ingram, DeVorss, Quality, or Unique.